# Accelerating Language Skills and Content Knowledge Through Shared Book Reading

# Accelerating Language Skills and Content Knowledge Through Shared Book Reading

by

**Sharolyn D. Pollard-Durodola, Ed.D.**
University of Denver
Colorado

**Jorge E. Gonzalez, Ph.D.**
Texas A&M University
College Station

**Deborah C. Simmons, Ph.D.**
Texas A&M University
College Station

and

**Leslie E. Simmons, M.Ed.**
Texas A&M University
College Station

·P A U L·H·
**BROOKES**
PUBLISHING CO.®

Baltimore • London • Sydney

**Paul H. Brookes Publishing Co.**
Post Office Box 10624
Baltimore, Maryland 21285-0624

www.brookespublishing.com

Typeset by Scribe Inc., Philadelphia, PA
Manufactured in the United States of America by
Sheridan Books, Inc., Chelsea, Michigan.

Cover images are ©istockphoto/Monkeybusinessimages, Photo-Dave, SHSPhotography, leonid_tit,
and Romanchuck

Interior images are © 2014 Jupiterimages Corporation.

**Library of Congress Cataloging-in-Publication Data**

The Library of Congress has cataloged the print edition as follows:

Pollard-Durodola, Sharolyn D., 1959-
  Accelerating language skills and content knowledge through shared book reading / by Sharolyn D.
Pollard-Durodola, Ed.D., University of Denver, Denver, Jorge E. Gonzalez, Ph.D., Texas A&M
University, College Station, Deborah C. Simmons, Ph.D. Texas A&M University, College Station,
Leslie E. Simmons, M.Ed., Texas A&M University, College Station.
     pages   cm
  Includes bibliographical references and index.
  ISBN 978-1-59857-257-5 (pbk.)—ISBN 978-1-59857-951-2 (ebook)
  1. Oral reading—United States.   2. English language—Study and teaching (Early childhood)—
United States—Foreign speakers.   3. Second language acquisition—United States.   I. Title.
  LB1573.5.P67 2015
  372.45'x2—dc23                                                                    2014038889

British Library Cataloguing in Publication data are available from the British Library.

2019   2018   2017   2016   2015

10    9    8    7    6    5    4    3    2    1

# Contents

# About the Authors

**Sharolyn D. Pollard-Durodola, Ed.D.,** Morgridge Endowed Associate Professor in Literacy, Child, Family, and School Psychology, Morgridge College of Education, University of Denver, Katherine A. Ruffato Hall 255, Denver, Colorado 80208.

Dr. Pollard-Durodola is an associate professor in the Child, Family, and School Psychology program at the University of Denver. Her scholarship attends to the prevention and intervention of language and literacy difficulties (Spanish and English) among students with identified disabilities or who are at risk of later academic difficulties. Central to her scholarship is an interest in developing intervention curricula that build on validated instructional design principles, evaluating their impact on the language and reading development of struggling readers (Spanish and English), and investigating how to improve the quality of language and literacy practices of teachers and parents of young English language learners (ELLs) and non-ELLs who are at risk for reading difficulties. She is specifically interested in bridging research and practice by examining the feasibility and usability of research-based practices in high-poverty classroom settings. She has received grants from the Institute of Education Sciences and the Mexican-American and U.S. Latino Research Center and published in peer-reviewed journals such as *Exceptional Children, Journal of Research on Educational Effectiveness, The Elementary School Journal, Language Speech and Hearing Services in Schools,* and *Bilingual Research Journal.* Prior to joining the University of Denver, Dr. Pollard-Durodola served as Associate Professor of the Bilingual Education Program in the Department of Educational Psychology at Texas A&M University and as Assistant Professor at the University of Texas–Houston Health Science Center (The Center for Academic and Reading Skills). Her undergraduate studies were in romance languages (Spanish and Portuguese) at Mount Holyoke College in South Hadley, Massachusetts. She has two master's degrees: a master of arts in teaching Spanish from Teachers College, Columbia University in New York City and a master of science in developmental and remedial reading from City University of New York. Her doctorate is in curriculum and instruction with an emphasis on second-language acquisition and bilingual education. She has 14 years of experience in public school settings as a school administrator, reading specialist, and teacher. Her favorite activities are visiting fine arts museums, both nationally and internationally, and photography—taking pictures of lighthouses on the coast of Michigan.

**Jorge E. Gonzalez, Ph.D.,** Associate Professor, Department of Educational Psychology, College of Education and Human Development, School Psychology MS 4225, College Station, Texas 77843.

Dr. Gonzalez is an associate professor in the School Psychology program, Department of Educational Psychology, College of Education and Human Development at Texas A&M University. Funded by the U.S. Department of Education, his work focuses on the causes and correlates of early language and literacy difficulties in young children with a focus on adult–child interactive reading in the context of dual-language learners. His scholarship addresses inquiries relevant to children's home literacy environments (HLEs), the effects of teacher talk around shared reading, longitudinal effects of evidence-based shared reading interventions, and investigating the heterogeneous nature language and literacy subtypes of at-risk children. His publications represent an array of journals with a focus on child development, including *Early Childhood Research Quarterly, Bilingual Research Journal, Journal of Educational Effectiveness, Early Education and Development, Journal of Special Education, Journal of Learning Disabilities, Journal of Emotional and Behavioral Disorders,* and *Journal of Early Intervention.* He has previously been the lead investigator on an Early Reading First (ERF) project titled Accelerating Children's Early Literacy and Language (ACELL), an Institute of Education Sciences (IES) development grant titled Words of Oral Reading and Language Development (WORLD), and a follow-up IES efficacy grant of the same name. In his spare time, Jorge enjoys hiking the Texas trails, exploring international cuisines, and spending time on the beaches of Mexico.

**Deborah C. Simmons, Ph.D.,** Professor, Department of Educational Psychology, College of Education and Human Development, Texas A&M University, College Station, Texas 77843.

Dr. Simmons is a professor of educational psychology in the College of Education and Human Development at Texas A&M University. Her professional career began as a speech-language specialist in public schools in Tennessee, where she experienced the importance of vocabulary and language development among the children she taught. Following her career in public schools, she earned her doctorate in reading and served on the faculties of Bowling Green State University, Vanderbilt University, and the University of Oregon. Since joining the faculty at Texas A&M University in 2004, she has directed or codirected research grants from the Institute of Education Sciences, U.S. Department of Education, that have developed and evaluated interventions to improve language and literacy outcomes for students with or at risk of academic difficulties. She is a standing panel reviewer for the Institute of Education Sciences. She was recognized by the American Educational Research Association and American Psychological Association with awards for outstanding articles in their journals. She was the recipient of the Jeanette Fleischner Award for Outstanding Contribution to the Field of Learning Disabilities from the Division for Learning Disabilities of the Council for Exceptional Children and the Faculty Mentoring Award in the College of Education and Human Development. Her current research focuses on prevention of and intervention in reading difficulties from kindergarten to high school and strategies to enhance reading programs and accelerate achievement for struggling readers. In her spare time, she enjoys hiking in the mountains of Oregon and Colorado and spending time with family and her "granddogs."

**Leslie E. Simmons, M.Ed.,** Research Assistant, Department of Educational Psychology, College of Education and Human Development, Texas A&M University, Mailstop 4225, 704 Harrington Tower, College Station, Texas 77843.

Leslie E. Simmons is a research assistant serving as the coordinator for federally funded research grants in the Department of Educational Psychology at Texas A&M University. She received her bachelor of arts degree from the University of Oregon and her master of education degree from Texas A&M University. Her research interests are in the areas of early reading, language assessment, and curriculum development. She has worked on projects evaluating the impact of shared book reading on preschool children's vocabulary development and the effectiveness of early reading interventions on at-risk kindergarten students. Currently, her work is focused on assessment as she coordinates a project examining the technical adequacy of early literacy measures commonly used to monitor the reading progress of kindergarten children and directs the assessment portion of a study on reading comprehension interventions for adolescent students. In her personal time, Mrs. Simmons enjoys spending time with her family, as well as with her two incomparable dogs adopted from the local animal shelter.

# Foreword

Readers are in for a treat as they delve into this book. Sharolyn Pollard-Durodola and her colleagues have masterfully unlocked the underlying principles and the power of shared book reading and its influence on vocabulary development, conceptual development, and content knowledge.

It could not come at a better time. Shared book reading has been known to be a key activity, if not the single most important activity, for enhancing school readiness. There is now a corpus of meta-analytic studies indicating that shared book reading improves language development, receptive and expressive vocabulary, and motivation to read. Nevertheless, it hasn't been until recently that we have begun to explore its power for learning content knowledge. In essence, these authors extend our understandings of the power of the book to enhance the development of networks of knowledge in science and social studies.

The authors' emphasis on knowledge *through* text is an extraordinarily important message. In the past, we have understood that listening to stories can help children learn new words outside of their day-to-day lexicon and recall and retell what they can remember, building a coherent story grammar for comprehending what they have learned. But to a great extent, this learning has been based on a single text in a single moment, each text representing a new set of words and conceptual challenges. In contrast, what Pollard-Durodola and her colleagues do is create a systematic plan—a cumulative set of experiences that support children's understanding of the connections between texts. By doing so, the texts and the talk that accompanies these texts build on one another, helping children develop "big ideas": interconnected core themes that represent knowledge networks.

This is why the book title so aptly describes their approach. By helping children develop concepts and big ideas, we are enabling children not only to accumulate content knowledge—facts and conceptual understandings—but to understand how knowledge is structured. When we provide a systematic intervention like this, we enable children to develop a mental model, a representation of the relationship between words and concepts. When we do so, we facilitate retention and recall. For example, knowing that a "cockatoo" is a type of bird and that all birds have feathers to keep them warm eases children's ability to remember the new word and to learn the relationship of cockatoos to other living things, like parrots. In this respect, learning words and concepts may accelerate children's language skills, promoting self-teaching in a fundamental way. Children develop important inferences and generalizations about categories and concepts, which will support more rapid word learning.

This book also comes at an exciting period in educational reform. There is greater access to early education and greater expectations for what children should learn in the early years. The Common Core and career-ready standards have "upped the ante" in terms of grade-level expectations and the goals we set for children's outcomes. To some scholars, these standards are to be avoided, but to others, like the authors here, the standards have challenged them to meet these expectations through meaningful instruction. What this book does brilliantly is demonstrate that it is possible to 1) teach complex ideas to young children, 2) to do so with integrity to the discipline, and 3) to engage in developmentally appropriate practice while motivating children to learn and want to learn even more.

No child is off the hook here in terms of learning expectations—as it should be. These researchers have had much practice in addressing the needs of special education students, children with language delays, and children who are second language learners. In the authors' years of practice preparing for larger random-ized control trials, they have worked collaboratively with teachers on formative design experiments, tweaking their intervention in ways that would promote chil-dren's learning. Their research, demonstrated powerfully in this book and in other articles, suggests that when we construct interventions that build on children's considerable strengths and scaffold appropriately, all children can be successful language learners and develop content expertise.

In this book, authors will provide essential guidelines, relying on their research and practice alongside teachers in classrooms. Readers will learn about the latest research on language, vocabulary, and content knowledge and impor-tant principles that may be derived from this research. These authors, however, go beyond just detailing the research. Throughout the book, readers will find exam-ples of what the instruction actually looks like, as if you were in the classroom with them. They deconstruct their intervention in ways that are highly readable, with rich descriptions of each part of the process, whether it is book (and genre) selec-tion, vocabulary selection (what words should be taught), or the extratextual dis-cussions that enrich children's learning and classroom organization (whole group, small group, or individual).

What readers will also find essential is the latest research on English lan-guage learners and how we can better address their development. Readers will find language strategies that can be used by teachers to facilitate book discussions with those who may have limited skills in their second language. Furthermore, the appendixes with additional practice strategies will be of great help to teachers as they engage in these content-rich exchanges.

In short, Pollard-Durodola and her well-respected colleagues have put together an extraordinary resource that is designed to inspire a paradigm shift in think-ing and teaching. Their work exemplifies the following principle: that children are highly capable of learning new words rapidly and comprehending big ideas that are tied to content domains. The authors' work shows that this can be true of all children regardless of family socioeconomic status or language background. They also vividly describe that young children need to be taught in a manner that is designed for their developmental level. Children learn through meaningful instruction, and when this is systematically, thoughtfully enacted and tied to their interests in learning about their world, as these authors so carefully do, we can realize all children's potential.

*Susan B. Neuman*
*Professor and Chair*
*Teaching and Learning Department*
*New York University*

# Preface

Shared book reading is a well-loved instructional strategy in early childhood education by teachers and students alike—and for good reason. Shared book reading can have profound and measurable effects on young children's oral language development, communication skills, and vocabulary knowledge. Despite the potential benefits, however, shared book reading is not necessarily standard practice in classrooms in which children are most at risk for comprehension difficulties (Neuman, 1999). One unintended outcome is that young children from high-poverty backgrounds have gaps in vocabulary knowledge that can negatively affect future reading comprehension. What can we do? How can early childhood educators address this issue in the classroom? The ideas and strategies presented in the coming chapters offer a compelling answer.

These ideas and strategies grew from Words of Oral Reading and Language Development (WORLD), an Institute of Education Services (IES) grant-funded research project headed by Jorge E. Gonzalez (Texas A&M University) and co-principal investigators Deborah C. Simmons (Texas A&M University), Sharolyn D. Pollard-Durodola (University of Denver), and Oiman Kwok (Texas A&M University). The purpose of WORLD was to evaluate an early curricular intervention for preschool children from high-poverty backgrounds. Specifically, the intervention was designed to mitigate the potential effects of limited socioeconomic resources and life experiences on oral language development. Over the course of 3 years, 16 preschool teachers used the shared book-reading process to accelerate both word and world knowledge in 197 children.

This text bridges WORLD research to classroom practice by providing early childhood educators with evidence-based strategies to intensify their daily shared book-reading practices. The shared book-reading framework will help guide educators in developing their own lessons, selecting books and vocabulary words, and using connected science and social studies themes and concepts. This book also may be used as a supplemental text to aid preservice teachers in planning instruction.

In Chapter 1, we review what we have learned from research about effective shared book-reading practices for young children at risk of future comprehension difficulties due to socioeconomic disparities. Despite the potential benefits of shared book reading for young children's word and world knowledge acquisition, observational studies suggest that shared book reading is not always a standard instructional feature in high-poverty preschools settings (Neuman, 1999). Thus this chapter presents a rationale and conceptual framework for integrating this type of instruction into the daily preschool classroom.

In Chapter 2, we describe the critical components of the empirically based WORLD shared book-reading pedagogical process. In this chapter, we refer to the WORLD design experiment and the primary ways in which preschool teachers' input shaped researchers' understanding of teaching and vocabulary learning as they field-tested the WORLD shared book-reading approach and materials with young children in Head Start and preschool settings. Teachers' recommendations were based on experiences implementing the WORLD intervention to develop content vocabulary knowledge of native English-speaking children and a smaller sample of children acquiring language and literacy in their native language, Spanish.

Young children who enter school with limited exposure to world and word knowledge can successfully learn content vocabulary via interactive book conversations in which an adult strategically implements a book-reading style that is conducive to dialogue and learning with adult feedback. Our pedagogical approach, therefore, acknowledges that young children bring to school an eagerness to learn about their world through relevant science and social studies topics and themes and that early childhood educators play a major role in ensuring quality instruction.

The objective of Chapters 3–5 is to provide a series of steps that preservice early childhood educators can follow to design and develop content-based shared book-reading lessons guided by the three instructional design principles integrated throughout the WORLD intervention. These chapters, therefore, shift the attention from shared book-reading research and instructional design theories to actual practice (e.g., designing a science and social studies unit of instruction), preparing future early childhood educators to accelerate vocabulary knowledge through research-based recommendations for preschool settings.

Within each chapter, we make instructional recommendations for applying the three instructional design principles to accelerate vocabulary and concept knowledge. The recommendations include opportunities for English language learners (ELLs) who may be listening and talking about books in their native language (Spanish) or in a second language (English). Instructional vignettes are woven throughout Chapters 3–5 to illustrate real-life applications of the concepts discussed. The following is a summary of the progression of instructional design experiences that are integrated in Chapters 3–5:

In Chapter 3, "Aligning Vocabulary Instruction with Content Standards and Objectives," you will do the following:

- Identify appropriate science, social studies, and language standards for preschool instruction

- Select content to guide the development of two corresponding thematic units of instruction (i.e., 2 weeks of shared book-reading instruction organized by content themes and topics)

In Chapter 4, "Creating Multiple Exposures to Content Words and Connected Concepts," you will do the following:

- Select complementary texts (i.e., a storybook and an informational text) that are thematically connected by a science and/or social studies theme

- Identify three content-related words from each text that are visually represented within and outside of the book

In Chapter 5, "Opportunities to Dialogue," you will do the following:

- Create a content map to summarize how content vocabulary instruction will be sequenced across the week and implemented with the repeated reading of complementary texts

- Develop open-ended questions to prime background knowledge before reading the book and to integrate content vocabulary use in postreading discussions

Chapter 6, "Instruction in Practice," provides an example of two science lessons. All lesson components in this chapter were implemented with children who entered school with limited vocabulary and world knowledge and who were at risk of future comprehension difficulties. This chapter serves as a culmination of the theories, instructional design principles, and recommendations for ELLs that are discussed throughout the book. As such, Chapter 6 provides a feasible representation of how to accelerate content vocabulary learning via a research-based shared book-reading process.

Chapter 7, "What Lies Ahead," accomplishes three goals. First, it summarizes some commonly held misconceptions about vocabulary teaching and learning. Second, it provides suggestions for how to support preschool teachers' shared book-reading vocabulary practices through opportunities for self-reflection and differentiation of professional development practices. Third, it discusses potential obstacles to student learning (e.g., misconceptions of book illustrations or other visuals, misuse of open-ended questions) that can be addressed through practical decisions (e.g., incorporating teacher modeling, extending background knowledge).

# Acknowledgments

We would like to acknowledge the many preschool teachers, parents, and students who participated in the Words of Oral Reading and Language Development (WORLD) project since 2005. We are also grateful to those pioneering school administrators and school district personnel who welcomed us into schools because they believed that our research could make a difference in improving the quality of instruction for young children from economically challenging settings.

We would also like to acknowledge, with gratitude, the long-standing guidance of Dr. Oiman Kwok and Dr. Aaron Taylor, methodologists and statisticians, as well as the many dedicated graduate research assistants, project coordinators, and project specialists who provided both their expertise and wisdom. We would like to especially thank the following individuals:

Graduate research assistants: Matthew Davis, Idalia Massa, Sophia Tani-Prado, Vivina Rivera, Erica Perez, Morgan Sowell, Alicia Darensbourg, Minjung Kim, Leina Zhu

Project coordinators: Becki Oakeley, Leslie Simmons, Catharina Carvalho, Denise Soares, Heather Davis

Project specialists: Kimberly Williams, Kristi Cleere

We also acknowledge our South Texas team (University of Texas–Pan American), organized by Dr. Laura Saenz, coprincipal investigator (2012–2014), and their tremendous effort to manage the WORLD study in approximately 140 classrooms with 800 Spanish-speaking preschool children in a dual-language instructional model:

Graduate research assistants: Iris Vasquez, Miguel Montemayor, Sonia Torres, Dakota Seale, Denise Garza, Meagan Perez, Gloria Cardona, Patty Lerma, Mari Cruz Luna, Joanna Webber-Norquest, Rica Ramirez

Project coordinator: Nora Resendez

We would also like to acknowledge the willingness of Dr. Teresa Satterfield Linares and Dr. José Benkí at the University of Michigan–Ann Arbor to implement the Spanish WORLD pedagogical approach in their En Nuestra Lengua Saturday School (*En Nuestra Lengua*: Proyecto de Alfabetismo y Cultura)

Thank you!

¡Gracias!

Preparation of this book was supported in part by Project WORLD, Grant R305G050121, Reading Comprehension and Reading Scale-Up Research and Grant R305A110638, Early Learning and Policies Research, U.S. Department of Education, Institute of Education Services. This material does not necessarily represent the policy of the U.S. Department of Education, nor is the material necessarily endorsed by the federal government.

# About the Forms

Purchasers of this book may download, print, and/or photocopy the blank forms in Chapter 6 for educational use. These materials are included with the print book and are also available at http://www.brookespublishing.com/pollard-durodola/materials.

# Shared Book-Reading Research and Content Learning

1

 **THE PURPOSE OF THIS CHAPTER IS** to establish the importance of interactive shared book reading as a tool for developing preschool children's oral language and comprehension abilities. We will summarize what we know about the most effective book-reading practices from the last 25 years of research and the purpose of shared book reading within the context of language development and content learning. The approach we introduce here was implemented with children from high-poverty settings in Project Words of Oral Reading and Language Development (WORLD). We will further describe Project WORLD in subsequent chapters.

 **KEY IDEAS |** The key ideas discussed in this chapter are as follows:

1. Gaps in children's language and world knowledge begin early and are evident in preschool.

2. Teachers can read and talk about books with children in ways that boost children's oral language abilities and conceptual knowledge.

3. Shared book reading is more effective when an adult listens to oral responses in book conversations and, in response to children's understanding, extends children's language and learning through a discussion with feedback and confirmation.

4. Building networks of knowledge and connected vocabulary concepts establishes a foundation for future academic learning and text comprehension.

*Shared book reading* is a process of talking about books that occurs between an adult and a child or children when reading or looking at books (What Works Clearinghouse [WWC], 2006). Also known as read-alouds, book sharing, and storybook reading, it is the primary instructional approach to promoting young children's vocabulary acquisition (Ezell & Justice, 2005; Hargrave & Sénéchal, 2000; Whitehurst & Lonigan, 1998), and it is a method that lends itself to the development of *content-related vocabulary and knowledge* (e.g., science, social studies; Gonzalez, Pollard-Durodola, Taylor, Simmons, Davis, & Simmons, 2011; Neuman & Dwyer, 2011; Pollard-Durodola et al., 2011). In the following excerpt from a shared book-reading dialogue, Ms. Thomas uses the informational text *Amazing Water* (Berger, 1996) as a springboard for a science discussion with a small group of preschool children. An informational text is a type of book that conveys facts and usually is written by an expert (Duke, 2003). It differs from a storybook, which is a type of text that usually has a character (e.g., person, animal) who resolves a problem through a sequence of events (plot; Mantzicopoulus & Patrick, 2011). Ms. Thomas has selected the informational text *Amazing Water* because it can be used to teach important concepts about water.

In this lesson, Ms. Thomas organizes book-reading content by a science theme (*nature*) and topic (*water*) that allow her to explicitly teach three new words (i.e., *liquid, frozen,* and *solid*) from *Amazing Water* that are related to important concepts that children will be learning that week. In this discussion, children learn about what water can do. They learn that water is a *liquid,* that a *liquid* can freeze, and that something *frozen,* such as ice, is a *solid.* When appropriate, Ms. Thomas also extends children's understandings of the science terms *liquid, frozen,* and *solid* beyond their application to water (e.g., *solid* objects in a classroom, other types of *liquid*).

This interactive discussion occurs before reading *Amazing Water* to expand children's knowledge of concepts and words to which they may not be exposed in daily life (Neuman & Roskos, 2007). In shared book-reading lessons, content-related book discussions can take place before, while, or after reading a selected text. In this scenario, Ms. Thomas explicitly previews important vocabulary concepts prior to reading *Amazing Water* so that children are better prepared to comprehend the content of the book as it is read.

In addition to extending their word and world knowledge, Ms. Thomas's goal is to extend the children's oral language abilities by encouraging them to use these science-related vocabulary words to talk about connected life experiences. Such language, word, and world knowledge extensions allow children to acquire new information and participate in academic discussions. These connections and extensions are especially important for children from low-income communities who enter school with vocabulary and knowledge gaps that place them at risk of comprehension difficulties.

## Instructional Science Vignette: What Can Water Do?

### Discussion Before Reading *Amazing Water*

Ms. Thomas: This week, we're going to read books that teach us about nature. Nature consists of things that are not made by people, such as water, air, and sunlight. Look at this picture about nature. Let's name and talk about the parts of nature that you see in these pictures. *[Children identify and talk about the sun, icicles, snow-covered trees, and swirling water.]*

In our new book, we'll listen for three new words. These new words will help us learn about water and what water can do. Let's practice them *before* reading the book.

---

⭐ **TEACHING STRATEGY:** Use a visual to depict a vocabulary concept.

---

*[She holds an 8½ × 11 picture/concept card of a glass filled with water.]*

Ms. Thomas: Look at this picture. Our first new word is *liquid*. A *liquid* is something such as water or juice. In this picture, water is a *liquid*. It is wet. What is this, everyone?

Children: *Liquid!*

Ms. Thomas: Let's point to the *liquid* in this picture. *[Everyone points.]*

---

⭐ **TEACHING STRATEGY:** Extend children's conceptual knowledge.

---

Ms. Thomas: Besides water, there are many other types of *liquids*. There is *liquid* paint, soup, and detergent for washing our clothes. And look at this *liquid* glue. Benjamin, I see that you want to say something! What is your favorite *liquid* and why?

Child: Juice.

Ms. Thomas: I like juice, too. Say, "My favorite *liquid* is juice."

Child: My favorite *liquid* is juice.

Ms. Thomas: Okay, why do you like juice?

Child: It's cold and sweet.

Ms. Thomas: That's a good explanation. You like juice because it is cold and sweet!

Can you think of a *liquid* that we use to soften our skin? What type of *liquid* is in this bottle?

Child: That's lotion.

Ms. Thomas: Yes, the *liquid* in this bottle is a lotion.

---

⭐ **TEACHING STRATEGY:** Use a visual to depict a vocabulary concept.

---

*[She points to a picture/concept card of icicles on a tree.]*

Here's our second new word. Look at this picture. Did you know this is *frozen* water? Everyone say, "It's *frozen* water." *[Children repeat.]*

If something is *frozen,* it is hard and cold. Ice is something that is *frozen,* or hard and cold. In this picture, the water on the branch is *frozen,* or cold and hard. Everyone, what is this?

Children:    *Frozen.*

Ms. Thomas:    What are some things you know that are *frozen?*

Child:    Popsicles!

Ms. Thomas:    Yes, Popsicles are *frozen.* Let's say that together: *Popsicles are frozen. [Children repeat.]* What are some other examples of *frozen* water?

Child:    The lake in the park.

Ms. Thomas:    Yes, the lake in the park is *frozen* this morning. In fact, there were geese sitting on the *frozen* lake this morning.

Child:    Water *frozen* on the sidewalk.

Ms. Thomas:    Yes, there is *frozen* water on the sidewalk. What do we call *frozen* water? *[There is a discussion about the ice on the sidewalk.]*

Ms. Thomas:    We have one more new word to learn that we will listen for in our book.

---

⭐ **TEACHING STRATEGY:** Use a visual to depict a vocabulary concept.

---

*[She holds a picture/concept card showing a brick wall.]*

Ms. Thomas:    This is a *solid.* A *solid* is something hard, such as wood or rocks. In this picture, the bricks are *solid.* They are hard. What is this, everyone?

Children:    *Solid.*

Ms. Thomas:    When water is *frozen,* it is a *solid,* so it feels hard. Besides *frozen* water, there are many other examples of *solid* objects. What do you see in this room that is a *solid? [Silence. The silence indicates that some children may need clarification or further explanation to understand the concept of* solid.*]*

Child:    Rocks.

Ms. Thomas:    Yes, the rocks on the science table are *solid.*

---

⭐ **TEACHING STRATEGY:** Scaffold with an explanation.

---

They are *solid* because they feel hard when you touch them. What else in the room is a *solid?*

---

⭐ **TEACHING STRATEGY:** Scaffold with additional examples.

---

I see maps on the walls that are *solids,* and I see lights on the ceiling that are *solids.* If I touched them, they would feel hard. What else in the room is a *solid?*

Child:          The table.

Child:          The little sticks in the bird's nest.

Child:          Coats and caps.

---

⭐ **TEACHING STRATEGY:** Model appropriate language use and more complex sentence structures.

---

Ms. Thomas:   Yes, the wooden table and the wooden chairs are also *solids.* Good observing that the bird's nest on the science table is made of small sticks or twigs that are *solid.* You are right, Jeremy! The coats and caps hanging by the door are also *solid.*

Today, in our new book, we will listen for three words: *liquid, frozen,* and *solid.* This week, we are learning about water and what water can do. We will learn that water is a *liquid* that can freeze and become a *solid.*

After previewing the three science-related words (i.e., *liquid, frozen,* and *solid*) and connected concepts (e.g., "Water is a liquid that can freeze and harden into a solid when the temperature is cold") before reading the book, Ms. Thomas is ready to read *Amazing Water.* While reading this informational text, she stops on specific pages to point to a picture and talk about the target word and connected science concepts that are depicted in the book. This teaching strategy ensures multiple opportunities to extend knowledge while expanding children's language abilities in the context of a book discussion.

## Instructional Science Vignette: What Can Water Do?

### Discussion While Reading *Amazing Water*

Ms. Thomas:   The title of our new book is *Amazing Water.* Melvin Berger is the author who wrote the book, and Robyn Lash is the photographer who took the pictures. As I read, you will listen to learn about water and our magic words: *liquid, frozen,* and *solid.*

*[She reads the first few pages of the book and stops to point to a picture of children swimming and children standing in the rain.]*

---

⭐ **TEACHING STRATEGY:** Stop and briefly talk about vocabulary within the context of the book using book pictures to scaffold instruction.

Ms. Thomas: This is a liquid. A liquid is something wet, such as water or juice. What is this, everyone?

Children: A liquid!

Ms. Thomas: Yes, here we see children playing in a pool. What liquid is inside the pool?

Child: I see blue water.

Ms. Thomas: Okay, the liquid water does look blue. What are the children doing in the liquid water in the swimming pool? [*There is a brief discussion. Then Ms. Thomas continues to read about water being a liquid that can change its shape. She reads that an iceberg is frozen water that may be found in the sea. She stops and points to the picture of the iceberg and engages children in a discussion about* frozen *water. She reads about ice being a* solid *and points again to the iceberg when explaining that ice is a solid.*]

Ms. Thomas: Yes, here is a big piece of ice, an iceberg, and it is solid. Remember, a solid is something hard, such as wood or rocks.

---

⭐ **TEACHING STRATEGY:** Make brief connections to life experiences using vocabulary.

---

Ms. Thomas: How do you think this solid ice would feel if you touched it with your fingers?

Child: Cold!

Child: Hard.

Ms. Thomas: I think that you are all right. If we touched this iceberg, it would feel cold because it is frozen water, and it would feel hard because it is a solid! [*She continues to read the book.*]

In these brief verbal exchanges before and while reading the text, Ms. Thomas makes it a daily routine to interject "knowledge-rich" (Hirsch, 2006, p. 6) science or social studies content into the book-reading discussions to expand children's life experiences—that is, Ms. Thomas explicitly engages children in an interactive discussion around three science concepts to boost children's content vocabulary and conceptual knowledge.

## PROJECT WORDS OF ORAL READING AND LANGUAGE DEVELOPMENT

In Project WORLD (Gonzalez, Simmons, Pollard-Durodola, & Kwok), preschool teachers like Ms. Thomas moved beyond teaching content vocabulary words in isolation and learned to be responsive to opportunities to build *networks of knowledge* (Nagy, 2005; e.g., "Water is a *liquid* that can *freeze* and harden into a *solid* when the temperature is cold. Both *frozen* and *liquid* water are crucial to our daily lives.") that can accelerate both vocabulary and content learning. By infusing content vocabulary instruction within the context of daily shared book-reading lessons, teachers progressively developed networks of words and connected knowledge with 197 preschool children from high-poverty backgrounds. The purpose of Project WORLD was to design and evaluate an early curricular intervention that accelerates the oral language abilities (e.g., vocabulary) and conceptual knowledge of children at risk for underachievement and comprehension difficulties due to limited life experiences and socioeconomic resources. The goal in writing this text, therefore, is to bridge research to practice by providing suggestions and examples of how early childhood educators can intensify their shared book-reading practices, as Ms. Thomas has done, to accelerate content vocabulary knowledge and learning in young children.

## Building a Foundation for Comprehension

The development of concept knowledge and related content-based word meanings is an important part of language and text comprehension (Hirsch, 2006; Verhoeven & Perfetti, 2011). Because word meanings do not exist in isolation, learning vocabulary is connected to acquiring sufficient world knowledge to be able to talk about broad experiences (Scarcella, 2003). Thus content vocabulary must be taught within the context of building extensive knowledge networks (Anderson & Freebody, 1981; Nagy, 2005; Neuman, 2006). Building a strong oral language foundation is specifically important to text comprehension because vocabulary is the true "carrier of meaning" (Verhoeven & Perfetti, 2011, p. 2).

## The Social and Economic Context

In a longitudinal study (2½ years) of 42 families that varied by socioeconomic status (SES; i.e., high-poverty, working-class, and professional backgrounds), Hart and Risley (1995) observed that families' language patterns varied considerably. Researchers noted that parents from higher socioeconomic backgrounds provided richer adult–child conversations in the home by talking more to their children and exposing them to both sophisticated words and connected world concepts. Thus children's oral language abilities at age 3 were found to be related to their life experiences and also were predictive of future academic success or failure. Based on these findings, Hart and Risley advocated for home- and school-based intervention approaches that would "equalize early experience" (p. 191) for children from high-poverty settings by addressing their oral language and conceptual knowledge needs early.

Beyond this study, there is further evidence that children's language abilities and conceptual knowledge are related to their life experiences. Children's experiences often are dictated by the family's SES and parenting practices, which have an impact on the quality and frequency of adult–child conversations in the home (Dickinson, 2011; Farkas & Beron, 2004; Lareau, 2003). For example, living in poverty may limit children's access to high-quality early child care, stimulating educational resources, varied print materials (e.g., books, newspapers) in the home, and other resources that parents use to support the development of oral language (e.g., vocabulary) and world knowledge in their children (Neuman, 2006; Neuman & Celano, 2001). Poverty also may affect parents' ability to interact with young children during periods of economic hardship (McLoyd, 1990) and may prevent children from being exposed to important "informal informational lessons" (Neuman, 2006, p. 25) in which knowledge about the world is transmitted during adult–child interactions. In contrast, children who enter school from families with higher socioeconomic resources demonstrate stronger language abilities (Barbarin et al., 2006; Lareau, 2003). These children may be accustomed to adult–child conversations that use more elaborate and analytical discourse with extensive discussions about the world (Lareau, 2003).

Limited home resources, life experiences, and adult–child verbal interactions ultimately may negatively affect children's acquisition of conceptual knowledge and comprehension skills (Biemiller, 2003; Hirsch, 2003) and hence their ability to benefit from academic learning, even through high school (NICHD Early Child Care Research Network, 2005). Equally important, these differences in children's initial abilities generate a "social stratification of knowledge" (Neuman, 2006, p. 32) that is initiated at home and perpetuated in school settings in which teachers of young children often have little guidance in how to accelerate oral language and vocabulary learning (Neuman & Dwyer, 2009; Neuman & Roskos, 2005). Yet research suggests that robust vocabulary instruction must begin early (e.g., preschool) when the highest rate of vocabulary growth occurs (Farkas & Beron, 2004; National Early Literacy Panel [NELP], 2009).

## Accelerating Oral Language and Vocabulary

Oral language development during preschool contributes strongly to a child's reading ability (NELP, 2009; Snow, Burns, & Griffin, 1998), including semantic (i.e., word knowledge and expressive and receptive vocabulary), syntactic (i.e., knowledge of grammar rules and word order), and conceptual knowledge (i.e., world knowledge and domain knowledge; Storch & Whitehurst, 2002). Oral vocabulary, a critical component of oral language, specifically appears to play a decisive role in the development of young children's ability to read (Adams, 1990; Biemiller, 2003; National Reading Panel [NRP], 2000; Scarborough, 2001; Storch & Whitehurst, 2002) and is important for building domain knowledge (e.g., science, social studies) and academic learning (Hirsch, 2003). Overall, the preschool years represent an important window for developing children's oral language and vocabulary.

Growth in specialized vocabulary is crucial for the development of *domain knowledge*, or content learning, which accelerates both listening and reading comprehension (Hirsch, 2003). Given that oral vocabulary acquisition is stimulated through interactions with adults and other children, closing the gap between children with sufficient vocabulary and conceptual knowledge and those with limited knowledge and life experiences is dependent on teachers' abilities to provide effective instructional practices that emphasize multiple, extended exposures (Coyne, McCoach, & Kapp, 2007) to specialized vocabulary associated with academic content domains (Stahl, 2003; Walsh, 2003).

In the opening vignette, Ms. Thomas's goal was to extend children's oral vocabulary abilities through explicitly teaching content-related (science) vocabulary concepts in the context of talking about books and connected life experiences. Ms. Thomas's preschool children benefit from an instructional method that organizes large amounts of content vocabulary and information into meaningful networks with plentiful opportunities for repeated practice and extended learning (Neuman, 2006; Neuman & Dwyer, 2009). This instructional method takes place during Ms. Thomas's daily 20-minute shared book-reading lesson.

## HOW WE READ BOOKS MATTERS

Shared book reading can occur in whole-class or small-group instruction and has been studied for the past 25 years in Head Start or subsidized child care settings established to meet the language, literacy, and cognitive needs of children from low-income backgrounds (Blok, 1999; Ezell & Justice, 2005; Hargrave & Sénéchal, 2000; Scarborough & Dobrich, 1994; Spycher, 2009; Wasik & Bond, 2001; Wasik, Bond, & Hindman, 2006; Whitehurst & Lonigan, 1998). In more recent years, investigators have sought to understand how specific strategies can be embedded in the book-reading process to promote children's early language and literacy abilities via prereading instruction, comprehension skills, and word meaning discussions (Diamond, Justice, Siegler, & Snyder, 2013).

Collectively, eight research syntheses (Blok, 1999; Mol & Bus, 2011; Mol, Bus, & de Jong, 2009; Mol, Bus, de Jong, & Smeets, 2008; NELP, 2009; Scarborough & Dobrich, 1994; Swanson et al., 2011; WWC, 2006) and four observational investigations (Dickinson & Keebler, 1989; Dickinson & Smith, 1994; Wasik & Bond, 2001; Wasik et al., 2006) have examined the effectiveness of reading books in terms of children's vocabulary outcomes. The value of word-learning activities around shared book reading is also underscored by correlational and experimental research showing a strong relationship between vocabulary and reading comprehension (Elleman, Lindo, Morphy, & Compton, 2009). Together, these school-based shared book-reading studies allude to a book-reading style and structure that depend on the expertise of a responsive adult and his or her ability to create a cycle of rich dialogue and feedback that is important for vocabulary acceleration and oral language expansion. Specifically, the efficacy of shared book reading is influenced by the way children are read to and the adult–child interactions that occur around and beyond the actual book-reading event (Reese, Cox, Harte, & McAnally, 2003).

Evidence suggests that an interactive book-reading style, in which an adult integrates open-ended questions in a cycle of feedback and confirmation, is necessary for accelerating vocabulary learning in children with limited language and literacy experiences (Arnold & Whitehurst, 1994; Hart & Risley, 1995; Huttenlocher, Vasilyeva, Cymermann, & Levine, 2002; NELP, 2009; Wasik et al., 2006). Interactive book-reading methods allow children to learn about their world through strategic and active engagement via telling and discussing a story and its characters, events, and vocabulary (Ezell & Justice, 2005). For example, *dialogic reading* is a method of interactive book reading that includes structured scaffolds (e.g., oral repetitions, expansions, modeling of grammatical structures) and feedback that extend children's oral responses via open-ended questions about a book or book pictures (Lonigan, Shanahan, & Cunningham, 2008). Dialogic reading was first studied in 1988 and has been associated with growth in children's expressive language abilities (Whitehurst et al., 1988). In a dialogic book-reading approach, an adult extends children's oral language abilities by progressively talking less so that children can increasingly talk more (Flynn, 2011).

Within the last 10 years, researchers have investigated the benefits of interactive book-reading interventions that integrated vocabulary instruction within the context of learning about science (French, 2004; Leung, 2008; Neuman & Dwyer, 2011). In these interactive content-based shared book-reading studies, science-related words (e.g., *prism*, *frequency*) and concepts were taught with informational text-reading content sometimes organized around themes (e.g., light, growth/change, healthy habits, living things) guided by appropriate science standards (e.g., Benchmarks for Science Literacy). Young children significantly grew in the acquisition of complex science vocabulary (e.g., *opaque*, *transparent*) and experienced higher gains on standardized vocabulary measures. In a third study, World of Words (WOW; Neuman & Dwyer, 2011), based on a multimedia approach (e.g., content-related videos, picture cards, take-home books) with content-related book discussions, low-income preschool children benefited from instruction on word taxonomies (classifying words into categories) to facilitate retention of difficult words.

Although these studies emphasize the importance of content learning for vocabulary building, they also yield two important insights related to intensifying vocabulary instruction for young children from low-income settings. First, results from these studies confirm that "many of the academic and linguistic delays shown by children from low-income families derive from the lack of broad-based experiences and that these experiences can be recreated using a content-focused preschool curriculum" (French, 2004, p. 148). Second, results from these investigations suggest that more effective vocabulary interventions emphasize the structure of knowledge with explicit opportunities for children to "integrate knowledge into larger categories and concepts" (Neuman, 2010, p. 302).

The key to all models of interactive shared book reading lies, therefore, in the instructional expertise of an adult who is able to push children's conversational abilities beyond what they can independently accomplish and, in the process, expand children's knowledge about words and the world. In the earlier vignette, Ms. Thomas extended children's conceptual knowledge (e.g., "Water is a *liquid*. . . . Besides water, there are many other types of *liquids*.") while modeling more complex sentence structures (e.g., in response to the child's response, "The table," Ms. Thomas said, "Yes, the wooden table and the wooden chairs are also *solids*."). This instructional approach during shared book reading generates adult–child informational conversations that allow children to say something about a specific topic (e.g., science—the nature of water) and allow the teacher to respond in a way that continues the dialogue while attending to vocabulary usage and knowledge (Hart & Risley, 1995).

As illustrated in the instructional vignettes throughout this book, there are two significant benefits of interactive book reading (Cabell, Justice, Vukelich, Buell, & Han, 2008). First, interactive reading provides a context for *scaffolding* children's language skills. In the scaffolding process, an adult listens to oral responses in book conversations; determines if children have learned the taught concepts or have sufficient background knowledge; and, in response to children's understanding, extends children's language and learning in a discussion. Second, interactive book reading moves children from being passive listeners to being active learners (e.g., asking questions, pointing to pictures, providing additional information, talking about life experiences)—a condition that is conducive to high vocabulary growth (Sénéchal, Thomas, & Monker, 1995).

For example, in the prior instructional vignette (before reading the text *Amazing Water*), Ms. Thomas understands that some children are not able to respond to her open-ended question, "What do you see in this room that is *solid?*" Children may remain silent because they may require additional clarification to understand the science concept, *solid*, or they may not understand how to clearly express their thoughts. Ms. Thomas thinks quickly on her feet and scaffolds instruction using the following strategies:

1. She provides an additional explanation of the concept:

   "They (rocks on the science table) are *solid* because they feel hard when you touch them."

2. She provides additional examples of *solids* that can be found in the classroom:

   "I see maps on the walls that are *solid*, and I see lights on the ceiling that are a *solid*. If I touched them, they would feel hard. What else in the room is a *solid?*"

3. She models appropriate language use and more complex sentence structures when the children require assistance in expressing their thoughts more completely:

   "Yes, the wooden table and the wooden chairs are also *solids*. Good observing that the bird's nest on the science table is made of small sticks that are *solid*."

In addition to scaffolding instruction, Ms. Thomas provides opportunities for *active learning* by encouraging children to point to pictures representing vocabulary and connected concepts, expand on their oral explanations, and talk about related life experiences. In sum, by scaffolding instruction and encouraging active student learning, this teacher is providing a foundation for cognitive growth.

## EFFECTIVE BOOK-READING PRACTICES

Mounting evidence shows that children from low-income settings require vocabulary instruction that is able to close both early word and knowledge gaps; however, research indicates that typical shared book-reading practices may not be intensive enough to support children's language development (Marulis & Neuman, 2011, 2013; Mol et al., 2009; Penno, Wilkinson, & Moore, 2002), especially if children enter school with limited word and world knowledge. For example, results from a synthesis of 31 shared book-reading studies indicated that the strongest effects for shared book reading occurred in interventions that were implemented not by teachers but by nonpractitioners (e.g., researchers; Mol et al., 2009). In a second investigation, Penno and colleagues (2002) concluded that although listening to and talking about books with repeated story readings and target word explanations are beneficial for young children, more intensive strategies are required for children with low language abilities. In addition, evidence suggests that young children and teachers typically spend little time engaged in conversations (Dickinson & Tabors, 2001). Interactive shared book-reading practices that allow children to respond to and discuss important connections between words and concepts are crucial.

In general, findings from the past 25 years of shared book-reading research indicate that effective book-reading practices can have a significant impact on the school readiness of children from low-income families (Zevenbergen & Whitehurst, 2003). This is especially the case when the following scientifically tested book-reading practices and structure are integrated into the shared book-reading process:

- *Multiple text genres* (i.e., narrative and informational text) provide frequent exposure to words, connected concepts, and prior knowledge to boost comprehension (Duke, 2000; Duke, Bennett-Armistead, & Roberts, 2003).

- *Repeated reading* of stories allows children to ask more questions and talk more about book-related content as they listen to a text multiple times (Justice, Meier, & Wadpole, 2005; McGee & Schickedanz, 2007).

- *Explicit teaching of high-utility vocabulary words* prior to reading the book and/or during the book-reading process exposes children to words that are important for later learning and text reading (Beck, McKeown, & Kucan, 2002; de Temple & Snow, 2003; Justice et al., 2005). Explicit teaching may include open-ended questioning, pointing to book pictures that depict words, and repeating words used in sentences (Sénéchal, 1997).

- *"Before" and "after" shared reading conversations with brief in-context definitions* allow instruction and talking points to be distributed so that new information can be taught in the context of the storybook or informational text (Reese et al., 2003; Wasik et al., 2006).

- *Multiple exposures to vocabulary and connected concepts* allow children to learn words incrementally and cumulatively so that information accumulates over time (Dickinson & Smith, 1994; Stahl, 1991). Multiple exposures can occur during and beyond book discussions.

- *High cognitive* instruction requires children to use complex thinking skills (e.g., explaining, summarizing, associating, connecting, synthesizing, analyzing) to deeply process vocabulary (Dickinson & Smith, 1994). Participation in higher level discussions improves oral language abilities and increases vocabulary depth as children make connections between words and factual knowledge (van Kleeck, 2008).

- *Priming background knowledge* is a brief scaffolding exercise in which the learner, through the guidance of a teacher, retrieves information drawn from personal experiences to better understand new knowledge (Baker, Simmons, & Kame'enui, 1998; Simmons et al., 2008). Priming background knowledge facilitates comprehension and broadens children's world knowledge (Simmons et al., 2008).

When used in tandem, these evidence-based instructional practices yield a type of "extended vocabulary instruction [which] is characterized by explicit teaching that includes both contextual and definitional information, multiple exposures to target words in varied contexts, and experiences that promote deep processing of word meanings" (Coyne et al., 2007, p. 74). These practices form the foundation for Project WORLD's shared book-reading approach that is highlighted in this text.

## READING BOOKS TO CHILDREN FROM DIVERSE LINGUISTIC BACKGROUNDS

The majority of interactive shared book-reading investigations have been conducted with children who were native English speakers, with fewer preschool center-based studies including children who speak another language at home (Cohen, Kramer-Vida, & Frye, 2012a; Collins, 2010; Roberts & Neal, 2004; Shanahan & Beck, 2006; Silverman, 2007; Spycher, 2009). Although we know much about effective instructional book-reading practices for native English speakers, we have less guidance from research on how interactive shared book reading might be used to accelerate the vocabulary and conceptual knowledge of children acquiring early language and literacy instruction in English as a second language and/or in another language, such as Spanish.

We focus on Spanish language and literacy instruction in this text because approximately 79% of English language learners (ELLs) in the United States are from Spanish-language backgrounds (Ballantyne, Sanderman, & Levy, 2008). In addition, evidence suggests that attendance in high-quality preschool instruction has a greater effect on reducing the achievement gap for Latino students than for any other ethnic group (National Clearinghouse for English

Language Acquisition, 2011); however, we acknowledge that intensified shared book-reading practices also may be a starting point for equalizing the language experiences for a range of students from diverse linguistic backgrounds, who are speakers of other languages or nonstandard English (e.g., African American vernacular; Foorman, Seals, Anthony, & Pollard-Durodola, 2003) and are acquiring English at school.

Findings of existing shared book-reading research have indicated that young language learners benefited from explicit interactive book-reading instruction when acquiring English vocabulary, regardless of initial English oral language proficiency (Roberts & Neal, 2004). ELLs grew in vocabulary knowledge whether they were read to in English or another language (e.g., Spanish, Portuguese; Cohen et al., 2012a; Collins, 2010). One study, which intentionally integrated interactive book-reading behaviors while building content-specific (science) academic knowledge, noted that young children from diverse linguistic backgrounds (e.g., Spanish, English, bilingual) grew in their vocabulary outcomes (Spycher, 2009). Findings from these investigations indicate that reading books to ELLs may be a promising practice; however, the "quality of evidence" is limited due to an insufficient number of studies (Shanahan & Beck, 2006).

The following scientifically based shared book-reading practices seem promising for young preschool ELLs:

- Repeated readings of texts, which is important for ELLs acquiring English as a second language (Espinosa, 2010; McGee & Schickedanz, 2007)

- Book-reading content that is organized by content themes (e.g., science; Spycher, 2009)

- Explicit instruction on specific target word use (Cohen et al., 2012a; Roberts & Neal, 2004)

- Strategic use of visuals (e.g., pictures of target words, book illustrations; Cohen et al., 2012a)

- Opportunities to use language for academic discussions (Spycher, 2009)

Note that some practices overlap with those that have been implemented in studies with native English speakers. The instructional implication is that, in general, these strategies may benefit all young learners who require explicit and multiple exposures to vocabulary concepts via interactive academic discussions.

Beyond the shared book-reading literature, vocabulary research summarized by the seminal review *Developing Literacy in Second-Language Learners: A Report on the National Literacy Panel on Language-Minority Children and Youth* (NLP; August & Shanahan, 2006) provides guidance on instructional practices that are associated with higher student vocabulary outcomes. After examining studies of ELLs (ages 3–18) acquiring English as a societal language, the NLP (August & Shanahan, 2006) found a positive benefit for explicit instruction of 1) native and/or second oral language skill development to build complex vocabulary for higher order cognitive tasks (Anderson & Roit, 1998) in addition to 2) elaborated word meanings illustrated with visuals (Vaughn-Shavuo,

1990). The latter strategy—the strategic use of visuals—is especially appropriate for instructing children from diverse linguistic backgrounds (Gersten & Baker, 2000; Wallace, 2007). Findings from intervention research also suggest that young ELLs benefit from early language and literacy interventions that boost vocabulary and maximize student-focused talk (Saunders & Goldenberg, 1999) first and also maximize opportunities for building concepts in the context of expository and traditional narrative texts (Vaughn, Linan-Thompson, Pollard-Durodola, Mathes, & Cárdenas-Hagan, 2005).

In our research, we have used the WORLD content-related shared book-reading approach in bilingual settings to accelerate English or native Spanish content vocabulary acquisition (Pollard-Durodola, et al., 2012) in Spanish-speaking preschoolers. In these ELL studies, children were able to learn content vocabulary and concepts that were explicitly taught using the shared book-reading approach initially implemented with monolingual English-speaking children; however, preschool teachers of ELLs were taught to use additional oral language scaffolds to address the range of English language abilities when book reading was conducted in English. There is mounting evidence of the significant role of oral language in the literacy development of young ELLs.

Overall, instruction that supports and builds native language acquisition for ELLs provides an important foundation for second-language vocabulary learning (August & Shanahan, 2006; Cummins, 1979). Research specifically suggests that ELLs who enter preschool with significant vocabulary gaps may require high-quality vocabulary instruction in their primary language without affecting future English language and literacy development (Durán, Roseth, & Hoffman, 2010). This "additive approach" to language learning promotes reading and discussing books in children's native language while promoting second-language acquisition (National Association for the Education of Young Children [NAEYC], 2009). Instructional practices (e.g., shared book reading) that develop native language and/or second oral language abilities should prioritize the explicit teaching of word meanings (August & Shanahan, 2006; Gutiérrez, Zepeda, & Castro, 2010; Silverman, 2007). In summary, the WORLD book-reading approach can be used when providing native and/or second-language content vocabulary instruction.

## A FRAMEWORK FOR INTENSIFYING SHARED BOOK READING INSTRUCTION

### Knowledge Connections

### Instructional Science Vignette: What Can Water Do?

### Discussion After Reading *Amazing Water*

Ms. Thomas:  Let's think hard. What is the *difference* between a *solid* and a *liquid? [Children are silent.]*

Ms. Thomas: Okay, let's look at this picture of a *liquid*. How would this *liquid* feel?

Children: It would feel wet!

Ms. Thomas: Great thinking! A *liquid* would feel wet. Now let's look at this picture of a *solid*. How does this *solid* feel?

Child: It feels hard!

Ms. Thomas: Yes, the bricks in this picture are *solids*, and they feel hard just like this wooden floor that we are sitting on. So something that is a *solid* usually feels hard, and it also has a shape; however, a *liquid* feels wet, and it does not have a shape. Look at the picture here *[pointing to a picture of a glass of water in the book]* of this *liquid* water. *Liquids* and *solids* feel *different*. Water can be a *liquid*, but when it becomes cold, it freezes and becomes a *solid* like the *frozen* ice cube in this picture. The difference between a *solid* and a *liquid* is that a *solid* is hard and a *liquid* is wet.

How can we design instruction to teach content words such as *solid, liquid,* and *frozen* to young children in ways that are effective and accelerate academic learning? We can begin by examining the *knowledge hypothesis*: a theory that suggests that children accrue vocabulary knowledge by understanding relationships between new words and their connected concepts (Anderson & Freebody, 1981; Nagy, 2005). For example, it would be difficult to understand the words *solid* and *liquid* without knowing something about what water can do. It would be equally difficult to understand the words *branch, twig,* and *woods* without knowing something about trees. Knowing a word's meaning, then, implies that one understands the "network of concepts" connected with the word (Stahl & Nagy, 2006). Because vocabulary knowledge is built on sets of word relationships or associations (Nagy, 1988), the development of content vocabulary is dependent on knowledge that is embedded in language (McKeown & Curtis, 1987).

Nagy, in his classic *Teaching Vocabulary to Improve Reading Comprehension,* refers to this conceptual framework of intensive vocabulary instruction as "integration" (1988, p. 10), emphasizing that children should learn "new words not as words but as new concepts" (p. 21). This approach, in turn, derives from *schema theory,* according to which knowledge consists of relationships and not independent facts. As a result, new information can be learned by relating it to what we already know (Nagy, 1988).

These units of relationships or networks affect comprehension (Stahl & Nagy, 2006). Therefore, more effective vocabulary instruction should 1) help young children understand relationships between new vocabulary and connected concepts while 2) deepening their knowledge of the world (McCardle, Chhabra, & Kapinus, 2008).

The instructional implication in interactive shared book reading is that the educator must make explicit connections between taught words from the text and concepts embedded in children's background knowledge. By constructing networks of knowledge via high-priority content themes (e.g., earth), topics (e.g., land, water), and related words (e.g., *shore, river, island, meadow, valley, mountain*), teachers can assist children in understanding relationships between words and concepts while building their background knowledge (e.g., "The earth is made of land and water"). This pedagogical approach provides a foundation for listening comprehension in the early years and text comprehension beyond preschool.

## Knowledge Acceleration

In addition, it is important to develop a book-reading style and structure that allows children to learn more (e.g., information, words, prior knowledge) in less time (Becker, 1992). For example, in the *Model of School Learning*, Carroll (1963) hypothesized that learning is a function of the time spent learning divided by the time needed to learn. For learners with significant oral language needs, the time needed to learn may exceed the time that is generally available. Quality instruction can actually reduce the amount of time needed, thereby increasing the probability of learning. We advocate that interactive book-reading time be enhanced and learning accelerated by designing high-quality instruction that focuses on the following three dimensions:

1. *Instructional dimension:* explicitly taught priority skills (e.g., deep processing of vocabulary knowledge by summarizing similarities and differences between concepts)

   *Instructional example:* Ms. Thomas: [*Holding a picture of a waterfall and a picture of a swimming pool.*] These are both examples of *liquids*. Now I'll tell you what is the same about the *liquids* in these pictures. They are both wet. Now you tell me what is the same about the *liquids* in these pictures. Now tell me what is different about the *liquids* in these pictures.

2. *Instructional dimension:* clearly communicated information

   *Instructional example:* Ms. Thomas: This is *frozen*. You know something is *frozen* if it feels cold and hard when you touch it.

3. *Instructional dimension:* strategic scaffolds for difficult tasks

   *Instructional example:* Ms. Thomas: What is the difference between something that is *frozen* and a *liquid*? Look at this picture of a glass of orange juice. If something is a *liquid*, it is wet, such as water. Now look at this picture of the hand holding the ice cube. If something is *frozen*, it is hard and cold. The difference between something that is *frozen* and a *liquid* is that if something is *frozen*, it is hard and cold, and if something is a *liquid*, it is wet, like water.

These dimensions of instruction are fundamental for children who enter school from high-poverty settings and have much to learn in a limited period of time (Simmons et al., 2008).

## Three Principles of Instructional Design

Based on what we know about designing a quality of instruction that can increase the probability of learning while developing networks of concepts within a limited amount of time (e.g., a typical school day), we propose three principles of instructional design. These principles should guide content-based instruction to accelerate science and social studies concepts and vocabulary via an interactive book-reading process that incorporates recommended practices from shared book-reading and vocabulary research:

- *Align vocabulary instruction with content standards and objectives.*
- *Create multiple exposures to words and connected concepts via content-related themes.*
- *Develop opportunities to dialogue about word and world connections.*

These guiding principles formed the basis for designing the WORLD preschool shared book-reading intervention and were used to organize book-reading content, intensify vocabulary instruction, and accelerate meaning-based skills such as oral language, content-related vocabulary, and world knowledge.

Unlike the majority of prior shared book-reading studies, ours approached lexical sets of related vocabulary using books as one context for introducing words. Lexical sets focus children's attention on vocabulary–concept connections before, during, and after reading texts. This instructional approach encouraged a deep understanding of relationships across words while discussing relevant life experiences.

## SUGGESTED FURTHER READINGS

Ezell, H.K., & Justice, L.M. (2005). *Shared storybook reading: Building young children's language and emergent literacy skills.* Baltimore, MD: Paul H. Brookes Publishing Co.

Hirsch, E.D. (2006). Building knowledge: The case for bringing content into the language arts block and for knowledge-rich curriculum core for all children. *American Educator, 30*(1), 8–18.

Neuman, S.B. (2006). The knowledge gap: Implications for early education. In S.B. Neuman, & D. K. Dickinson (Eds.), *Handbook of early literacy research* (pp. 29–40). New York, NY: Guilford Press.

# Design and Development of the Words of Oral Reading and Language Development Shared Book-Reading Approach

2

**THIS CHAPTER SUMMARIZES THE PURPOSE OF** the WORLD investigation and introduces a pedagogical approach that early childhood educators can use to design vocabulary instruction to accelerate oral language and comprehension skills in young children. We first describe how the shared book-reading intervention was designed and developed in collaboration with preschool teachers who provided feedback on the vocabulary lessons. We then summarize the instructional implications for designing more intensive vocabulary instruction for young children.

**KEY IDEAS |** The key ideas discussed in this chapter are as follows:

1. Children require additional background knowledge to deeply understand critical science and social studies vocabulary and related knowledge *prior* to reading books and introducing new information.

2. Children who enter school with limited vocabulary and conceptual knowledge benefit from instructional extensiveness in which there are planned opportunities to use words in and beyond book discussions.

3. Children may require extensive background knowledge to facilitate learning abstract vocabulary concepts.

4. It is easier to monitor and extend children's learning and oral responses with meaningful feedback when shared book reading occurs in smaller group settings (five or six students).

## WHAT IS A DESIGN EXPERIMENT?

A design experiment is a methodology used to develop and refine an instructional intervention or curriculum. In this type of research, researchers conduct systematic observations and analyses to determine the conditions under which the intervention functions and is effective in real educational settings (Cobb, Confrey, diSessa, Lehrer, & Schauble, 2003; Collins, Joseph, & Bielaczyc, 2004; Gersten & Baker, 1998). Although design experiments have been used in non-educational settings (e.g., aeronautics, architecture, engineering, medicine) for a number of years, it only recently has received widespread interest in the field of teaching and learning as a means to improve educational practices (Bannan-Ritland, 2003; Cobb et al., 2003; Gorard, Roberts, & Taylor, 2004; Kelly, 2003). In the context of early childhood settings, this systematic, methodological approach allows researchers to better understand conditions that may hinder or facilitate the implementation of novel instructional practices (Bradley & Reinking, 2011).

In the WORLD shared book reading study, we designed instructional vocabulary tasks and small units of content-based shared book-reading lessons and field-tested them with teachers who subsequently provided feedback (e.g., focus group discussions) on their feasibility and usability within real classroom settings. Such feedback led to modifications in the instructional approach and materials.

The intervention was then tested in two randomized experiments in which preschool teachers were randomly assigned to implement the WORLD intervention or to continue with their typical shared book-reading practices as usual (comparison teachers). The purpose of the two experiments was to examine the effects of this shared book-reading approach on preschool children's receptive and expressive vocabulary outcomes on standardized tests—such as the Peabody Picture Vocabulary Test (PPVT; Dunn & Dunn, 1997) and the Expressive One-Word Picture Vocabulary Test (EOWPVT; Brownell, 2000)—and two researcher-developed curriculum-based measures. The two researcher-developed, curriculum-based measures were modeled after the PPVT-III and the EOWPVT to assess children's receptive and expressive knowledge of the content-related words taught during the WORLD shared book-reading intervention.

Overall, the design experiment was important for three reasons: First, it allowed researchers to use a systematic method of developing and modifying curricular lessons based on field-testing the lessons in real preschool classrooms. Second, it allowed researchers to investigate the efficacy of this interactive content-based shared book-reading approach with children who exhibited low vocabulary knowledge at the beginning of the school year and were at risk for future comprehension difficulties. Third, it allowed researchers to understand the feasibility and usability of empirically based shared book reading and vocabulary instructional practices.

In this chapter, we describe the preliminary WORLD intervention design. We also summarize the primary ways in which preschool teachers' input shaped researchers' understanding of teaching and vocabulary learning as they implemented the *preliminary* and 12-week shared book-reading intervention. Last, we discuss what we learned from teacher–researcher collaborations.

## COLLABORATION WITH TEACHERS

Our pedagogical approach was developed in collaboration with preschool teachers to better understand the feasibility of the evolving shared book-reading vocabulary tasks. Traditionally, teachers' knowledge, ideas, or insights have rarely been validated and used in meaningful ways in educational research (Nevárez-La Torre, 1999). Our initiative to include teachers as collaborative partners, interventionists, and participants in focus groups gave teachers an opportunity to reshape our understanding of teaching and vocabulary learning (Nevárez-La Torre, 1999). That is, as preschool teachers implemented the shared book lessons to build lexical sets of content vocabulary knowledge, we were able to make changes to the shared book-reading intervention and materials based on their feedback, thus allowing a deeper understanding of the critical features that contribute to teaching and/or learning success with students in real-world contexts (Klingner, Vaughn, & Schumm, 1998; Malouf & Schiller, 1995). To our knowledge, this is the only research-based approach to date that uses preschool teacher feedback to shape intervention strategies.

## PROCEDURES OF THE WORDS OF ORAL READING AND LANGUAGE DEVELOPMENT STUDY

### Shared Book-Reading Observations

Prior to beginning curriculum design, we as researchers wanted to observe shared book reading in Head Start and preschool classrooms with 4-year-old children from low-income families to better understand typical shared book-reading practices. Our observations occurred in a school district in the southwest in which 85% of the preschool students qualified for free and reduced-cost lunch and in which teachers implemented a published preschool curriculum aligned with state prekindergarten (pre-K) standards. Each classroom contained a class library of teacher-selected storybooks (approximately 200). The shared book-reading lessons were conducted with the entire class. Sessions generally averaged 5–7 minutes in length with minimal student engagement and adult–child talk, included little or no attention to vocabulary and connected concepts, and provided limited background knowledge for students. For the most part, preschool teachers read from storybooks but did not discuss book content.

### Evaluation of Preschool Curricula

We next reviewed three common preschool curricula and materials to better understand typical language- and literacy-focused instruction for young children. We found that existing preschool book-reading interventions or vocabulary tasks were somewhat consistent with research-based practices but provided limited resources for the teacher. There was little information on scaffolding instruction for difficult tasks, developing background knowledge related to new words, and opportunities for multiple exposures to target words and connected concepts.

Overall, we found that preschool teachers' typical shared book-reading vocabulary practices were not interactive. The existing curricula furthermore did not always guide teachers toward a better understanding of how to teach vocabulary, especially content-related vocabulary, to young children (Beck & McKeown, 2007; Neuman & Dwyer, 2009; Neuman & Roskos, 2005).

## Shared Book-Reading Research

Last, we reviewed the shared book-reading literature from the past 25 years, specifically focusing on effective shared book-reading practices for children raised in high-poverty settings. We found that certain book-reading styles (e.g., interactive) and shared book-reading features (e.g., repeated reading of text, brief in-context definitions, multiple exposures to words and connected concepts, explicit instruction on target words) were effective with children who required intensive instruction to close existing word and knowledge gaps. Because many previously conducted shared book-reading interventions do not examine the feasibility of this instructional approach, however, this was an impetus for including teacher feedback in our study.

Based on teacher observations, preschool curricula, and shared book-reading studies, we developed a conceptual framework for intensifying shared book-reading instruction (see Chapter 1). We then created a *design experiment*, or teaching experiment, to develop and refine the shared book-reading vocabulary intervention in cycles or phases of development: implementation/field-testing, evaluation, and modification. As stated previously, the design experiment included collaboration with preschool teachers who agreed to implement or field-test the intervention in their classrooms.

## Preliminary Words of Oral Reading and Language Development Intervention: Thematic Science Instruction

One goal in instructional design is to create curricular coherence by organizing information and connecting learning experiences through meaningful schemes so that children can be personally engaged in the learning process (Beane, 1995). With this goal in mind, we were guided by previous shared book-reading research (Wasik & Bond, 2001; Wasik et al., 2006; Sénéchal et al., 1995) and preschool state and national standards in our selection of important content themes: broad, universal ideas about life, nature, or society. These themes were used to organize shared book-reading content and to provide opportunities to use vocabulary in a broader context of conceptually related knowledge networks.

The preliminary 2-week thematic science units contained scientifically tested book-reading practices and structures (e.g., repeated reading of texts, explicitly teaching high-utility vocabulary words, brief in-context discussions of word meanings) that were integrated into a 5-day scope and sequence. Within this instructional cycle, explicit vocabulary instruction was distributed before, during, and after reading a book.

## Five-Day Scope and Sequence

In a 5-day scope and sequence, one theme and one smaller topic was introduced and reviewed in-depth with a storybook and informational text. Days 1 and 3 of the 5-day cycle introduced a new book, three new theme-related words, and new science concepts. Days 2 and 4 included a second reading of the book and reviewed word meanings and concepts. Lessons on Days 1 and 2 focused on reading a storybook, whereas lessons on Days 3 and 4 focused on reading an informational text. Finally, Day 5 activities were designed to review all words and concepts. In sum, specific days were used to introduce, review, and integrate new words and science concepts across varied text genres. The instruction was designed, in this manner, to routinely integrate multiple exposures to content vocabulary and concepts and to build and extend children's background knowledge with briskly paced explicit instruction. We anticipated that daily WORLD lessons would last 15–20 minutes.

## Before, During, and After Reading Discussions

The WORLD book-reading routine was designed to distribute vocabulary and related content instruction before, during, and after reading the text with interactive discussions primarily occurring before and after reading. This instructional routine was important because it increased the number of exposures to words and content and allowed teachers to integrate a range of lower and higher cognitive tasks throughout the book-reading process. Before reading a text, teachers previewed three new words, using pictures embedded in the lesson material. While reading the book, teachers then provided brief in-context explanations of the target words by pointing to a related book picture/illustration to clarify word meaning (e.g., "These are twigs. Twigs are small sticks that have fallen off a tree. Here we see the owls in their home made of twigs, leaves, and owl feathers. Why do you think they use these things to make their home?"). Finally, after reading the book, target words and book content were reviewed in a discussion about related life experiences.

## SELECTION OF CONTENT-RELATED VOCABULARY

Content vocabulary selected 1) was visually represented in the text, 2) was thematically related to the science theme, 3) could be used to build important background knowledge, and 4) was applicable to higher order concepts and thinking skills (e.g., making predictions and associations). Words selected were typically nouns, followed by verbs, all selected because they were likely to appear in a wide variety of texts and were less likely to be learned by children in everyday conversations (Beck et al., 2002; Stahl, 1991). Because we wanted to build children's life experiences, vocabulary selection included high-frequency words that could increase their ability to use more sophisticated language to talk about familiar topics (e.g., *twigs* instead of *sticks*; Beck et al., 2002), as well as words that would increase children's conceptual understanding of the world—specifically, content vocabulary that was semantically related (e.g., *twig, cone, trunk, branch, woods*) and could be utilized to build networks of knowledge that would facilitate future text comprehension.

## DETERMINING THE CONTINUATION OF QUESTIONS TO PROMPT INTERACTION

Building on Dickinson and Smith's (1994) research, tasks were designed along a cognitive continuum from less complex cognitive tasks to more complex higher cognitive tasks that required deep processing of learned knowledge. The following examples reflect the range of instructional opportunities in the WORLD shared book-reading curriculum. The continuum of questions recognizes that different question types prompt different types of information; therefore, it was important to specify questions to promote a rich dialogue.

- Labeling/identifying/recalling: "What are some things in nature? What is the name of this picture? What is the girl doing in this picture?"
- Defining/describing: "Be the teacher and tell us about branches."
- Predicting: "What do you think you will learn in this book? What do you think will happen in this story?"
- Sequencing/retelling: "Retell this story using the pictures. What happened first? What happened last?"
- Associating: "Look at these pictures [woods and branches]. What is the same about these pictures? What is different about these pictures? What is the difference between a *bulb* and a *stem*?"

## YEAR 1: TEACHER RECOMMENDATIONS AFTER IMPLEMENTING THE PRELIMINARY SCIENCE UNITS

In the first year of the study, four preschool teachers and two instructional assistants at an early childhood center implemented lessons organized into 2-week thematic science units. We provided all books and materials to teachers and provided 4 hours of professional development (PD) prior to implementing the intervention. In this PD session, researchers modeled instructional strategies and provided opportunities for teachers to role-play and practice the lessons in pairs with feedback.

During this year of field-testing lessons, teachers talked with researchers on an ongoing basis and participated in two focus groups in which they made recommendations to increase the feasibility of the shared book-reading instructional materials and approach. Among the instructional issues discussed and adopted, the following are four of the primary recommendations that were integrated into the WORLD shared book-reading approach.

## Recommendation 1: Elicit Individual Child Responses

Preschool teachers suggested that when reading and talking about books, instruction should allow for attention to individual child responses in addition to group responses and discussions. Child-centered activities would encourage children to talk to each other in pairs, using target words and providing opportunities for individual children to talk about an important concept using target words. We integrated more student-centered tasks so that when a child responded to a partner or provided an individual response, the teacher would listen, provide corrections or extensions of information, and ask questions to assist children in making important connections to words, concepts, and life experiences before reading the book.

## Example of Paired Practice

Ms. Thomas:  Look at the cover of our book *Trees Are Terrific.* In this book, we'll learn about trees and that trees are living things. Look at this picture.

On this page, you'll learn about our magic word *trunk.* What do you think we'll learn about the tree *trunk* on this page? Tell your partner what you think you will learn about a tree *trunk,* and try to use the word *trunk* when you talk.

## Example of Individual Practice

Ms. Thomas:  Today, as I look into the magic mirror, I see that we are all outside. In the mirror, I'm looking at the big part of a tree. Hmm, it is standing straight and tall, and it is holding up all the tree branches. It looks like the *stem* of a tree. Does anyone know what word the magic mirror is showing me today?

Children:  *Trunk!*

Child:  It's a tree *trunk.*

Ms. Thomas:  Good thinking. Yes, I see a tall, strong tree *trunk* when I look into the magic mirror. Gloria, it's your turn to look into the magic mirror and tell us about the *trunk* that you see. Everyone, let's listen to Gloria.

## Recommendation 2: Build Background Knowledge Extensively

Teachers confirmed that children with limited knowledge require additional background knowledge to deeply understand critical science and social studies vocabulary and related knowledge prior to reading books and introducing new information. Providing more background information would allow teachers to create a new schema or conceptual framework so that children would be able to make connections between familiar and unfamiliar concepts (Hickman & Pollard-Durodola, 2009).

To facilitate interactive discussions and prime background knowledge in a 15–20 minute shared book-reading lesson, researchers created standalone visuals (i.e., theme posters and picture/concept cards) that would allow teachers to introduce and review new information as well as scaffold discussions of abstract concepts that are difficult for young children.

## Example of Thematic Posters

An 8½ × 14-inch poster consisting of a carefully selected collage of content-related photographs was created as a focus for introducing the theme on the first day of the 5-day lesson cycle before reading the book. In the following discussion, the teacher modeled how to talk about the theme using complete sentences and encouraged children to do the same.

Ms. Thomas: This week we're going to read books and learn about living things! Living things include plants, animals, and people. Living things are special because they need water, air, and sunlight to help them live and grow.

Everyone, look at these pictures *[holding a poster, a collage of photographs representing living things]*. I'll tell you about some of the living things that you see in these pictures. *[This is a modified version of the poster used in the actual lesson.]*

Look *[pointing to pictures of trees and woods]*, I see a kind of plant. It is a tree. Trees are living things because they live and grow. They also need sunlight and water. Trees can grow to become very tall and they grow from the ground. Now it's your turn to tell us about the living things that you see in these pictures.

## Example of Picture/Concept Cards

Ms. Thomas: *[Before reading the book, the teacher points to a picture/concept card of a pine* cone.*]* Everyone, look at this picture. This is a *cone*. A *cone* is the part of the tree that holds the seeds. What is this?

Child: It's a *cone!*

Children: A *cone!*

Ms. Thomas:  Yes, it's a *cone*. Now let's talk about this *cone*. Here we see a *cone* for an evergreen tree that is a pine tree. Where do you think the seeds are on the *cone*? *[A discussion follows, and children ask questions about the* cones *and the evergreen trees.]*

In the remaining 2 years of the study, preschool teachers emphasized the benefits of using visuals during the WORLD shared book-reading approach because they provide a visual representation of abstract concepts and can be used to solidify, reinforce, and develop new word and world knowledge. In general, the visual tools proved beneficial for scaffolding instructional tasks requiring higher order thinking, such as discussing similarities and differences of concepts and words. Due to potential pitfalls in relying on visuals to teach content vocabulary and connected concepts (e.g., misinterpretation of illustrations, narrowly associating vocabulary with specific visual representations; Schickedanz & Collins, 2012), teachers also provided feedback on visual representations that might be confusing for young children. We eventually created two picture/concept cards for each vocabulary concept (e.g., Day 1 picture/concept card to introduce the word and Day 2 picture/concept card to review the word) to assist children in generalizing knowledge across word representations.

### Recommendation 3: Provide More Scaffolding Suggestions for More Difficult Tasks

The language development activities were challenging for both students and teachers, as they often contained tasks that required higher cognitive skills, which contribute to vocabulary acquisition. The teachers in our study were not used to talking about books in an interactive style or employing scaffolding opportunities to increase student talk within the context of higher cognitive tasks. However, at the same time, teachers expressed a preference for less scripted shared book-reading lessons. The original lessons contained explicit teacher-response suggestions and scaffolds to extend children's thinking and oral language responses.

We decided to limit the amount and type of embedded scaffolding procedures (e.g., explicit strategies for providing feedback, extending oral responses) in the shared book-reading lessons based on teacher feedback. We continued to discuss with teachers ways to provide more effective instructional scaffolding, especially during interactive discussions around high-cognitive tasks (e.g., "What is the difference between an *island* and a *meadow*?"). Ultimately, we provided more scaffolding suggestions in ongoing PD discussions at targeted times throughout the year when researchers met with teachers to provide feedback (based on videotaped observations) on their intervention implementation practices.

## Recommendation 4: When Appropriate, Read Select Passages from Informational Texts

Although the use of informational texts provides opportunities to build children's background knowledge on broad themes (e.g., learning more about living things, the earth, places in which we live on the earth) and smaller topics (e.g., plants, trees, ocean animals, cities, schools), preschool teachers found that some texts contained lengthy passages, complex terminology, and complicated syntax. To address this problem, we modified some shared book-reading lessons so that teachers only read select passages from challenging informational texts that contained too many facts for children to learn. We also eliminated those texts with too many unfamiliar vocabulary concepts. For example, when selecting an informational text on farm animals in the *living things* theme, we eliminated texts that contained too many labeled photographs of farm animals (e.g., "This is a cow. This is a horse. This is a rooster. This is a pig.") in favor of a text with fewer but richer concepts that allowed the animal topic to be taught in depth (e.g., "This animal has a hoof. A hoof is the hard foot that some animals have, such as cows and horses. Here we see the lamb's hoof. How does a lamb use his hoof?").

These teacher recommendations were used to guide the modification of existing instructional tasks and the development of a 12-week science-based shared book-reading intervention with supporting visual materials.

## YEAR 2: TEACHER RECOMMENDATIONS AFTER IMPLEMENTING 12 WEEKS OF SCIENCE INSTRUCTION

During the second year of the study, 11 randomly assigned teachers implemented a 12-week version of the content-based shared book-reading intervention with a group of approximately 9–10 children. These children were selected to participate in the study because they exhibited low vocabulary knowledge at school entry, as evidenced by their scores on the PPVT-III, form A (Dunn & Dunn, 1997). The intervention lessons were implemented daily for 15–20 minutes and replaced teachers' typical shared book-reading instructional practices. In this preliminary intervention, 24 books were selected and used. From these, a corpus of 72 vocabulary words was taught via lexical sets (e.g., *trunk, branch, woods*) to assist children in understanding two science themes (i.e., *nature* and *living things*). Topics in the *nature* theme included water, air, light, and seasons. For *living things,* the topics included plants, animals, and our body.

Three of the primary teacher recommendations were integrated into the WORLD book-reading approach to improve the feasibility of vocabulary tasks.

### Recommendation 1: Clarify Abstract Vocabulary Knowledge

Teachers confirmed that knowing a word's meaning is dependent on understanding the knowledge units that are connected with the word (Stahl & Nagy, 2006). Thus some vocabulary words are difficult to teach due to the abstract nature of the connected concept(s). The following example illustrates the instructional complexity of teaching abstract word knowledge to young children.

Teachers introduced the word *year* in the *nature* theme and the topic of seasons. Using the informational text *A Book of Seasons/Un libro de las estaciones* (Provensen, 2008), the word *year* was described "as the time that passes from one birthday to the next." The following vignette summarizes how the concept of *year* was developed and taught.

Ms. Thomas: This week, I want you to pay attention to two new magic words. The first magic word is *year*. Look at this photograph [*a picture of a calendar with 12 months is displayed*]. This photograph of a calendar shows 1 *year*. A *year* is the amount of time that passes from one birthday to the next. If you are 4 *years* old, in another *year* you will be 5 years old. The calendar in this photograph shows 1 *year*. It shows all the months that are in a *year*. [*Students then discuss how old they are and how old they will be in 1 year.*]

On Day 2 of this lesson, the vocabulary concept, *year,* is reviewed prior to rereading the informational text *A Book of Seasons/Un libro de las estaciones.* The following vocabulary review process was implemented:

Ms. Thomas: Look at this photograph [*pointing to a photograph of a yearly planner with 12 months*]. What do you think this calendar shows us? [*A discussion follows, and individual children are selected to talk about the term* year.]

Ms. Thomas: You're right; a year is the time that passes from one birthday to the next. Look at this photograph. What is happening here? [*There is a discussion about a photograph of a boy with a birthday cake with three candles.*] These two photographs both show an example of a *year*. In this picture, the candles on this cake show how old the boy is. Each candle is 1 *year*. Let's count to see how old this boy is. [*The children count the three candles.*]

Ms. Thomas: How old do you think the boy will be on this birthday? How old do you think the boy will be on his birthday in one *year*? [*There is a discussion about the boy's age, and children say how old they are and how old they will be in one year.*]

Although various methods were used to facilitate the teaching of the concept of *year,* including the illustration of the calendar and the birthday cake, teachers in the study ultimately indicated that it was difficult for young children to understand the concept of the passage of time, although they had discussed the concept of *change* when talking about the changing seasons. The word *year* and a few other vocabulary words that were difficult to teach via *scaffolding* eventually were eliminated from the intervention. Other abstract word meanings were refined and clarified; however, we also discussed how abstract concepts could be clarified and taught if additional *background knowledge* was provided to children.

In Year 2, it became clearer from discussions between teachers and researchers that the final criteria for selecting content words should include the following:

- High-utility words that are important for later learning
- Words related to important science concepts and topics
- Words depicted within and outside of the book (e.g., photographs from various sources) in ways that are clearly understood by children to ensure that concepts and words are not misinterpreted

### Recommendation 2: Utilize a Smaller Group Size

Teachers shared that they found it difficult to manage the behavior of the large group of young children (9–10 students) during the 15-minute book discussions, even with the help of an instructional aide, who engaged students in the class who were not participating in the shared book-reading intervention with other activities (e.g., computer time, preschool center-based activities). In addition, they noted that it was easier to monitor and extend children's learning and oral responses with meaningful feedback in a smaller group setting. As a result, they recommended a smaller group size (five or six students).

### Recommendation 3: Discuss the Rationale for Scientifically Based Strategies

It became evident from discussions with teachers that although they received initial professional development on critical intervention design and delivery features of the shared book-reading process, they did not always understand the rationale or importance of novel practices (e.g., repeated text readings, brief in-context definitions, distributed teacher behaviors while reading the text) and the use of informational text. It was decided, based on this finding, that professional development for the following year would not only address how to build lexical sets of knowledge and content words in the WORLD approach but also make clear the scientific rationale supporting the instructional strategies that could foster more vocabulary building during an interactive shared book–reading process.

### YEAR 2: STUDENT VOCABULARY OUTCOMES AND FINAL CURRICULAR MODIFICATIONS

After 12 weeks of content-based shared book-reading instruction, preschool students in the WORLD intervention ($n = 69$) significantly outperformed students in the comparison condition ($n = 56$) on researcher-developed measures of receptive and expressive vocabulary that assessed children's knowledge of the concepts that were *taught* in the WORLD approach.

There were, however, no significant effects on standardized vocabulary measures, in this first experiment, which meant that preschool children's vocabulary learning did not generalize to standardized receptive (PPVT; Dunn & Dunn, 1997) and expressive (EOWPVT; Brownell, 2000) measures (Pollard-Durodola, Gonzalez, Simmons, Kwok, Taylor, Davis, and Simmons, 2011). This finding is not unexpected, given the possibility that standardized measures often are insensitive to vocabulary growth (Elleman, Lindo, Morphy, & Compton, 2009).

We specifically hypothesized that in the first experiment, the brief intervention period (12 weeks) and large group size (9–10 children) contributed to *insufficient dialogue opportunities* for preschool children with limited vocabulary and world knowledge (Pollard-Durodola et al., 2011). Based on the study's results and teacher recommendations, the goal at the end of the second year was to increase the *instructional extensiveness* of the intervention in the following ways:

1.  Additional themes (i.e., science and social studies) and books were integrated into the intervention for a total of *18 weeks of lessons,* organized by lexical networks of knowledge. This included a) two science themes (i.e., *nature* and *living things*) around ten smaller science topics (e.g., plants, animals) and b) two social studies themes (i.e., *places where we live and go* and *earth: land and water*) around six smaller social studies topics (e.g., city, grocery store).

2.  Greater instructional emphasis was placed on *higher cognitive tasks* (e.g., making associations) that occurred mostly after reading the book.

3.  Intervention *group size was reduced.*

In the more extensive curriculum, preschool teachers would continue to introduce a new unit of instruction every 5 days within the 5-day instructional cycle. However, this routine was intensified so that more time would be spent priming students' background knowledge using the thematic poster and previewing vocabulary using the picture/concept cards before reading the texts. See Figure 2.1.

## YEAR 3: RESULTS AFTER IMPLEMENTING 18 WEEKS OF CONTENT INSTRUCTION WITH EMPHASIS ON HIGHER COGNITIVE THINKING

In the second experimental study, we evaluated the effectiveness of the refined intervention on the vocabulary outcomes of 96 preschool students. Twenty-one preschool teachers were randomly assigned to either implement the WORLD intervention ($n$ = 13) or use their usual shared book-reading practices (comparison, $n$ = 8) with smaller groups (five to six students). As in previous years, student participants exhibited low vocabulary knowledge at school entry, as evidenced by their scores on the PPVT-III, form A (Dunn & Dunn, 1997). In this year, students in the WORLD intervention significantly outperformed students in the comparison condition on researcher-developed measures of receptive and expressive content-related vocabulary. This indicated that children in the shared book-reading intervention learned the vocabulary concepts that were taught. However, unlike in the previous 12-week study, treatment students also outperformed students in the comparison condition on a standardized

| | Day 1 | Day 2 | Day 3 | Day 4 | Day 5 |
|---|---|---|---|---|---|
| Title | *The Adventures of Maxi the Taxi Dog* | | *Taking a Walk* | | *The Adventures of Maxi the Taxi Dog* and *Taking a Walk* |
| Text structure | Story | | Information book | | Story and information book |
| Before reading | 5 minutes<br><br>Talk about the theme.<br><br>Preview magic words.<br><br>Discuss text structure and prediction. | 3–4 minutes<br><br>Talk about magic words. | 5 minutes<br><br>Preview magic words.<br><br>Discuss text structure and prediction. | 3–4 minutes<br><br>Talk about magic words. | 15 minutes<br><br>Discuss magic words pages (both books).<br><br>Play the Same Game.<br><br>Play Ready, Set, Go!<br><br>Play Magic Mirror.<br><br>Talk about the theme.<br><br>Wrap up. |
| While reading | 5 minutes<br><br>Summarize listening goals.<br><br>Introduce magic words within the book.<br><br>Read the book. | 6 minutes<br><br>Summarize listening goals.<br><br>Read the book. | 5 minutes<br><br>Summarize listening goals.<br><br>Introduce magic words within the book.<br><br>Read the book. | 6 minutes<br><br>Summarize listening goals.<br><br>Read the book. | |
| After reading | 5 minutes<br><br>Review magic words.<br><br>Answer book questions with magic words.<br><br>Wrap up. | 6 minutes<br><br>Play Ready, Set, Go!<br><br>Answer challenge questions with magic words.<br><br>Play Magic Mirror.<br><br>Wrap up. | 10 minutes<br><br>Review magic words.<br><br>Answer book questions with magic words.<br><br>Wrap up. | 6 minutes<br><br>Play Ready, Set, Go!<br><br>Answer challenge questions with magic words.<br><br>Play Magic Mirror.<br><br>Wrap up. | |
| Cards | Theme card A: Places where we live and go<br><br>1: City<br><br>2: Building | 3: City<br><br>4: Building<br><br>(1–4 for Ready, Set, Go!) | 5: Neighbor<br><br>6: Bridge | 7: Neighbor<br><br>8: Bridge<br><br>(1–8 for Ready, Set, Go!) | Theme card A: Places where we live and go<br><br>Vocabulary cards: 1–8 |
| Total time | 15 minutes | 15–16 minutes | 20 minutes | 15–16 minutes | 15 minutes |

**Figure 2.1.** Lesson content map.

receptive vocabulary measure (PPVT-III; Gonzalez, Pollard-Durodola, Taylor, Simmons, Davis, & Simmons, 2011).

Overall, results from this year revealed that teachers' use of higher cognitive vocabulary tasks (e.g., *Challenge Questions*) or association questions around vocabulary and comprehension (e.g., concepts) positively predicted growth in generalized vocabulary. Specifically, the more time spent on vocabulary-related association talk (e.g., talking about connections and relationships between words and concepts), as described in the following vignette, the more children benefited in terms of general receptive and expressive vocabulary (Gonzalez, Pollard-Durodola, Simmons, Taylor, Davis, Fogarty, & Simmons, 2013).

## Instructional Social Studies Vignette: Land and Water

### Discussion After Rereading *The Runaway Bunny*

Ms. Thomas: It is time for our challenge questions. Let's sit tall and think big! We have learned about *streams* and *rivers* on the earth. What do you think is the difference between a *stream* and a *river*? *[There is silence.]*

Ms. Thomas: What's a stream? Let's look at this picture of a *stream*, and let's look at this picture of a *river*.

Child: A *stream* is a little water *[pointing to the picture]* here.

Ms. Thomas: You're correct. A *stream* is a little bit of water that moves slowly between the land. Let's compare the *stream* in this picture with the *river* in this picture *[pointing to an adjacent picture]*.

Children: The *river* is bigger.

Child: The *stream* is smaller than the *river*.

Ms. Thomas: Yes, a *stream* is smaller than a big, wide *river*. Would we need a *bridge* *[bridge was taught in a previous lesson]* to cross a big *river*? Why or why not?

Child: A *bridge* would get you to the other side.

Child: We could walk across the *bridge*!

Child: The *bridge* would keep you dry.

Ms. Thomas: Yes, it would, and yes, we could walk across the *bridge*—going from one side of the river to the other. Let's all say this together, "A *bridge* can help us get to the other side of a river." *[Students respond.]*

Now it's time for our "big-kid question." Let's see who can figure it out.

Could a really big boat float on a *river* or on a *stream*? Why or why not?

### Instructional Implications

Conversations and collaborations with teachers in the WORLD study confirmed that preschool instruction can support young children's vocabulary learning through multiple opportunities for children to hear and use content-related words and connected concepts while building networks of domain knowledge.

The instructional implication is that words that are important for building domain knowledge must be encountered in multiple ways and experiences (e.g., thematic instruction, center-based instruction) and is the consequence of a vocabulary instruction method that is "intentional and preplanned" (Christie, 2008, p. 30), resulting in a series of connected learning experiences for young children.

Our observations of typical shared book-reading practices in preschool settings confirmed that these connected learning experiences must be driven by advance decisions, such as which words to teach, which texts are conducive to generating rich conversations about world and word connections, and how to more effectively organize children's experiences and book-reading content to accelerate learning and language development while building world knowledge.

Although children's learning (e.g., oral vocabulary, language abilities, content knowledge) can be stimulated and extended in a variety of ways, research indicates that at-risk children benefit from systematic instruction and organization of content so that vocabulary acquisition is not left to chance.

In the following chapters, we provide specific guidance on how daily book-reading vocabulary routines can be planned and intensified by integrating three instructional design principles. The goal is to provide a feasible framework for making decisions about what and how to teach young children in ways that ultimately build a strong oral language foundation through adult–child interactions and shared conversations about words, life, and the world.

## SUGGESTED FURTHER READINGS

Gonzalez, J.E., Pollard-Durodola, S.D., Taylor, A., Simmons, D.C., Davis, M., & Simmons, L. (2011). Developing low income preschooler's social studies and science vocabulary through content-focused shared book reading. *Journal of Research on Educational Effectiveness, 4,* 25–52.

Pollard-Durodola, S.D., Gonzalez, J.E., Simmons, D.C., Kwok, O., Taylor, A.B., Davis, M.J., Kim, M., & Simmons, L. (2011). The effects of an intensive shared book reading intervention for preschool children at-risk for vocabulary delay. *Exceptional Children, 77,* 161–183.

Simmons, D.C., Pollard-Durodola, S.D., Gonzalez, J.E., Davis, M., & Simmons, L. (2008). Shared book reading interventions. In S.B. Neuman (Ed.), *Educating the other America* (pp. 187–212). Baltimore, MD: Paul H. Brookes Publishing Co.

# Aligning Vocabulary Instruction with Content Standards and Objectives

## Selecting and Organizing Book-Reading Content

3

**THIS CHAPTER FOCUSES ON HOW TO** use preschool content and language standards to guide the selection and thematic organization of shared book-reading content. We first discuss the importance of designing thematic instruction that begins with what students should learn. We then provide examples of content themes and language objectives that guided the development of the WORLD curriculum. Last, we discuss how to generate high-priority themes from science and social studies standards.

**KEY IDEAS |** The key ideas discussed in this chapter are as follows:

1. Big-idea standards can provide a starting point for content learning.

2. Aligning preschool instruction with standards ensures that young children are equipped with content knowledge and language skills that are necessary for kindergarten and beyond.

3. When designing shared book-reading instruction, science and social studies standards can be used to generate relevant themes and connected topics that guide the selection and organization of book-reading content.

4. Oral language objectives also should be considered because they are important for language acquisition in all children.

## BIG-IDEA INSTRUCTION

To close gaps in language learning and accelerate the development of conceptual knowledge in young children, it is important first to identify domains of knowledge that preschoolers need. Big-idea instruction suggests that some domains of knowledge, or "big ideas," are more important than others and should be taught more thoroughly to accelerate academic learning (Brophy, 1992; Carnine, 1994; Simmons et al., 2008). Big ideas are important because they focus attention on high-priority content that serve as anchors for smaller ideas or topics.

Identifying the big ideas is the initial step of backward curriculum mapping, an instructional design process by which one begins with the "end in mind" (Covey, 2013, p. 102; McTighe & Wiggins, 1998, p. 7) of what the students should learn. This approach to designing an instructional framework contrasts sharply with instructional approaches that are anchored to teaching materials or topics. For example, McTighe and Wiggins noted that "many teachers begin with textbooks, favorite lessons, and time-honored activities" (1998, p. 7) rather than making instructional decisions based on what knowledge is important for students to know and understand. Although we acknowledge that there is a time and place for "favorite books" and reading for pleasure, instructional decisions designed to accelerate conceptual knowledge should be guided by what students need to learn. There will always be more content than can be taught in one lesson, day, or academic year. Identifying big-idea concepts helps teachers establish instructional priorities.

In early vocabulary and language development, the environmental and experiential conditions in low-income homes often result in significant disparities in young children's breadth and depth of vocabulary (Simmons et al., 2008). The question then becomes what the big ideas are that can be integrated into shared book reading to provide a threshold for accelerating world and word learning. Hirsch suggested that classroom instruction should expose children to big ideas related to the "worlds of nature and culture" (2006, p. 17) because these domains of knowledge represent concepts that are commonly understood by literate adult readers. Within the context of reading books to children, Hirsch posited that big ideas about nature (e.g., science) and culture (e.g., social studies) can be accelerated via "'topic immersion,' in which adults read a sequence of books organized by relevant topics over a period of days and weeks instead of selecting 'stand-alone'" (2006, p. 20) texts and materials that are read and discussed in a single occasion.

In a topic immersion approach to conceptual knowledge building, children are immersed in rich, deep discussions on the same topic or big idea for a period of time so that learning new words becomes easier as the context becomes more familiar (Landauer & Dumais, 1997). Within this approach to teaching and learning, content-related topics are organized under the umbrella of bigger themes—broad universal ideas about life, nature, and society. For example, the broader nature theme includes smaller topics, such as plants and animals. The broader culture theme might include the study of places where we live and go with smaller topics on cities and houses.

The following WORLD shared book-reading vignette illustrates how big ideas can provide a threshold—a starting or entry point—for content learning. In this lesson, preschool children are studying the topic of cities and learning two new words—one of the words is *neighbor,* a person who lives in a building or house close to you. Students have read the storybook *The Adventures of Maxi the Taxi Dog* (Barracca & Barracca, 1990) on the first and second days of this instructional unit and discussed what the dog character saw and did in a city (e.g., "He saw many people crossing the street in busy intersections."). Today, Ms. Thomas introduces a new book, *Taking a Walk* (Emberley, 1990), to expand children's knowledge about what they might see if they were taking a walk in a city.

## Instructional Social Studies Vignette: Cities

### Discussion Before Reading *Taking a Walk*

#### Day 3

Ms. Thomas:  Look at the cover of the new book that we are reading today, *Taking a Walk.* We'll continue to learn about cities in this book. This book is an information book, and it teaches us information about cities. One of the magic words that you will listen for as we read the book is the word *neighbor.*

*[Ms. Thomas points to two houses in a picture/concept card.]* A *neighbor* is a person who lives in a building or house close to you. *[There is a discussion about who children's neighbors are and what they like to do with their neighbors.]*

Okay, everyone, sit next to your partner. *[Ms. Thomas waits for children to sit in pairs.]* Let's look at the pictures to find out what we will learn about cities before reading the book. *[Ms. Thomas slowly shows the book pages, and there is a discussion based on what children notice in the pictures. She then stops on one page.]*

On this page, we will learn about *neighbors.* What do you think we will learn about *neighbors* on this page? Tell your partner.

*[Ms. Thomas then reads the book and asks questions about what children learned about cities while scaffolding instruction to ensure that the children can respond to and discuss concepts, using the word* neighbor.*]*

The next day, children read the book again.

### Discussion Before Rereading *Taking a Walk*

#### Day 4

Ms. Thomas:  Yesterday, we read an information book called *Taking a Walk,* and we learned two new magic words. Let's look at some pictures of the words that we learned.

Okay, let's look at this picture of a house. If this is your house, then this *[pointing to the house next door]* is your neighbor's house. How do you know that people are neighbors?

| | |
|---|---|
| Child: | Close by. |
| Child: | When they live near you. |
| Ms. Thomas: | Yes, a *neighbor* is someone who lives close to you. When people live in a house or apartment that is close by, we can say they are *neighbors*. |
| | In cities, people may live close to each other because there is limited space. |
| | What are some things that people can do with their *neighbor?* |
| Child: | They can play in the park. |
| Child: | Eat at their house. |
| Ms. Thomas: | Yes, *neighbors* can invite you next door to their home to have dinner, to play with toys . . . |
| Child: | To see their pet and play with their dog. |
| Ms. Thomas: | Yes, you could visit your *neighbor* and play with their pet. |
| | Can a teacher be your *neighbor?* Why or why not? |
| Children: | No! |
| Ms. Thomas: | If the teacher lives close to you, can the teacher be your *neighbor?* |
| Children: | Yes! |
| Ms. Thomas: | Now it's time for our "big-kid question." Let's see if you can figure it out. |
| | What can *neighbors* do to help each other? |
| Children: | Give you a ride to school. |
| Ms. Thomas: | Oh, I really like that answer! Let's say that together: "A *neighbor* can give you a ride to school." [*The students repeat the information, and the dialogue continues.*] |

By organizing the shared book lesson by the topic *cities*, children learned the following information and were able to make important connections between the previously taught words—*city* and *building*—and the new vocabulary word, *neighbor:*

- In the world, there are places where we live and places where we go.
- A city is a place where we live and go.
- In cities, we may go to places like schools, theatres, libraries, hospitals, and stores.
- These places are examples of *buildings.*
- A *building* is a place with rooms where people live and/or work.
- In cities there are many *buildings,* and sometimes people live near or close to each other in these *buildings.*
- A *neighbor* is a person who lives in a *building* or house close to you.

In this example, big-idea instruction expands children's conceptual understanding of the topic, *city*, and provides a platform for word acquisition and future learning that will become richer, deeper, and more complex in later years (e.g., future knowledge about ancient Mayan cities, the evolution of the Greek city-state).

The instructional implication is that vocabulary learning can be accelerated in interactive shared book-reading experiences when book content is intentionally organized by themes, in this case, related to nature (science) and culture or society (social studies). In this process, children benefit from thematically organized knowledge that is important for academic discussions that highlight word–world relationships.

## STANDARDS FOR PRESCHOOL LEARNING

Our research suggests that big-idea themes and smaller topics used to organize shared book-reading content can be identified within state and national standards for preschools. Such standards specify expectations not only for science and social studies but also for language development. Although state standards often are extensive and detailed, early childhood educators can use standards to identify the "big ideas" or "enduring understandings" (Herczog, 2010, p. 1) to build domains of knowledge important for preschool and later learning. In our shared book-reading approach, we specifically utilized oral language, science, and social studies standards as a way to integrate "conceptual and cultural knowledge, vocabulary, and verbal reasoning abilities" (Stipek, 2006, p. 457) in shared book-reading vocabulary experiences.

Our recommendation that preschool content vocabulary instruction be guided by relevant standards does not de-emphasize the importance of designing preschool instruction that is responsive to individual differences in child development and attends to nonacademic dimensions (e.g., socioemotional well-being, self-regulation, cultural diversity) that are important for young learners (NAEYC, 2002; Neuman & Roskos, 2005). Aligning instruction with content standards, however, ensures that young children are equipped with academic knowledge and language skills that are necessary for preschool and beyond.

In addition to state/national standards and local school district benchmarks, several organizations provide direction on learning objectives for young children. In the context of teaching social studies, for example, there is the National Council for Social Studies (NCSS) and its publication *National Curriculum Standards for Social Studies* (2010). In the context of teaching science, there is the National Association for the Education of Young Children (NAEYC) and the Core Knowledge Foundation. Additionally, although the Common Core State Standards for English Language Arts were created for grades K–12, these standards are important because they provide some guidance in text selection (balance of informational and storybooks) for shared book reading with the implication that children learn to talk about connections across text genres and are able to integrate content knowledge and literacy (Neuman & Wright, 2013). This is a significant objective in the WORLD shared book-reading approach.

## ORGANIZING BOOK-READING CONTENT BY STANDARDS

In the process of reading this text, you will use relevant preschool standards to develop the framework for designing two thematic instructional units (one instructional unit is one week of lessons): science and social studies. We provide examples of appropriate preschool standards or big ideas to guide your content decisions. At the end of this chapter, in the section "Designing Instruction," you will select science and social studies standards that will serve as book-reading themes with smaller topics. Because the primary instructional goal of the shared book-reading approach that we describe in this text is to accelerate young children's oral language abilities while developing content knowledge, we will first consider oral language development standards.

### Oral Language Standards

Prior to selecting appropriate science and social studies standards to organize thematic book-reading content, it is important to identify oral language standards that are important for language acquisition in children from high-poverty settings. These oral language objectives can begin with simple expectations and gradually include more challenging objectives to expand children's linguistic abilities.

The examples of big ideas for oral language development and acceleration in Table 3.1 are recommendations from the Core Knowledge Foundation (2013) that describe appropriate language experiences and expectations that may be important for building interactive adult–child preschool discussions.

In addition to these recommendations from the Core Knowledge Foundation (2013), NAEYC (1998) advises that young children should be engaged in a range of oral language skill development—this is especially the case for young children who may be raised in homes with limited life experiences. These

**Table 3.1.** Oral language standards

| | |
|---|---|
| Use language to communicate. | Interact in conversations by responding to or initiating talk. |
| Use language to think and analyze concepts. | Classify pictures by categories that represent concepts. |
| Use complex vocabulary and language structures. | Answer with elaborated responses, moving beyond simple subject/verb statements (e.g., "I see the stream in the green valley" instead of merely "I see the stream"). |
| Listen to and engage in storybook-reading discussions. | Listen to texts of varying genres (e.g., storybooks, informational texts). |

*Source:* Core Knowledge Foundation (2013).

language skills and experiences should be integrated into high-priority academic content that is explicitly connected to prior learning. NAEYC (1998) also recommends that shared book-reading instruction and learning should occur in small groups that support analytic discussions (e.g., making predictions), dialogues about book pictures and content, and higher cognitive thinking and discussions (http://www.naeyc.org/files/naeyc/file/positions/PSREAD98.PDF).

Ultimately, the big oral language ideas that guided the WORLD topic immersion approach were aligned with preschool standards (e.g., Core Knowledge Foundation, 2013) and allowed preschool children to

- Show a steady increase in listening and speaking vocabulary
- Use new content vocabulary in everyday communication
- Refine and extend understanding of known content words
- Link new content and vocabulary to previously discussed topics

To guide your selection of appropriate oral language objectives, we provide the following examples of three oral language standards from Core Knowledge Foundation (2013) with specific expectations for language use that could provide a starting point for the first weeks of shared book-reading thematic instruction. These standards can continue to guide oral language expectations throughout the year with the gradual addition of more challenging language objectives.

## Examples of Big Ideas for Oral Language Development

### WEEKS 1 THROUGH 4

**Objective 1:  Use language to communicate.**
- Respond to or initiate talk in conversations about books while using new vocabulary knowledge.
- Describe a personal experience.

**Objective 2:  Listen to and engage in book discussions (i.e., storybooks and informational texts).**
- Make predictions.

**Objective 3:  Use language to think about and analyze science and social studies concepts.**
- Classify pictures by categories that represent science and social studies concepts.

### WEEKS 5 AND BEYOND

*Weeks 5 and beyond include Objectives 1–3 plus an additional, more challenging objective.*

**Objective 1:  Use language to communicate.**
- Respond to or initiate talk in conversations about books while using new vocabulary knowledge.
- Describe a personal experience.

Objective 2: **Listen to and engage in book discussions (i.e., storybooks and informational texts).**

- Make predictions.

Objective 3: **Use language to think about and analyze science and social studies concepts.**

- Classify pictures by categories that represent science and social studies concepts.

Objective 4: **Use complex vocabulary and language structures.**

- Answer with elaborated responses.

## Science Standards

Young children are inherently curious about the natural world, and that curiosity can be used to expand their knowledge of science-related concepts (French, 2004). Most children love to observe, explore, and interact with the environment. Indeed, an understanding of science concepts develops as early as infancy and continues as children develop with age (Kuhn & Pearsall, 2000). Developmental research indicates that long before children enter kindergarten, "they have begun to reason in ways that form foundations for later scientific thinking" (Duschl, Schweingruber, & Shouse, 2007, p. 1).

Early science learning experiences allow children to understand fundamental science concepts, provide a foundation for understanding more complex science thinking in later years, and complement the natural way that young children enjoy and explore the environment (French, 2004; Patrick, Mantzicopoulus, Samarapungavan, & French, 2008; Trundle & Saçkes, 2012). Unfortunately, despite the benefits, early science learning in young children is often sacrificed in favor of literacy and math (Early et al., 2010).

Only 12 states, to our knowledge, have adopted preschool science content learning standards, with most state science standards focusing on learning in kindergarten through grade 12 (Saçkes, Trundle, & Flevares, 2009; Trundle & Saçkes, 2012). Three common, broad science content themes with related topics are suggested for preschool learning across these 12 states (Trundle & Saçkes, 2012):

- Life science: the life cycle of plants and animals, plant and animal habits, plant and animal classification, needs of plants and animals, heredity

- Physical science: physical properties of materials, classification of materials (e.g., weight, shape, height), movement of objects, sound, light, physical changes

- Earth and space science: weather, day and night, earth materials, seasons

It is recommended that young children be provided opportunities to learn the difference between living and nonliving things, life cycles (e.g., butterflies, humans), physical changes in the earth and sky (e.g., seasons, weather), the properties of matter, and the behavior of materials (e.g., changes in liquids and solids through melting).

Within preschool science standards, the most commonly emphasized *process skills* for young children include developing their ability to ask questions about science content, explaining cause and effect, making predictions, describing events, discussing and drawing conclusions, and making comparisons (Trundle & Saçkes, 2012). These process skills are parallel to early language and literacy expectations (e.g., predicting how the story's problem will be resolved) for young children and exemplify the important role that language—especially syntax and vocabulary—plays in acquiring conceptual knowledge (Charlesworth & Lind, 2013). Science-related literacy instruction and interventions, therefore, should develop scientific vocabulary and concepts, beginning with knowledge about the world and building on and extending children's experiences (Hirsch, 2006; Leung, 2008).

To guide your selection of appropriate science objectives, we provide the following examples of big ideas that are important for preschool science instruction.

## Examples of Big Ideas in Life and Physical Science

**Objective 1:**  **Demonstrate an understanding of the living world.**
- Identify and describe basic human needs (e.g., food, drink, shelter from temperature and weather).
- Identify basic body parts and organs (e.g., heart, lungs).
- Observe the needs and life cycle of an animal.
- Observe parts of the plant, its needs, and its life cycle.

**Objective 2:**  **Demonstrate an understanding of the material world.**
- Describe basic properties of water and its effects in the physical world.
- Describe basic properties of air and its effects in the physical world.
- Describe basic properties of light and its effects in the physical world.

## Social Studies Standards

There has been a gradual decline in the teaching of social studies in the United States, primarily due to an increase in language arts and mathematics instruction in response to accountability standards and assessments (Borba, 2007; National Council for Social Studies [NCSS], 2007). With limited time allocated for social studies instruction, shared book-reading discussions present an optimal opportunity for learning important social studies concepts and vocabulary (Borba, 2007). Although 12 states have adopted science standards, as mentioned previously, few sources are available to guide our understanding of expectations of social studies knowledge.

The primary objective of teaching social studies is to talk about the human experience in a diverse world (NCSS, 2010). Children as young as 5 years of age can learn about history, geography, conceptions of work, relationships, and their immediate environments (NCSS, 2007).

Overall, 10 themes or big idea standards are recommended by the NCSS for social studies teaching in general (Herczog, 2010). Other appropriate topics include the study of family, self, and the community (Mindes, 2005). Following are some examples of social studies standards.

## Examples of Big Ideas in Social Studies

- Culture and cultural diversity
- Time and change
- People, places, and the environment

### THE INTEGRATION OF LANGUAGE, SCIENCE, AND SOCIAL STUDIES STANDARDS

Figure 3.1, which was used to guide the development of the WORLD shared book-reading intervention, summarizes examples of standards-based science and social studies themes, topics, and language expectations that are appropriate for young children.

### DESIGNING INSTRUCTION: SELECT ORAL LANGUAGE, SCIENCE, AND SOCIAL STUDIES STANDARDS

#### Oral Language Standards

First, identify oral language standards.

1. Identify areas of strength and weakness in children's oral language abilities (e.g., vocabulary knowledge, ability to talk about personal experiences, elaborated versus limited response). This process begins during the first few weeks of school through observations of child talk and conversational interactions with children throughout the day.

2. Identify three to four oral language objectives that can be integrated during the shared book-reading time that will provide opportunities for expanding children's linguistic abilities. Write your selected standards in the "What Do Children Need to Learn?" section in the Instructional Unit Planner in Appendix 6A.

#### Science Standards

To align shared book-reading vocabulary instruction with preschool science standards, complete the following steps:

| Language concepts | | Science and social studies domains | | | |
|---|---|---|---|---|---|
| | | Themes | | | |
| | | Human | Animal | Plant | Physical elements |
| World/concept knowledge <br> • Identify <br> • Describe <br> • Predict <br> • Classify similarities and differences | Human | Health (e.g., habits, hygiene, nutrition, exercise, rest) <br> Senses | | | |
| | Growth | Life cycles | Life cycles | Seeds <br> Life cycles | |
| | Living things | Needs (e.g., food, water, air) | Needs (e.g., food, water, air) | Needs (e.g., water, food, air, light) | |
| | Insects | | Types <br> Growth | | |
| | Animals | | Home <br> Farm <br> Zoo <br> Dinosaur | | |
| | Earth | | | | Seasons <br> Weather <br> Rocks, soil, water, land, river, ocean <br> Cities <br> Places to live, work, and go to school |
| | Sky | | | | Planets <br> Sun, moon <br> Stars <br> Shadows <br> Light and dark |
| | Properties of matter | | | | Hard and soft <br> Floating <br> Solid and liquid |

| Objectives | Text structure and/or literary forms |
|---|---|
| • Shows a steady increase in listening and speaking vocabulary <br> • Uses increasingly precise vocabulary in describing his or her immediate environment at home, in the neighborhood, and at school <br> • Uses new vocabulary in everyday communication <br> • Refines and extends understanding of known words <br> • Attempts to communicate more than current vocabulary will allow, borrowing and extending words to create meaning <br> • Increases listening vocabulary and begins to develop a vocabulary of object names and common phrases in English (ESL) | • Becomes increasingly familiar with narrative form and its elements by identifying characters and predicting the events, plot, and the resolution of the story <br> • Asks questions and makes comments about the information and events from books <br> • Connects information and events to real-life experiences <br> • Retells a story that has been read aloud, including the characters, setting, and plot of the story <br> • Predicts events in a story; that is, what will happen next <br> • Reads and/or tells a story based on the illustrations of a book with text that has been read aloud previously |

**Figure 3.1.** Alignment of language, science, and social studies themes and topics.

1. Identify one big science idea or standard that will serve as a book-reading theme and three connected topics. Early childhood educators might select a learning objective that is complementary to other instructional goals and activities (e.g., learning centers, science lessons, field trips) so that children will have several opportunities to be deeply immersed in knowledge acquisition about the topic in multiple contexts. Write your selected standard, theme, and initial topic in the "What Do Children Need to Learn" section in Appendix 6A.

2. Next, sequence the topics that will be anchored to the broader theme for extended units of instruction (one unit is equivalent to one week of instruction). Immersing young children in one or several weeks of instruction ensures multiple exposures to concepts and connected vocabulary. Write your selected theme and sequenced topics in Appendix 6B/Extended Instructional Unit Planner.

3. To guide your selection, we have provided examples of two science objectives that are appropriate for preschool children in Table 3.2 (Core Knowledge Foundation, 2013).

## Social Studies Standards

To align shared book-reading vocabulary instruction with preschool social studies standards, complete the following two steps. These are the same steps used to align vocabulary instruction with preschool science standards.

1. Identify one big social studies idea or standard that will serve as a book-reading theme and three connected topics. The selected social studies standard should be complementary to other instructional goals and activities (e.g., center-based activities) so that children will have several opportunities to make connections between word and world knowledge across multiple contexts. Write your selected standards, themes, and initial topic in the "What Do Children Need to Learn" section in Appendix 6A.

2. Next, sequence the topics that will be anchored to the broader theme for one or two units of instruction (one unit is equivalent to one week of

**Table 3.2.** Science themes and topics

| *Science theme 1:* The living world or "living things" | *Science theme 2:* The material world or "nature" |
| --- | --- |
| *Living things are plants, animals, and people. Living things need water, air, and sunlight to help them grow.* | *Nature is things that are not made by people, such as water, air, and sunlight.* |
| (3–6 weeks) | (3–6 weeks) |
| Topic 1: plants (1–2 weeks)<br>Topic 2: animals (1–2 weeks)<br>Topic 3: humans—our body (1–2 weeks) | Topic 1: water (1–2 weeks)<br>Topic 2: air (1–2 weeks)<br>Topic 3: light (1–2 weeks) |

instruction). Write your selected theme and sequenced topics in Appendix 6B/Extended Instructional Unit Planner.

3. To guide your selection, we have provided examples in Table 3.3 of two social studies objectives related to geography and living on the earth (Herczog, 2010; NCSS, 2008).

All science and social studies themes and topics, derived from recommended standards, were used to guide our selection of storybooks and connected informational texts, as well as the vocabulary words that became the foci of the weekly lesson. In Chapter 4, you will continue to develop your two instructional units by selecting theme-related texts and content-related vocabulary concepts.

## RECOMMENDATIONS FOR ENGLISH LANGUAGE LEARNERS

Due to the increasing ELL school population, it is important that early childhood educators are familiar with the instructional implications of landmark U.S. court rulings because of the likelihood that educators will be responsible for the future instructional planning for an ELL child (Zehler et al., 2003). Between 1991 and 2001, for example, at least 43% of U.S. teachers were responsible for providing instruction to an English language learner (Zehler et al., 2003).

U.S. court rulings have mandated that schools must address the academic and linguistic needs of children who speak a non-English language at home. Explicit English language development (ELD) instruction is specifically required in school settings, in addition to general academic content instruction, so that school districts are addressing both linguistic and academic instructional needs of ELLs. These court decisions collectively imply that both academic and English language proficiency standards play a major role in designing high-quality instruction for ELLs who may be educated in a range of bilingual instructional models (e.g., dual-language, transitional, structured immersion).[1]

The Teachers of English to Speakers of Other Languages (TESOL; http://www.tesol.org) and the organization of World-Class Instructional Design and

1. For more information, see http://www.colorincolorado.org/article/49704/ and http://www.nabe.org/Resources/Documents/Advocacy%20page/LauvNichols.pdf.

**Table 3.3.** Social studies themes and topics

| *Social studies theme 1:* how and where humans live or "places where we live and go" | *Social studies theme 2:* the earth or "our earth" |
| --- | --- |
| *Cities are places where we live and go.* | *Our earth is where we live. It is made of land and water.* |
| (3–6 weeks) | (3–6 weeks) |
| Topic 1: cities (1–2 weeks)<br>Topic 2: home (1–2 weeks)<br>Topic 3: school (1–2 weeks) | Topic 1: land (1–2 weeks)<br>Topic 2: water (1–2 weeks)<br>Topic 3: land and water (1–2 weeks) |

Assessment (WIDA; http://www.wida.us) have been instrumental in establishing ELL standards to ensure academic success for children who enter school with varying degrees of second-language proficiency. The latter represents the collaborative effort of state and local education agencies, researchers (e.g., Center for Applied Linguistics), and policy makers. We will now discuss big ideas recommended by TESOL and WIDA that guide ELL language and content learning.

The 2006 TESOL English language proficiency standards address a range of oral, listening, speaking, and writing abilities of ELL children and reflect two important communication goals for English language acquisition: 1) Children should use language and vocabulary to support *social interactions,* and 2) children should use language and more specialized vocabulary and complex sentence structures to support *content and academic learning* (e.g., making predictions, summarizing, analyzing; Teachers of English to Speakers of Other Languages, Inc. [TESOL], 2006).

The two communication goals can be achieved via four English language proficiency standards that support preschool content-based shared book vocabulary learning. These TESOL (2006) English language proficiency standards are as follows:

Standard 1: Communicate for social and instructional purposes.

Standard 2: Communicate information and talk about concepts that are important for reading and language arts learning (e.g., vocabulary knowledge).

Standard 4: Communicate information and concepts important for science learning.

Standard 5: Communicate information and concepts important for social studies learning.

(Standard 3 was omitted here because it addresses mathematical learning.)

Scaffolding during thematic shared book-reading discussions can support children's linguistic abilities as they develop along the following five-level continuum of English proficiency (TESOL, 2006).

The child will be able to

1. Use smaller phrases and rely on nonverbal communication during the *starting level* of English acquisition.

2. Use some academic vocabulary and short, simple sentences during the *emerging level* of English proficiency.

3. Use longer sentences during the *developing level* of English proficiency.

4. Use more complex syntax structures and language to discuss abstract concepts in the *expanding level* of English proficiency.

**Table 3.4.** Examples of World-Class Instructional Design and Assessment (WIDA) descriptions of student abilities by proficiency in English

| | Level 1<br>Entering or starting (TESOL) | Level 2<br>Beginning or emerging (TESOL) | Level 3<br>Developing (TESOL) |
|---|---|---|---|
| Listening | Point to visuals or words that are referred to orally. | Match information that is stated orally (i.e., descriptions) with appropriate visual representations (i.e., pictures and illustrations). | Sequence or categorize information when provided orally by using pictures. |
| Speaking | Respond to *what, when, where, which, why,* and *who* questions. | Talk about previously learned information and facts. | Discuss stories and concepts. |

*Source:* Wisconsin Center for Education Research (2014a).
*Key:* TESOL, Teachers of English to Speakers of Other Languages.

5. Use longer oral statements, technical vocabulary, and fluent speech when approaching native-like English proficiency during the *bridging level* of English proficiency.

In conjunction with the TESOL (2006) English proficiency standards, the *Can Do Descriptors for WIDA's Levels of English Language Proficiency* (Wisconsin Center for Education Research, 2014a) provide examples of pre-K–12 student performance (e.g., listening, speaking, reading, writing) based on the individual child's linguistic ability. Additionally, *Early English Language Development* (E-ELD; Wisconsin Center for Education Research, 2014b) has recommendations for English proficiency expectations for young children. Table 3.4 summarizes several WIDA examples of listening and speaking expectations for ELL learners who may enter school with more limited English proficiency at the beginning of the school year because they have not been exposed to extensive English discussions. In the WORLD ELL studies, for example, Spanish-speaking preschool children primarily entered school with Levels 1 and 2 speaking abilities, although their English proficiency advanced across the academic year.

In Chapter 5, we again refer to the emerging English-language abilities and instructional expectations for ELLs and how this information should guide shared book-reading instruction and planning. We also offer suggestions for what teachers should understand about second-language acquisition and instruction in general and offer specific examples of how the WORLD thematic shared book-reading approach encourages young ELLs to demonstrate their listening and speaking abilities in English. The important point here is that oral language expectations for ELLs in the book-reading experience must be scaffolded so that children can successfully progress in second-language proficiency.

## SUGGESTED FURTHER READINGS

Core Knowledge Foundation. (2013). *Core knowledge preschool: Content and skill guidelines for preschool.* Charlottesville, VA: Core Knowledge Foundation.

Neuman, S.B., & Wright, T. (2013). *All about words: Increasing vocabulary in the Common Core classroom, prek-2.* New York, NY: Teachers College Press.

Teachers of English to Speakers of Other Languages, Inc. (2006). *Pre-K–12 English language proficiency standards: Augmentation of the world-class instructional design and assessment (WIDA) consortium English language proficiency standards.* Alexandria, VA: Author.

# Creating Multiple Exposures to Content Words and Connected Concepts

## Selecting Complementary Texts and Vocabulary

**THIS CHAPTER DISCUSSES HOW TO** use thematically related storybooks and informational texts to organize shared book-reading content that facilitates frequent knowledge building and vocabulary acquisition. We first summarize text structure differences between storybooks and informational texts. We then suggest criteria for selecting books and content-related vocabulary and provide examples of thematically paired WORLD texts and connected vocabulary concepts.

**KEY IDEAS |**    The key ideas discussed in this chapter are as follows:

1.  Children need sufficient practice and application opportunities during shared book reading to be able to retrieve and apply new vocabulary effortlessly.

2.  Pairing storybooks with informational texts by science and social studies themes and topics provides multiple opportunities to deeply process new information.

3.  Informational texts used during content-based shared book reading allow young children to analyze and discuss concepts using discipline-related terms and vocabulary that are characteristic of the academic world.

4.  Teaching from informational texts may require instructional scaffolding (e.g., pointing out text features such as graphs, diagrams, figures, and graphic organizers) to facilitate listening comprehension during the book-reading process.

## MULTIPLE EXPOSURES

The term *multiple exposures* refers to opportunities to see and use words in a variety of contexts (Nagy, 1988). These exposures are made possible when teachers strategically integrate sufficient practice opportunities for children to master newly learned concepts in the shared book-reading experience (Simmons et al., 2008). In addition, multiple exposures to words and concepts facilitate in-depth word knowledge (Nagy, 1988). In-depth word knowledge is specifically generated through frequent opportunities for children to first think deeply about taught information and then articulate perceived word and concept associations across networks of knowledge. Frequent application of new information during interactive book discussions ensures retention of knowledge as it is used in meaningful conversations.

The instructional implication is that integrating multiple exposures in thematic shared book-reading lessons allows young children with limited oral language and conceptual knowledge sufficient time to develop and demonstrate *verbal efficiency* while learning about the world around them. According to the *verbal efficiency hypothesis* (Perfetti & Lesgold, 1979), limited word knowledge (e.g., knowledge of word meanings) without sufficient practice and application opportunities does not ensure that new information can be quickly retrieved and appropriately used. In thematic shared book-reading discussions, frequent exposures to vocabulary concepts can occur through strategies that enable fast- and slow-mapping cognitive processes through the use of complementary twin texts.

## MULTIPLE EXPOSURE STRATEGIES

### Fast and Slow Mapping

During interactive shared book reading, the teacher can design thematic instructional opportunities that integrate both *fast and slow mapping*—two cognitive processes that accelerate vocabulary learning (Horst, Parsons, & Bryan, 2011; Swingley, 2010). *Fast mapping* occurs, for example, when a child hears the target word while observing an illustration of the word. By hearing the word and looking at the illustration simultaneously, the child develops a quick but basic understanding of the word's meaning. *Slow mapping,* which allows a child to slowly develop and store "a robust memory representation of the name-object association" (Horst et al., 2011), is then possible. Repeated exposures, such as rereading the storybook the next day and discussing the word's meaning with visual prompts that are both contextual (e.g., book picture) and decontextual (e.g., different pictures of the word beyond the book) can assist storing and retrieving new word and content knowledge.

### Use of Twin Texts

Teachers in the WORLD intervention used varied text genres or *twin texts*— the pairing of an informational text and a storybook by theme and topic—to integrate frequent exposures to new words and concepts during the shared book-reading process. Twin texts generally can be used during thematic shared book-reading instruction to strategically integrate multiple opportunities to do the following:

- *Familiarize young children with the differences and similarities in text structures* and prepare them for later informational reading (Dickinson, 2001; Duke, 2000; Hirsch, 2006; van Kleeck, 2003)

- *Cultivate an awareness of the various ways a text can be read, understood, and discussed* (e.g., storybook discussions focus on characters, whereas informational texts attend to facts) to accelerate listening comprehension (Gersten, Fuchs, Williams, & Baker, 2001; Meyer, Brandt, & Bluth, 1980)

- *Allow children to use target words and varied syntax structures* in both narrative and scientific discourse (Mantzicopoulus & Patrick, 2011)

Overall, twin texts that are paired by content themes generate frequent opportunities to deepen children's understanding of science and social studies topics by first introducing new knowledge via the familiar structure of a storybook (e.g., character, plot) and then extending this knowledge with additional facts through a complementary informational text. In the following section, we summarize text structure differences between storybooks and informational texts. We also provide suggestions for selecting texts followed by examples of thematic book pairings to facilitate multiple exposures, as well as narrative and scientific talk.

## TEXT TYPES

### Storybooks

The basic text structure of storybooks consists of a story grammar or structure (e.g., characters, plot), which assists students in understanding the sequential and causal events about a main character faced with a conflict (Mantzicopoulus & Patrick, 2011). For young children, storybooks lend themselves to discussions about the main idea, character, plot, and setting. The language of storybooks contrasts sharply with informational texts by exposing how characters think, feel, and are motivated to solve life problems (Varelas & Pappas, 2006). For this reason, storybook discussions can expand children's analytical, problem solving, and sociolinguistic skills (Cook-Gumperz, 1993).

A discussion based on the storybook *Moonbear's Shadow* (Asch, 1999) illustrates this point well. In this storybook, the main character, Moonbear, is annoyed that, when trying to fish, his shadow appears and frightens the big fish away. Moonbear attempts repeatedly, though unsuccessfully, to rid himself of his shadow. He tries to run from it, hide from it, climb high so that it won't reach him, nail it to the ground, and lock it outside of his door; however, it is impossible to get rid of his shadow.

To solve the problem, Moonbear makes a deal with the shadow: "If you let me catch a fish, I'll let you catch one too" (Asch, 1999, p. 24). In the storybook illustration, the shadow nods in agreement. When the main character returns to fish in the pond, the sun is now in a different place in the sky (because it is midday), making it easy for "Shadow to keep his part of the deal" (Asch, 1999, p. 26). In the book, children see an illustration of Moonbear successfully catching fish in the pond during a time of day in which there is no longer a shadow of him. In the afternoon, however, the text illustration shows the sun projecting a shadow of Moonbear on the ground so that when he catches a fish, so does his shadow.

In the WORLD intervention, teachers used this storybook to introduce the concept of *light* in the broader theme of *nature* (tying into the science standard, "demonstrate an understanding of the material world") while introducing two target words: *shadow* and *sky*.

## Instructional Science Vignette: What Do We Know About Light?

### Discussion Before Reading *Moonbear's Shadow*

Ms. Thomas:  This week we're going to read books that teach us about nature. Nature is made of things that are not made by people, such as water, air, and sunlight.

---

⭐ **TEACHING STRATEGY:** Use a visual to depict theme.

---

Look at this picture *[poster]* about nature. Let's name and talk about the parts of nature that you see in these pictures. *[Children identify and talk about the sun, ice, and so forth.]*

Ms. Thomas:  Look at the cover of our book, *Moonbear's Shadow*. We'll learn about *light* in this book.

---

⭐ **TEACHING STRATEGY:** Introduce text genre and predict the big thing that will happen in the story that is related to the topic, light.

---

This book has a big thing that happens because this is a storybook. Let's look at the pictures in this book to find out what happens with *light*. Remember that *light* is a part of *nature*.

The children in the class made various predictions. On one page, children predicted that the bear would see his shadow. On another page, children predicted that the sun would be high in the sky and that the day would be sunny with a lot of *light*. On another page, the children predicted that the bear would fish with the sun high in the sky. The children then identified Moonbear as the character in the story and listened to find out what would happen to him in the book and what they would learn about light.

While reading the book, the teacher stopped briefly to define words when they first appeared on the page and to ask open-ended questions to stimulate children's thinking about *light* in the context of the target word, *shadow.*

## Discussion While Reading *Moonbear's Shadow*

⭐ **TEACHING STRATEGY:** Point to the picture in the book while defining the target word.

Ms. Thomas: This is a *shadow [pointing to picture in the book].* A *shadow* is a dark spot that appears when something gets in the way of light. Here we see Moonbear looking over the water, and there is a dark spot right here in front of him. What do you think is making the *shadow* here? *[The teacher waits for a response and then continues to read the book, stopping to discuss the word* sky.*]*

After reading the book, the discussion pivots around the idea that shadows occur when something gets in the way of light, causing a dark spot to appear. Articulating the main idea requires that children use their cognitive and linguistic abilities. With the guidance of the teacher, they first must understand how the position of the sun in the sky at noon, when the sun is directly overhead, assists Moonbear so that the shadow no longer appears when he is fishing. (The text illustration shows that as the sun moves directly overheard, the shadow disappears.) Understanding and articulating how Moonbear's dilemma is resolved also depends on children's linguistic ability, again with guidance from the teacher, to talk about the nature of light and how shadows are formed.

The following vignette is a simplified version of this rich discussion, which took place after reading the book.

## Discussion After Reading *Moonbear's Shadow*

⭐ **TEACHING STRATEGY:** Review storybook content by referring to storybook features (e. g. characters and setting).

Ms. Thomas: Who are the characters in the story?

Children: A bear.

Child: Moonbear.

Ms. Thomas: Yes, Moonbear is a character because the story is about this bear. Where does this story take place?

Child: At the pond.

Child: His house.

Ms. Thomas: Yes, part of the story takes place at his house. You are all correct. We find Moonbear in many places because he moves around from place to place trying to get rid of his *shadow.*

⭐ **TEACHING STRATEGY:** Use target vocabulary and storybook illustrations to review book content and science concepts.

| | |
|---|---|
| Ms. Thomas: | Look at this picture *[pointing to a book page]*. What do we call the dark spot when something gets in the way of light? |
| Children: | A *shadow!* |
| Ms. Thomas: | Look at this picture *[pointing to a book page]*. What do we call the air that is up high with the sun and clouds? |
| Children: | It's the *sky.* |
| Ms. Thomas: | Good. How does Moonbear try to get rid of the *shadow*? *[There is a discussion.]* |

⭐ **TEACHING STRATEGY:** Use target vocabulary to make connections to life experiences.

| | |
|---|---|
| Ms. Thomas: | Have you ever tried to make your *shadow* disappear? *[There is a discussion.]* |
| | Where have you seen your *shadow*? Are you afraid of your *shadow*? |
| Child: | No—I'm not afraid of my *shadow!* |
| Child: | I see my *shadow* outside. |
| Child: | On the playground. |
| Child: | In the park. |
| Child: | I see my *shadow* on the sidewalk. I like my *shadow!* |
| Ms. Thomas: | Yes, we can see our *shadow* in many places outside. What was the big thing that happened in this story? |
| Child: | The bear saw his *shadow*. |
| Child: | The bear ran from his *shadow*. |
| Child: | He didn't like the *shadow*. |
| Ms. Thomas: | Why didn't he like his *shadow*? |
| Child: | He was scared of his *shadow*. |
| Child: | The *shadow* scared the fish away! He couldn't catch anything. |

⭐ **TEACHING STRATEGY:** Summarize the big thing that happened in the story.

| | |
|---|---|
| Ms. Thomas: | Okay, let's put all this information together. The big thing that happened in the story was that Moonbear wanted to get away from his *shadow* because he thought it frightened the fish away while he was fishing at the pond. He tried many ways to make his shadow disappear, but he was not successful. The *shadow* only disappears when the sun is directly overhead in the *sky* at noon. |

In this example, multiple exposures to both words and science concepts are integrated into the book-reading experience. By utilizing the more familiar structure of the storybook to organize the lesson content, children can engage in narrative talk about a character, the character's problem, the problem's resolution, and the main event as it relates to the science topic *light* and the two new words: *sky* and *shadow*. A second reading of *Moonbear's Shadow* the next day allowed students to do two things: 1) review words and 2) engage in deeper ways of critical and analytical thinking about the concepts prior to reading the thematically paired informational text.

## Informational Texts

Informational texts can provide frequent exposures to a topical theme (e.g., *nature*) and subthemes (e.g., *light, plants, animals, cities*) and summarize relevant characteristic features of a concept (Duke & Bennett-Armistead, 2003; Pappas, 2006). After reading and discussing *Moonbear's Shadow* for two days, for example, preschool teachers read the informational text *Light* (Parker, 2006), which summarizes important features of the science topic *light:*

1. Light derives from varied sources (not just from the sun but also from light bulbs and candles).
2. Light emits heat or warmth.
3. Light is necessary because it provides visual clarity, warmth for the human body, and vitamin D (in the case of sunlight) to keep people healthy.

Informational texts are highly appropriate for conveying factual information about the social or natural world and also allow teachers to make connections among books, new vocabulary knowledge, and children's lives (Dickinson, 2001; Duke, 2004). Informational texts can also be used to build background knowledge that is essential for accelerating comprehension (Duke & Bennett-Armistead, 2003). Lack of exposure to informational texts in early grades may limit children's interest in and ability to comprehend these texts later during content instruction (Mantzicopoulus & Patrick, 2011). Though all children benefit from instruction that systematically includes informational texts, young children from high-poverty settings who enter school with limited vocabulary and concept knowledge generally require greater access and more opportunities to interact with informational texts (Duke, 2000).

Despite the benefits of using informational texts during shared book-reading lessons, in a study of conventional book-reading practices among preschool teachers, Dickinson (2001) found that only 5% of observed teachers considered informational texts to be a criterion for book selection when reading out loud to 4-year-olds. In 2012, Wright reported that 17% of shared book-reading kindergarten observations included talk about informational texts. Although informational texts provide opportunities for discussing theme-related content in depth, "they typically are not seen as a vehicle for introducing new information" (Dickinson, 2001, p. 187).

One barrier that explains teachers' reluctance to incorporate more informational texts in early language and literacy instruction is the belief that informational texts are too difficult for young children because they contain complex content and language structures (Duke & Bennett-Armistead, 2003); however, there are many appropriate informational text selections for children, and evidence suggests that young children can successfully interact with this text genre (Duke, 2003; Duke & Bennett-Armistead, 2003; Maduram, 2000). Some experts suggest that when provided a choice, young children may prefer informational texts because they tap into their natural curiosity about the world (Duke, 2003; Neuman & Roskos, 2007)—especially their interest in the world of science (Mantzicopoulus & Patrick, 2011). Last, there is some evidence that children who engage in informational text discussions may become better informational writers (Duke & Bennett-Armistead, 2003).

In the WORLD study, preschool teachers were not accustomed to reading informational texts but learned to value the depth of content information contained in these books. They learned that children's background knowledge could be expanded and deepened through informational text discussions in a way that is not possible with storybook discussions. Overall, WORLD preschool teachers learned that informational texts can support and enrich content-related vocabulary learning in the following manner:

- Informational texts increase children's background knowledge through discovery of new specialized words and concepts to which some children may not be exposed in daily life (Duke & Kays, 1998; Neuman & Roskos, 2007; Purcell-Gates & Duke, 2001).

- Informational texts allow children to understand cause–effect relationships and to compare and contrast facts (Duke, 2003). Both skills provide the foundation for making inferences, a higher-level comprehension skill that is important during beginning and later reading.

- Informational texts expose children to new conceptual understandings and perspectives and also give them language to discuss what they have learned (Pappas, 2006).

A major distinction between informational texts and storybooks is that the former provide insight into the language used by scientists—or social scientists in the case of books that focus on social studies concepts. This distinction allows children to see that different disciplines present and talk about knowledge in distinct ways (Pappas & Pettegrew, 1998). Understanding how scientific knowledge is discussed (e.g., causes and effects, technical words) is important for content vocabulary learning, especially for children from high-poverty settings who would especially benefit from multiple opportunities to discover and articulate new conceptual understandings about the world around them. Informational texts used during content-based shared book reading allow young children to analyze and discuss concepts using discipline-related terms and vocabulary (e.g., *sprout, cone, herd*) that are characteristic of the academic world.

When this occurs multiple times and in multiple instructional tasks, children have opportunities to begin to develop a scientific (and social studies) discourse and way of thinking, which is important for later text comprehension and academic learning (Pappas & Pettegrew, 1998).

Overall, informational texts differ from traditional storybooks in their use of linguistic (e.g., complex sentence structures) and visual features (e.g., diagrams, semantic maps, bar and line graphs); presentation of abstract concepts, especially through comparisons and contrasts; frequency of academic word use; and their summary of the factual topic (Pappas, 2006). Informational texts also rely on "illustration extensions" (Pappas, 2006, p. 232), or labels, dialogue bubbles, and other explanations, which are provided to clarify visuals, abstract concepts, and technical language. Because of these more complex linguistic, visual, and lexical features (e.g., technical and academic vocabulary), teaching from informational texts may require instructional scaffolding during the book-reading process (e.g., pointing to graphs, diagrams, and other figures that organize data) to enhance comprehension about a topic or theme.

## Instructional Units Organized by Twin Texts

Table 4.1 exemplifies how twin texts were used in the world study to organize book-reading content in an instructional unit on the science topic of *light* within the theme of *nature*. This theme and topic derive from the preschool science standard (Core Knowledge Foundation, 2013, pp. 84–87) discussed in Chapter 3: "Demonstrate an understanding of the material world" (e.g., demonstrate an understanding of the properties of light, water, and air).

By pairing the informational text *Light* with the storybook *Moonbear's Shadow*, young children receive frequent exposure to five content words that are semantically related (e.g., the words are conceptually related), clearly depicted (e.g., illustrations, photos), and important for broadening young

**Table 4.1.** Complementary science texts

*Science standard:* Demonstrate an understanding of the material world.

*Science theme:* nature

| Topic | Book title | Author | Sample content vocabulary |
|-------|-----------|--------|---------------------------|
| Light | Storybook: *Moonbear's Shadow* | Asch (1999) | *Shadow:* a dark spot when something gets in the way of light |
| | | | *Sky:* the air that is up high with the sun and clouds |
| | Information book: *Light* | Parker (2006) | *Light:* what the sun and lamps make that helps us see |
| | | | *Dark:* when there is no light, and it is hard to see |
| | | | *Shade:* a cool place with little sunshine |

children's network of knowledge about light, nature, and the material world. In this unit, students will learn that the topic and content words are related in the following ways:

1. There is a difference between light and dark.

2. There is a relationship among shadow, light, and dark.

3. Shade is connected to the word *shadow*, and both words and concepts imply a quality of darkness or condition of no or limited light.

The following example in Table 4.2 pairs a popular storybook, *No Jumping on the Bed!* (Arnold, 1987), with a complementary informational text, *House* (Schaefer, 2003). This pairing facilitates multiple exposures to content-related words and connected concepts about the social studies topic *homes*, which is part of the broader theme, *places where we live and go*. As discussed in Chapter 3, this theme and topic derive from the social studies standard (Herczog, 2010; NCSS, 2008) that children should understand how and where humans live.

In this instructional unit, shared book-reading content, which is organized around twin texts, deepens children's knowledge network about how humans live. Children will learn the following:

1. People live in shelters (e.g., homes, apartments) that protect them from the rain, sun, and other elements.

2. Homes and apartments have ceilings and roofs that further protect people from the rain, sun, storms, and other elements.

3. Homes and apartments have rooms that allow people to take care of specific needs (e.g., cooking, sleeping, storing goods, taking baths).

## SEQUENCING MULTIPLE INSTRUCTIONAL OPPORTUNITIES THROUGH TWIN TEXTS

The following instructional sequence demonstrates how complementary texts can 1) generate multiple opportunities for content exposure and rich discussions while 2) introducing and reviewing new information through repeated readings. In this instructional approach, one day is used to read and discuss

**Table 4.2.** Complementary social studies texts

*Social studies standard:* Demonstrate an understanding of how and where humans live.

*Theme:* places where we live and go

| Topic | Book title | Author | Sample content vocabulary |
|---|---|---|---|
| Homes | Storybook: *No Jumping on the Bed!* | Arnold (1987) | *Apartment:* a building where many people have their own place to live |
| | | | *Ceiling:* the part of the room that is on top |
| | Information book: *House* | Schafer (2003) | *Roof:* the top part of the building that is on the outside |
| | | | *Basement:* the part of the building that is underground |

the storybook or informational text for the first time, introducing new thematic concepts and words. A second day is used to read the book again to review, discuss, and extend children's understanding of previously taught information. The last day of the instructional unit is used to cumulatively review the concepts, theme, and topic using both the storybook and the informational text. This 5-day scope and sequence allows teachers with limited class time to distribute vocabulary instruction across 15–20-minute daily lessons. Teachers in the WORLD study successfully implemented this effective scope and sequence (see Figure 2.1 on Chapter 2).

## SELECTION CRITERIA: HOW TO PAIR TWIN TEXTS

When creating complementary pairs of books to facilitate thematic teaching with frequent exposures to concepts, several factors should be taken into consideration. First, facts presented via the twin texts must be consistent and not contradictory. Second, book illustrations and visuals across texts should be connected to the book content and include sufficient clarifying details across texts. Storybook illustrations, for example, can clarify a character's actions, whereas pictures in informational texts should accurately depict behavior patterns (e.g., the life cycle of a butterfly) with clearly presented diagrams that are not misleading. Third, book pairs should contain sufficient, semantically related content vocabulary that will be important for later academic learning.

Overall, when selecting books for shared book-reading instruction, consider doing the following:

1. Select storybooks that have visuals that can be used to scaffold story narration sequentially and assist young children in making predictions.

2. Select informational texts that present facts clearly without complicated explanations, lengthy sentence structures, or overly simplified concepts.

3. Select storybooks and informational texts that contain unambiguous illustrations, pictures, or photographs, depicting important science and social studies concepts and words.

4. Select storybooks and informational texts in which target vocabulary and concepts appear multiple times.

In the WORLD intervention, we also selected twin texts that were one grade level above the students' current placement (e.g., kindergarten level for preschool children) to expose children to text structures and content vocabulary that would be important for later learning.

Sudol and King offered several recommendations for selecting informational texts, including 1) checking the content of the book for accuracy (e.g., is the information current?); 2) previewing books to see if the text is organized in the most appropriate way for children to perceive "relationships among concepts" (1996, p. 422) via comparisons and contrasts, cause and effect, and chronological order; and 3) considering the cognitive load of the book's content by noting whether abstract concepts are presented individually and supported by a reasonable number of concrete examples.

In general, select books that

- are not excessively long to increase the likelihood of adult–child interactions,
- contain content that is age-appropriate and of interest to young learners,
- do not include an excessive amount of new vocabulary words (e.g., lists of many animal names, plant names, transportation types) and irrelevant details that can distract from key concepts,
- contain content that will not cause anxiety in young children and are not overly negative, and
- employ an appropriate format (e.g., length of book or number of pages, number of pictures).

Text selection can be especially challenging when children's books lack sufficient, rich content that is appropriate for vocabulary acceleration. Text selection is, therefore, dependent on the availability of content-related words that are 1) likely to be encountered in multiple contexts and texts, 2) of high utility for mature language learners, and 3) not likely to be learned through everyday conversations (Beck et al., 2002; Stahl, 1991; Stahl & Nagy, 2006).

## SELECTION CRITERIA: HOW TO CHOOSE CONTENT-RELATED VOCABULARY

Vocabulary from storybooks and informational texts generally should be selected because the words are important for accelerating conceptual knowledge, allowing teachers to teach target vocabulary not as words but as concepts (Nagy, 1988), which is a more effective method of vocabulary instruction. For this reason, when we refer to visuals used in the WORLD intervention, we use the term *picture/concept cards*, because the photos not only are visual representations of vocabulary but also convey important science and social studies concepts. Shared book-reading complementary texts should each contain two to three content words that are important for teaching a science or social studies concept and that are depicted inside and outside the book (e.g., photographs from varied sources) so that vocabulary instruction can be scaffolded with appropriate visuals.

In order to teach vocabulary words as concepts, the selected words should, as much as possible, also be semantically or conceptually related, allowing broad themes and smaller topics to be taught with breadth, depth, and clarity. Semantically related words generally are more often encountered in informational texts than in storybooks (Armbruster & Nagy, 1992; Wright, 2013).

This approach to word selection is important because it assists young children in organizing and storing new information and generates networks of knowledge in which new words can be linked to previously taught information. Semantically related words, therefore, provide an important cognitive framework or schema for accelerating listening and future text comprehension. This method of vocabulary selection ultimately benefits young children from high-poverty settings by greatly decreasing the "information-processing load" (Neuman, 2006, p. 32), making it easier to acquire new information and build more expansive knowledge networks.

Tables 4.3 and 4.4 present examples of words that were semantically related and taught by thematically paired twin texts in the WORLD study to extend social studies and science knowledge.

## A TIERED APPROACH TO VOCABULARY INSTRUCTION

Beck, McKeown, and Kucan (2002, 2013), recognized experts in the field of vocabulary instruction, recommend a tiered approach to vocabulary instruction. In their text *Bringing Words to Life: Robust Vocabulary Instruction,* Tier I words are described as the most basic words (e.g., *dog, water, shoe*) that are learned primarily via life experiences. These words may not require formal explicit school instruction. Tier II words (e.g., *liquid, cashier, thermometer*) should be explicitly taught in school settings and are recommended for shared book vocabulary instruction because they allow young children to talk about familiar concepts (e.g., water) in more sophisticated ways (e.g., liquid) and are used by more mature language learners (see Beck et al., 2013 for more details). Tier II words are especially important for children from high-poverty settings because they extend children's general word knowledge to allow greater "precision and specificity" (Beck et al., 2002, p. 19) in talking about a concept. Tier III words, in contrast, are associated with specific domains of knowledge, are used less frequently by most learners, and are best taught when it is necessary to understand a broader concept. *Apastron*—when two stars that typically orbit each other are far apart—is an example of a Tier III word and would be taught during an astronomy lesson.

In the WORLD intervention, we aimed to include Tier II words but noted, as does Beck et al. (2002, 2013) in *Bringing Words to Life: Robust Vocabulary Instruction* that there is sometimes a *fine* distinction among the three tiers. Some words

**Table 4.3.** Social studies topics and related vocabulary

| *Social studies standard:* how and where humans live | |
| --- | --- |
| *Social studies theme:* places where we live and go | |
| Topic | Semantically related words that are visually represented in the text |
| Homes | *Apartment, ceiling, roof, basement* |
| School | *Gymnasium, cafeteria, principal, custodian* |
| Stores | *Department, escalator, customer, groceries, bakery, cashier* |
| Earth | *Meadow, shore, pond, earth, island, river* |

**Table 4.4.** Science topics and related vocabulary

*Science standard*: Demonstrate an understanding of the material world or "nature."

*Science theme:* Nature is things that are not made by people, such as water, air, and sunlight.

| Topic | Semantically related words that are visually represented in the text |
|---|---|
| Water | *Pour, puddle, liquid, frozen, solid* |
| Storms | *Storm, raindrop, lightning, wind, spin, tornado* |
| Light | *Shadow, sky, light, dark, shade* |

that might be considered basic (Tier I) for children from higher socioeconomic families that engage in rich discussions to accelerate knowledge-building and self-expression (Lareau, 2003) might not be known by children with more limited life experiences and resources.

In the first experimental WORLD study, for example, most preschool children in the treatment and comparison condition had little prior knowledge of basic words, such as *season* (a time of year). Although this word could be considered Tier I, or basic vocabulary, for families that engage in extensive adult–child conversations about wide-ranging topics and life experiences (e.g., camping in national parks, visiting a natural science museum, international/ national travel, adult–child workshops), children in the WORLD study did not initially exhibit an understanding of this concept and, therefore, benefited from explicit exposure/instruction on some Tier I words in addition to more challenging Tier II words.

Using a tiered approach to vocabulary selection, however, provides a starting point for deciding which words should be taught to young learners so that preschool teachers have a rationale for the words that are selected (Beck et al., 2002) and become more attentive to word-level difficulty during shared book-reading instruction. Teaching more abstract or challenging Tier II and III words, for example, may require more intensive scaffolding and/or priming of important background knowledge to facilitate learning and comprehension. A review of 10 commercially developed curricula for young learners indicated that it is common for discussions of word-level difficulty and suggestions for vocabulary selection to be absent from instructional units and tasks (Neuman & Dwyer, 2011). Early childhood educators, however, should be knowledgeable about these issues in order to maximize learning and vocabulary acceleration.

## DEVELOPING WORD MEANINGS FOR CONTENT VOCABULARY

In the WORLD intervention, word meanings were developed by first attending to the meaning of the word as it was used contextually in the informational text or storybook and then using explicit child-friendly language to clarify the essential features of the word and its related concept. Beck and colleagues refer to this process as using "language that is readily accessible so students can understand the concepts with ease" (2002, p. 36) and avoid false assumptions about word meanings.

In the *birds* topic within the *living things* theme, for example, WORLD preschool teachers read the storybook *Ruby in Her Own Time* (Emmett, 2004) and introduced the word *hatch* with the following explanation: "When something hatches, it breaks out of an egg." This explanation is clearly stated and visually represented in the text (with a picture of a hatching egg) and in picture/concept cards. From these pictures and the child-friendly explanation of the word, children learn the essential features of the concept *hatch*: "Some living things (e.g., young animals) begin their life cycle in an egg consisting of a hard protective shell that is broken by the baby animal when it is strong enough to live in the world."

In this lesson, the teachers pointed to the book page and discussed how baby ducks use their hard beaks to crack open the egg. The meaning of the word was then used to generalize children's knowledge about hatching eggs beyond the text: "What kinds of animals *hatch* from eggs?" (turtles, ostriches, alligators, and many other reptiles); "Where do baby birds hatch?" (nest); "How do you know if something is *hatching*? Could *a cloud hatch* from an egg?" Table 4.5 presents examples of word meanings that summarize the essential features of concepts that were depicted in storybooks and informational texts used in the WORLD intervention.

Content-related vocabulary may represent challenging concepts that are completely new for young children (Hiebert & Cervetti, 2012). These words also may represent multiple meanings that may be confusing. Multiple meanings for a science concept may include one meaning that is more familiar (e.g., *bank*, a place where people can keep their money) and one that is more conceptually complex and unknown (e.g., *bank*, the side of a river or stream; Wright, 2013). For this reason, in the WORLD shared book-reading intervention, teachers did not

**Table 4.5.** Examples of child-friendly word meanings

*Social studies standard:* Demonstrate an understanding of how and where humans live.

*Social studies theme:* places where we live and go

*Topic:* stores (People go to stores.)

| Vocabulary | Word meaning |
| --- | --- |
| Department | A department is a place in a store with things that are alike. |
| Escalator | An escalator has steps that move people up and down in a building. |
| Customer | A customer is a person who buys things at a store. |
| Groceries | Groceries are food that you buy from the store. |
| Bakery | A bakery is a place in which bread, cakes, and cookies are made. |
| Cashier | A cashier is a person who takes the money when people buy things. |

introduce multiple meanings for a word. Some experts suggest that although a definition may not capture all word applications, "explanations that attempt to be all inclusive sacrifice explanatory strength" (Beck et al., 2002, p. 35). It is preferable to introduce a single, clearly focused word explanation until children learn to use the word appropriately and are ready for an additional meaning.

Overall, more cognitively complex vocabulary may require instructional support and scaffolding beyond child-friendly definitions (Wright, 2013). The most effective approach is to teach challenging content vocabulary words (e.g., *meadow*, a place outside with lots of grass where animals can live) while discussing related concepts (e.g., Theme: The earth has land and water.) to solidify comprehension and accelerate learning.

## DESIGNING INSTRUCTION

In this chapter, we have given examples of how twin texts can be used to provide multiple exposures to content-related words and connected concepts in a science and social studies instructional units. Preschool standards were used as a starting point for selecting storybooks and informational texts that were appropriate for science and social studies shared book-reading discussions. Using the science and social studies standards that you selected after reading Chapter 3, you will continue to design a science and a social studies instructional unit. For each unit, you will do the following:

1. Select twin texts (i.e., one storybook and one informational text) that are connected by a theme and topic.

2. Select three content-related words from each text that are represented visually inside and outside of the book (e.g., photos), resulting in six words to be taught in the science unit and six words to be taught in the social studies unit. Follow the guidelines for selection of content-related words, making sure they are semantically related to help young children develop networks of knowledge important for later academic learning.

3. Develop child-friendly definitions that help children understand the broader science and social studies concepts. Think about the essential features of the selected word and how the word or concept is used in the text. Then summarize this information briefly in a sentence.

Use the printable outline in Appendixes 6A and 6B to organize the content of your instructional units. You can use the latter to add future thematic books and vocabulary concepts to extend your science and social studies theme over several weeks of instruction.

## RECOMMENDATIONS FOR ENGLISH LANGUAGE LEARNERS

English language learners also benefit from multiple opportunities to see and use semantically related content words in a variety of contexts and text genres. In the ELL school-based WORLD investigations, the instructional scope and sequence described in this chapter also was used to pair a complementary storybook and informational text by science and social studies themes and topics with the purpose of generating multiple exposures to words and concepts in Spanish (e.g., children receiving native language instruction) and/or English as a second language. Table 4.6 provides examples of parallel complementary book titles and content vocabulary in Spanish for the social studies theme *los lugares donde vivimos* (places where we live and go): *las ciudades* (cities) *y la casa* (house). Table 4.7 provides examples of book titles and content vocabulary for the science theme *la naturaleza* (nature): *luz* (light).

In general, text selection for ELL shared book-reading discussions should include texts that are culturally relevant, be one grade level above the students' current grade (e.g., kindergarten level for preschool ELLs), and include content vocabulary at varied levels of complexity to encourage language skill development and proficiency whether instruction is provided in English or Spanish (Hickman & Pollard-Durodola, 2009). Selecting books that are culturally relevant means that books (e.g., storybooks) reflect values, belief systems, and worldviews that are familiar to ELL children. This, in turn, allows children to draw from their prior cultural knowledge in interactive book discussions, which facilitates comprehension (Anderson & Roit, 1996). In addition, selecting texts that are one grade level above the students' current placement exposes children to text structures, linguistic patterns (e.g., idiomatic expressions, complex sentence structures and lengths, a variety of verb tenses), and vocabulary

**Table 4.6.** Complementary Spanish social studies texts

*Social studies standard:* Demonstrate an understanding of how and where humans live.

*Social studies theme:* places where we live / *los lugares donde vivimos*

| Topic | Book title | Author | Sample content vocabulary |
|---|---|---|---|
| Las ciudades | Storybook: *Las Aventuras de Maxi el perro taxista* | Barracca and Baracca (1990) | *Ciudad:* un lugar donde hay muchas personas y edificios<br>*Edificio:* un lugar con muchos cuartos, donde las personas viven y trabajan |
| | Informational text: *Caminando* | Emberley (1990) | *Vecino:* una persona que vive en un edificio o en una casa que queda cerca de la tuya<br>*Puente:* algo que ayuda a las personas a cruzar agua y lugares muy altos |
| La casa | Storybook: *¡No se salta en la cama!* | Arnold (1987) | *Apartamento:* una parte de un edificio en donde vive una persona o una familia<br>*Techo:* la parte más alta de un edificio o de una casa |
| | Informational text: *Casa* | Schafer (2003) | *Alcoba:* el cuarto donde dormimos<br>*Sótano:* la parte de un edificio que se encuentra debajo del suelo |

**Table 4.7.** Complementary Spanish science texts

*Science standard:* Demonstrate an understanding of the material world.

*Science theme:* Nature / *La naturaleza*

| Topic | Book title | Author | Sample content vocabulary |
|---|---|---|---|
| La luz | Storybook: *La Sombra de Moonbear* | Asch (1999) | *Sombra:* el sitio oscuro que vemos cuando algo se coloca frente a la luz |
| | | | *Cielo:* el aire que se encuentra en todo lo alto, donde están el sol y las nubes |
| | Informational text: *Luz* | Parker (2006) | *Luz:* lo que el sol y las lámparas nos dan para ayudarnos a ver |
| | | | *Oscuridad:* cuando no hay luz y es difícil ver |

that may improve their use and understanding of academic language and prepare them for future learning (Hickman & Pollard-Durodola, 2009).

Because of the oral language demands on young ELLs whose vocabulary networks and word connections are still developing (Beck et al., 2013; Verhoeven, 2011), complementary text selection should consider appropriate word-level difficulty (August, 2003) to ensure that shared book reading provides frequent opportunities for children to use English vocabulary of varied complexity while learning and discussing academic content. In shared book–reading discussions, ELLs should be exposed to Tier I and II words and cognates that are relevant for text comprehension and academic learning.

## Word-Level Difficulty for English Language Learners

Tier II words are important for ELLs because they extend children's general word knowledge, allowing the use of more sophisticated vocabulary to talk about concepts (Beck et al., 2002). ELLs also benefit from frequent opportunities to use Tier I words (August, Carlo, Dressler, & Snow, 2005; Beck et al., 2013), however, especially during shared book reading (Hickman & Pollard-Durodola, 2009) and as Spanish-speaking children transition from Spanish to English instruction and discussions (Calderón et al., 2005). Tier I words represent basic concepts in ELL children's native language (e.g., in Spanish, *correr,* to run; *comer,* to eat), although the term or label for the word may be unfamiliar in English (Beck et. al., 2013). Because second-language vocabulary acquisition is easier when concepts are familiar to children in their native language (DeKeyser & Juffs, 2005), teaching some Tier I concepts in the native language may facilitate the transfer of familiar knowledge across languages by explicitly pointing out semantic similarities. Transfer, the process that takes place when there are similarities among languages, is important for second-language learning (August et al., 2005; Odlin, 1989).

Although Beck et al. (2013) suggest that ELL children will continue to develop Tier I knowledge in daily life without explicit instruction in school settings, Calderón et al. (2005) have modified Beck's tiered approach to vocabulary instruction. Calderón suggests that ELLs who are still developing English proficiency may need oral language experiences with Tier I words to help them talk about familiar concepts that were acquired previously in their native language. Other experts recommend that extensive vocabulary instruction should include opportunities for ELLs to learn words that may not be included in the school curriculum but are commonly used by native English-speaking children (Gersten et al., 2007; Hickman & Pollard-Durodola, 2009). Some commonly used Tier I words (e.g., *shoe*) can be easily introduced by using simple pictures or providing a brief explanation during shared book reading (August et al., 2005).

## Cognates

Cognates (e.g., in Spanish, *animal,* animal; *hospital,* hospital) should also be considered when selecting vocabulary for ELL shared book-reading practices. Cognates are words across languages that are similar in spelling, meaning, and etymology or word history/origin (Montelongo, Hernández, Herter, & Cuello, 2011). Cognates provide an important semantic resource for ELLs developing second-language proficiency (August, Calderón, & Carlo, 2002; August et al., 2005; Bravo et al., 2007; Calderón et al., 2005; Nagy, García, Durgunolgu, & Hancin-Bhatt, 1993) by facilitating some transfer of vocabulary knowledge across languages (e.g., from Spanish to English) when they share a large quantity of cognate pairs (August et al., 2007). In the WORLD Spanish shared book-reading intervention, 27% of the content vocabulary words selected were Spanish–English cognates and were high-frequency words in Spanish and English (e.g., *apartamento,* apartment) or high-frequency Spanish words with lower English frequency (e.g., *edificio,* edifice or "building"; see Bravo et al., 2007 for further discussion on cognate difficulty level). These words were explicitly taught because they were important for understanding book content and related science and/or social studies concepts, and they would provide a foundation for future academic and English language learning.

Table 4.8 lists examples of the Spanish–English cognates that were explicitly taught in the Spanish shared book-reading WORLD curriculum. Words noted with an asterisk are examples of high-frequency words in Spanish that are linguistically more complex for native English speakers. Most cognate vocabulary selected were science-related concepts.

Although most studies on cognates and transfer have been conducted on older students with mixed results (Hancin-Bhatt & Nagy, 1994), ELL students benefit from attending to the linguistic similarities and differences across their native and second language (August & Shanahan, 2006; Graves, August, & Mancilla-Martinez, 2013). For example, it may be a good practice to explicitly point out both true cognates and false cognates—words that may be similar in spelling but do not share the same meaning (e.g., Spanish *sopa* means "soup" and

**Table 4.8.** Spanish–English cognates

| Spanish | English |
| --- | --- |
| *líquido* | liquid |
| *sólido* | solid |
| *apartamento* | apartment |
| *gimnasio* | gymnasium |
| *\*edificio* | edifice (building) |
| *naturaleza* | nature |
| *\*congelar* | to congeal (to freeze) |
| *flotar* | to float |
| *productos* | product |
| *\*ascender* | to ascend/to rise |
| *\*oscuridad* | obscurity/dark/darkness |
| *oceano* | ocean |

*Denotes high-frequency words in Spanish that are linguistically more complex for native English speakers.

not "soap"; Spanish *carpeta* means "folder or file" and not "carpet")—when appropriate. Overall, intentional instruction on important cognates is one way of using the native language as an instructional support for second-language learning.

## SUGGESTED FURTHER READINGS

Beck, I.L., McKeown, M.G., & Kucan, L. (2013). Differentiating vocabulary instruction. In *Bringing words to life: Robust vocabulary instruction* (2nd ed., chap. 9, pp. 153–171). New York, NY: Guilford Press.

Duke, N.K. (2003). Informational texts in early childhood. National Association for the Education of Young Children. Retrieved from http://journal.naeyc .org/btj/200303/InformationBooks.pdf

Nash, R. (1997). *NTC's dictionary of Spanish cognates thematically organized.* Chicago, IL: National Training Center.

Pentimonti, J.M., Zucker, T.A., Justice, L.M., & Kaderavek, J.N. (2010). Informational text use in preschool classroom read-alouds. *The Reading Teacher, 63*(3), 656–665. doi:10.1598/RT.63.8.4

# Opportunities to Dialogue

## Word and World Connections

5

**THIS CHAPTER ADDRESSES THE IMPORTANCE OF** integrating intentional opportunities for language interactions throughout content vocabulary shared book-reading instruction. We first discuss how to integrate opportunities to dialogue about words and concepts throughout the shared book-reading process (e.g., a 5-day scope and sequence). We then provide suggestions for varying opportunities for students to respond (e.g., small-group versus individual responses) while integrating a range of simple to more complex tasks.

**KEY IDEAS |** The key ideas discussed in this chapter are as follows:

1. Teacher modeling (e.g., higher order thinking and responding, appropriate language use) is one way to scaffold interactions during the book-reading process.

2. Vocabulary discussions should be integrated throughout the preschool day so that young children have sufficient opportunities to engage in conversations with peers and adults who are able to provide feedback.

3. Reading a text twice provides additional exposures to words and thematic concepts and prepares children to engage in higher cognitive tasks.

4. Children and their families should be encouraged to continue content vocabulary discussions at home through simple daily life experiences.

5. Small-group instruction can facilitate greater adult–child interactions with opportunities to provide individual feedback.

## MAXIMIZING TIME TO DISCUSS AND RESPOND

Sophisticated talk during shared book reading is important. In brief shared book-reading lessons, the challenge becomes how to increase sophisticated student talk in adult–child conversations for children who may not have had sufficient opportunities to engage in rich discourse in the community or at home (Hart & Risley, 1995; Lareau, 2003). These children enter school with a language base that may limit their participation in deep discussions and academic discourse.

These children may be specifically accustomed to adult–child conversations that use less elaborate discourse (e.g., more verbal directions) with most discussions focusing on the familiar (e.g., familiar events, objects, people) with limited opportunities to learn about and discuss knowledge about the world (Beck & McKeown, 2001; Lareau, 2003). Children may not have a strong foundation of language learned in home environments that prepares them to benefit from explicit vocabulary instruction at school (Beck & McKeown, 2007).

Because our shared book-reading intervention was piloted with preschool teachers, we were able to observe whether the instructional activities in school promoted responses and discussion. Some activities were modified over time, or new ones were created, to increase the amount of instructional time spent in interactive discussions. Specifically, a range of opportunities were strategically scheduled within the lesson sequence to facilitate talk about content vocabulary words, critical story grammar elements (e.g., character, main idea, setting), and thematic book content and to assist students in applying new concepts to lively discussions about life.

In the WORLD intervention, preschool teachers were taught to increase student involvement and language engagement briefly during 15–20 minutes of shared book-reading conversations by implementing the following strategies: 1) distributing language interactions across a 5-day thematic unit and throughout the daily book-reading lesson (before, during, and after reading the text), 2) integrating discussions and tasks that ranged from simple to more complex ones, and 3) intentionally designing opportunities for young children to discuss and respond via small-group instruction, in addition to group, peer-practice, and individual turns. These strategies allowed preschool teachers to maximize time for rich science and social studies discussions by increasing the rate at which information could be presented and practiced during a brief lesson and actively engaging students in tasks that were highly relevant to the content of instruction (Gonzalez et al., 2011; Pollard-Durodola et al., 2011; Simmons et al., 2008).

We elaborate on each of these strategies in the sections that follow.

## DISTRIBUTING OPPORTUNITIES TO TALK

### Five-Day Scope and Sequence

Interactive content-based shared book-reading discussions can be distributed across the week in a 5-day instructional sequence to provide frequent opportunities for rich adult–child interactions and thematic discussions using storybooks paired with complementary informational texts by theme and topic. The following instructional process was initially discussed in Chapter 4 and integrates adult–child conversations around repeated text readings to allow more time for depth of understanding and use of target vocabulary.

- *Day 1:* Read the storybook for the first time, and introduce the big ideas and two or three new semantically related words that are important for understanding the science or social studies concepts. This includes introducing the theme, topic, and related background information to facilitate learning new information and vocabulary.

- *Day 2:* Read the storybook again, and discuss previously taught information—vocabulary and connected concepts. Integrate two or three instructional tasks to creatively review lexical sets of words and concepts with greater emphasis on higher order thinking tasks that integrate knowledge and words from previous lessons.

- *Day 3:* Read the informational text for the first time to further develop the topic introduced by the storybook and introduce the big ideas and two or three new, semantically related words that are important to understanding book concepts. This discussion includes extending and broadening children's background knowledge about the theme and topic and summarizing new information and facts learned about the topic.

- *Day 4:* Read the informational text again, stopping to discuss previously taught information—vocabulary and concepts. Integrate two or three instructional tasks to creatively review lexical sets of words and concepts with greater emphasis on higher order thinking tasks that also integrate knowledge and words from previous lessons.

- *Day 5:* Cumulatively review words and concepts by discussing similarities across the two complementary texts in the context of the theme and topic. More time can be devoted to extending children's language and providing instructional scaffolding as children are taught how to talk about what is the same and/or different across the two texts.

## Before, During, and After Book Reading

Thematic science and social studies discussions can maximize student engagement when interactive adult–child dialogues are distributed across the daily shared book-reading lesson and occur before, during, and after reading the book.

Prereading tasks generally focus on building children's background knowledge on the week's theme and topic. As discussed in Chapter 1, background knowledge refers to explicit instruction in which the teacher either builds new knowledge or guides children to retrieve information from personal experiences to better understand new knowledge—for example, making connections between life experiences and new words and concepts introduced in the shared book-reading text (Baker, Simmons, & Kame'enui, 1998). Discussions that occur while reading the book are brief and contribute to understanding the topic while focusing on in-context definitions of target words or reviewing information on a topic in the context of the story. These interactions should be brief to avoid disrupting the meaning of the text. Postreading discussions can be longer, allowing time for extended conversations while using the target vocabulary to discuss thematic book content.

Overall, integrating interactive adult–child thematic discussions throughout the shared book-reading session is influenced by the teachers' ability to scaffold instructional support that builds linguistic engagement and learning. Instructional support includes a combination of strategies such as the following:

1. Providing feedback to students' comments to extend learning and to correct inappropriate vocabulary use or conceptual misunderstandings

2. Modeling higher order thinking, which is a skill that is important for concept development

3. Modeling and/or demonstrating appropriate language use during instruction and conversations (Modeling how to talk about a topic is one strategy that can be implemented to extend children's oral language abilities and to engage children conversationally when they may not be able to discuss and respond independently using appropriate vocabulary and/or grammatical structures.)

Previous research has shown that these methods of responding to and expanding young children's language and cognitive abilities are persistently related to preschool children's early language and literacy acquisition (Pianta, LaParo, Payne, Cox, & Bradley, 2002).

Here we provide practical suggestions for how thematic science and social studies discussions and instruction can occur in a 15–20 minute lesson using complementary twin texts and visuals that depict words and concepts during instructional scaffolding. We first describe how adult–child dialogues can be integrated and distributed throughout the first reading of a storybook or informational text to introduce science and social studies concepts. First readings focus primarily on lower cognitive tasks (e.g., identifying, labeling, defining; "This is a liquid. A liquid is ___") as children learn new information and vocabulary. For children with limited language experiences, beginning with lower cognitive demand tasks sets an important foundation for later engagements with more cognitively complex dialogues. We next discuss how the second reading of the text can be used to generate higher cognitive thinking (e.g., summarizing, analyzing, associating; "What is the difference between a liquid and a solid?") about words and world knowledge to generate deep processing of content vocabulary and connected concepts that were previously introduced. Throughout the repeated reading process, we provide several examples of open-ended questions and examples of how the teacher can model language use in the discussion through the use of instructional scaffolds. Modeling how to respond to questions is important for young children who may not have the linguistic ability or vocabulary necessary to engage in interactive science and social studies discussions.

# First Reading of the Book

## OPPORTUNITIES TO TALK BEFORE READING THE BOOK

### 1. Introduce the Theme

*Using a visual or visuals to prime children's background knowledge and to provide the focus for a discussion on the week's theme and topic, develop two or three open-ended questions that can be used to stimulate children's thinking about the theme and to extend their knowledge of the topic. During this discussion, encourage students to respond in complete sentences, model how to talk about the theme, and extend children's language use. The following examples demonstrate how to introduce the theme, ask open-ended questions to build important background knowledge, and model language use to stimulate linguistic engagement when children find it difficult to respond to questions during a discussion.*

*The goal is to create a back-and-forth discussion between students and the teacher as they talk about the week's theme.*

### Introduction to a Theme

This week, we are going to read two new books and learn about living things. Living things are plants, animals, and people. Here's what we know about living things. Living things may need water, air, food, and sunlight to help them live and grow. People are living things because they need water, air, and food to live and grow.

Look at these pictures, and tell us what living things you see here *[displaying a poster with pictures of plant roots, gardens, a forest, tree roots, a gardener planting seeds in soil, humans and whales swimming under water, and animals grazing in a meadow]*.

Note: In the WORLD intervention, this thematic poster was used to extend children's background knowledge on different types of living things. It was, therefore, used for several weeks of instruction on smaller related topics (plants, trees, and ocean animals) that are depicted in the poster.

### Examples of Open-Ended Questions to Build Background Knowledge

a. Look at this tree. A tree is a living thing. It needs air, water, and sunlight. What other living things do you see?

b. Tell me more about the flowers here. What do the flowers need to live and grow? Why are they living things?

### Examples of How Teachers Can Model Language Use

a. I see flowers here. Flowers are living things because they need air, water, and sunlight. This flower receives water from the rain that is falling.

b. I see a tree. Trees are living things because they need air, water, and sunlight.

c. Let's say this together: "The whale is a living thing. A whale lives in the ocean and breathes in air from a hole on its back."

d. *[To an individual child]* Say, "A tree is a living thing because it needs _____."

## 2. Preview Two to Three Semantically Related Content Vocabulary Words

*Preview two to three semantically related content vocabulary words to be taught from the book using a visual (picture/concept card for each target word) that depicts each word's meaning and the connected concept. This same visual can be used to review words after reading the book. Introducing target words prior to reading the book further builds background knowledge about the theme and the week's topic. Encourage children to say each new word to generate a "phonological representation" (Beck et al., 2002, p. 51). Next, ask one to two open-ended questions to encourage a discussion in which children can use the target words to describe their life experiences in the context of the theme and topic.*

### Preview Vocabulary

This week, we will learn about plants because plants are living things. You will listen for two words in our book today that help us to learn more about plants. Look at this picture *[a garden with rows of vegetables].*

This is a garden. A garden is a place where people grow plants.

### Examples of Open-Ended Questions to Build Background Knowledge

    a. Everyone, what is this? What do you think can grow in a garden?

    b. What plants would you like to grow in a garden?

### Examples of How to Model Language Use

    a. Plants can grow in a garden. This cabbage is a plant, and it is growing in this garden.

    b. Let's say this together: "Zucchini is a plant, and it can grow in a garden."

    c. We see many types of vegetables growing in this garden. These vegetables can only grow if they have enough water, air, and sunlight.

    d. *[To an individual child]* Say, "I would love to grow _____ in a vegetable garden."

## 3. Introduce the Text Structure in Simple Language

*The following examples demonstrate how to introduce a storybook and informational text.*

### Storybook

Let's look at the cover of our book *Mr. Greg's Garden* (Brennan, 2006). We will learn about plants in this book. This is a storybook. This book has characters and a big thing that happens. It also has a setting where the story takes place. Everyone, what kind of book is this?

### Informational Text

Let's look at the cover of our new book *How a Seed Grows* (Jordan, 2006). This is an informational text, and it teaches about things. In this book, we will learn more about the topic, plants. Everyone, what kind of book is this?

### 4. Use the Text Structure to Make Predictions

*Use the text structure to make predictions about what children will learn from the book content. Preview the book pages and pictures to encourage children to predict what the story is about (storybook) or what information will be learned (informational text). This technique is similar to conducting a "picture walk," a strategy used to generate interest in book content by flipping through each page of a book to infer what might take place in the book or what information will be learned (Reading to Kids, 2002). This strategy is implemented without referring to words in the text.*

### Examples of Open-Ended Questions to Facilitate Storybook Predictions

a. Look at the pictures. *[Turn to each page in the book.]*

b. What do you think will happen in this story? Who is the character in this story? Where does the story take place? What do you think will happen to the character in this story? What do you think will happen to the character on this page?

### Examples of How to Model Language Use

*[Point to pictures in the book.]*

a. I think the man will make a garden.

b. I think the man will grow vegetables in the garden.

c. Let's make a prediction together. I think the animals will _____.

d. *[To an individual child]* Say, "I think the man will put a scarecrow in the garden to _____."

### Examples of Open-Ended Questions to Facilitate Informational Text Predictions

a. Let's look at the pictures in *How a Seed Grows* (Jordan, 2006) to find out what we will learn about plants. *[Turn to each page in the book.]*

b. What do you think you will learn in this information book? What do you think you will learn about seeds? What do you think we will learn about trees and flowers?

### Examples of How to Model Language Use

a. I think we will learn about planting seeds in a garden.

b. I think we will learn that trees and flowers grow from seeds.

c. Let's make a prediction together. I think we will learn about _____.

### 5. Monitor Paired Predictions and Discussions

*After briefly previewing the book and making general predictions, use specific book illustrations and pictures that depict target words to generate predictions related to the new vocabulary and connected concepts. This brief discussion can take place between pairs of students. It is important that while children are talking with their partners, the teacher is actively listening to their responses, asking additional questions when appropriate to clarify concepts and extending children's oral responses when they are only able to respond with brief phrases or words.*

**Examples of Paired Discussion and Predictions**

    a. Everyone, let's look at this page *[pointing to picture in the book]*. On this page, we will learn about the new word, *soil*. What do you think you will learn about soil on this page? Turn and tell your friend what you will learn about the soil that you see on this page.

    b. Now look at this page *[pointing to picture in the book]*. On this page, we will learn about the new word, *root*. What do you think you will learn about roots on this page? Turn and tell your friend what you will learn about the roots that you see on this page.

**Examples of How to Model Language Use**

    a. When I look at this page, I think I will learn that plants grow in the soil.

    b. *[To an individual child]* When you talk to your friend, say, "I think I will learn that plants _____."

## OPPORTUNITIES TO TALK WHILE READING THE BOOK

### 1. Summarize the Goal for Reading the Book

*Summarize the goal for reading the book referring to the topic, theme, and new vocabulary.*

As I read *Mr. Greg's Garden,* you will learn about plants and two important words: *garden* and *plant*. Remember, plants are living things, and they can grow in a garden.

### 2. Read the Book and Provide In-Context Word Meanings

*Read the book and provide in-context word meanings for the target vocabulary. Stop briefly when the target word first appears in the text to discuss the word meaning while pointing to a book picture or illustration that clearly depicts the concept. This approach allows children to understand the word in the context of the book and aids in understanding the connected information (Beck et al., 2002). Have students say the word.*

**Storybook:** *Mr. Greg's Garden*

Look at this picture. On this page, a plant is a living thing that grows from dirt like a flower, grass, or trees. Let's say our new word. What is this? Yes, a plant.

**Informational Text:** *How a Seed Grows*

Look at this picture. This is a root. *[Point.]* A root is the part of the plant that grows in the ground. Let's say our new word. What is this? Yes, it is a root.

### 3. Talk About the Concepts and Extend Children's Knowledge

*Talk about the concepts and extend children's knowledge while using the target word to discuss the information depicted on the page.*

**Storybook:** *Mr. Greg's Garden*

Look at this picture of a plant. Some plants make fruits and vegetables for people to eat. These plants are vegetables—bean plants. The rabbits here are eating the leaves off Mr. Greg's bean plants. What do you think Mr. Greg can do to stop the rabbits from eating the bean plants?

### Examples of How to Model Language Use

    a. I think Mr. Greg will build a fence so they will not eat his plants.

    b. I think Mr. Greg can build a _____.

### Informational Text: *How a Seed Grows*

Here we see the roots of the plant spreading out in the soil. Why do you think the roots spread out in the soil?

### Examples of How to Model Language Use

    a. I think the roots spread out because they are seeking water and food from the soil.

    b. Everyone, let's say this together, "I think the roots spread out because they help the plant to grow big and strong."

## OPPORTUNITIES TO TALK AFTER READING THE BOOK

### 1. Review Content Vocabulary and Related Key Concepts

*Review content vocabulary and related key concepts using the same visuals (picture/ concept cards) that were used prior to reading the book. Ask two to three open-ended questions that will allow children to use the words to talk about related life experiences. Remember, the goal is not to ask a series of open-ended questions but to create a back-and-forth discussion between the children and the teacher.*

Let's look at this picture. This is a garden. What is this? Yes, this is a garden. Remember, a garden is a place where people can grow plants. What kinds of plants grow in a garden? Where would you find a garden? Where have you seen a garden?

    This is a seed. What is this? Remember, a seed is a living thing from which plants grow. Are seeds big or small? What things grow from seeds?

### Examples of How to Model Language Use

    a. Vegetables and flowers can grow in a garden.

    b. You can find a garden of flowers in a city park. You can find a garden in someone's backyard.

    c. *[To an individual child]* Say, "I saw a garden with _____."

    d. Yes, corn and beans can grow from seeds.

    e. Everyone, let's say this together: "Plants can grow from seeds."

### 2. Discuss Book Content

*Discuss book content by asking open-ended questions to generate a dialogue using target words while referring to the text's genre. This discussion can be used to assess if children understood what happened in the storybook and what new information was learned in the informational text. Use pictures from the book to scaffold the discussion.*

Who are the characters in the storybook *Mr. Greg's Garden*? What is the big thing that happened? Where did the story take place?

    In the informational text *How a Seed Grows,* what did we learn about plants?

### 3. Integrate Opportunities for Instructional Extensions Beyond the Book During the School Day

*Integrate opportunities for instructional extensions beyond the book during the school day. Although the WORLD intervention focused solely on interactive thematic discussions that occurred within the shared book-reading group, there are numerous opportunities throughout the preschool day that could support and extend content vocabulary learning and oral language development.*

*Table 5.1 lists some examples of thematic content-based learning centers that extend oral language abilities and knowledge building. Scheduling one center-based activity is preferred to planning too many activities within a short school day. Ideally, instructional extensions should be scheduled across the week to increase depth of learning, as well as frequency of exposures to content vocabulary and connected concepts.*

**Table 5.1.**   Instructional centers at school

*Science standard:* Demonstrate an understanding of the living world or "living things."

*Science theme:* Living things are plants, animals, and people.
Living things need water, air, food, and sunlight to help them grow.

*Topic:* plants

*Storybook: Mr. Greg's Garden*

*Vocabulary:* garden, plant

| | |
|---|---|
| *Sequencing:* Children review the story by indicating what happened at the beginning, middle, and end of the story. | Children can work as a team to talk about what happened in the book *Mr. Gregg's Garden*. Children can look at specific book pictures identified by the teacher to talk about what happened at the beginning, middle, and end of the story. This activity may require adult scaffolding. |
| *Dramatic role playing:* Children role play to reenact the plot using simple props. For young children, dramatic role playing is central to thematic content instruction because it allows further development of conceptual knowledge while children are trying out adult roles (Charlesworth & Lind, 2013). | In a small group, one child can pretend to be Mr. Greg, a gardener, and plant a bean garden while other children pretend to be the animals that eat the planted vegetables. Children can learn more about gardening by using *realia* (real-life objects) related to gardening while discussing how specific tools are beneficial to gardening and growing plants. After role playing, open-ended questions can address children's emotions (e.g., "How did you feel when the animals ate your plants? Why? How did you feel when Mr. Greg built a fence around the garden or placed a scarecrow in the garden? Why?"). |
| *Hands-on application:* Children participate in an experience that allows them to apply the concepts to life experiences. | Children work in small groups to create a terrarium of plants. They can document weekly plant growth on a chart. |
| *Thematic picture dictionary:* Children create a picture dictionary using visuals (e.g., magazine photographs) of vocabulary concepts. The dictionary allows cumulative discussions about concepts. Pages can be assembled with a bracket to allow words to be used in games, word sorts, and so forth. | An individual photograph for each word/concept (garden and plant) is provided for children. Each week, children add new vocabulary pictures. |

### 4. Encourage Children to Use the Target Words at Home

*Encourage children to use the target words at home. Design an activity that strengthens home and community connections so that children can use target vocabulary to engage in conversations about the week's theme and topic with individuals beyond the school setting. The following examples demonstrate opportunities for adult–child conversations that can take place at home and/or in the community. In these extended experiences, the family and child can be encouraged to do the following:*

    a. *Take a walk through their neighborhood or home and talk about the plants that can be seen. Use a thematic journal (pages are labeled by theme/topic to correspond with school-based shared book-reading instruction) to draw a picture of a plant that was discovered.*

    b. *Discuss why a community garden might be useful for a neighborhood (e.g., growing vegetables for consumption, flowers for beautification, large trees to provide shade during the summer when it is hot). Talk about how to design a garden for the neighborhood—what kinds of plants would be grown and why? In a thematic journal, draw a picture and/or design for a garden that would be beneficial for a neighborhood.*

These adult–child conversations could also be recorded by the parent, using a simple cassette player and collected and played back by the parent and/or child over time to remember the shared experiences and to note growth in children's language abilities.

## Second Reading of the Book

*The second reading of the storybook or informational text is used to review previously taught information, provide additional exposures to the words and thematic concepts, and extend children's knowledge through more complex activities that require higher order thinking. Because students have acquired a basic understanding of the new words and concepts, they are now ready to engage in higher cognitive tasks that require deeply processing taught information by making connections across words, content, and concepts. Adult–child conversations can now 1) discuss what is similar or different about word features or concepts, 2) make inferences, and 3) manipulate word sets or networks in which selected vocabulary words share semantic attributes (Beck, McKeown, & Omanson, 1987; Beck, Perfetti, & McKeown, 1982; Kame'enui, Dixon, & Carnine, 1987).*

### OPPORTUNITIES TO TALK BEFORE READING THE BOOK

### 1. Review the Topic, Vocabulary, and Concepts

*Review the topic, vocabulary, and concepts using new visuals (picture/concept cards) so that children generalize their knowledge to new contexts. Ask two to three open-ended questions (what, where, when, and how) about the topic.*

This week, we are learning about living things. Let's look at some new pictures of living things *[plants growing in a forest]*. This is a plant. Tell me something you know about plants? How do you know if something is a plant?

**Examples of How to Model Language Use**

> *[Pointing to the picture, the soil, and so forth to scaffold instruction and assist children in thinking about what they have learned]*

a. I learned that plants are living things.

b. I learned that plants can grow in a garden.

c. *[To an individual child]* Say, "I learned that plants _____."

d. I know something is a plant if it grows from the soil.

e. I know something is a plant if it has leaves or grows from a seed.

## OPPORTUNITIES TO TALK WHILE READING THE BOOK

### 1. Read the Book and Provide Brief In-Context Discussions

*Read the book, and provide brief in-context discussions using vocabulary to talk about concepts by stopping to encourage children to talk about what they learned in a brief paired discussion. Stop briefly when the target word first appears while pointing to a book picture or illustration that clearly depicts the concept.*

Look, we learned this word yesterday! Look at the picture here and say what is happening. Try to use the word *garden*. Turn and tell your friend what you learned about the garden here.

Look at this picture. What is this? Yes, this is soil. Turn and tell your friend what you learned about the soil on this page.

### 2. Monitor Paired Discussions

*Monitor paired discussions. Provide feedback and model language use. It is important that while children are talking with their friend, the teacher is actively listening to children's responses, asking additional questions when appropriate to clarify concepts and extending children's oral responses when they are only able to respond with brief phrases or words. Also confirm student responses and provide feedback to deepen children's understanding of the topic.*

**Examples of How to Model Language Use**

a. When you talk to your neighbor, say, "I learned that _____."

b. Yes, Mr. Greg is planting a garden in his backyard.

c. What kinds of plants did he grow in the garden?

d. Yes, we learned that plants grow from seeds that are planted in the soil.

## OPPORTUNITIES TO TALK AFTER READING THE BOOK

### 1. Review Words and Concepts Quickly

*Review words and concepts quickly (1–2 minutes) using visuals (e.g., picture/concept cards). This instructional task also serves as a brief evaluation of whether students have mastered word meanings. In the WORLD intervention, this activity is referred to as Ready, Set, Go! The goal of this type of quick review is for children to correctly identify, with 100% accuracy, the word meanings taught within the current and previous 2–3 weeks. By flashing the picture/concept cards, the teacher can quickly determine if children have understood rudimentary concepts, confirm correct responses, and correct errors (recycling the misidentified concept card three cards back so that it will reappear in the card stack) until all concepts are accurately identified.*

## 2. Challenge Children's Thinking About the Topic, Vocabulary, and Connected Concepts

*Challenge children's thinking about the topic, vocabulary, and connected concepts by integrating the use of content vocabulary and related concepts into higher cognitive questions and discussions. The goal of this deep processing task is to encourage children to see important connections between words and concepts in real life experiences and, consequently, to expand their knowledge about the world. Because these open-ended questions are challenging, one to three for each vocabulary word and concept is sufficient.*

*One question, for example, can encourage children to talk about the differences between two concepts. A second question can encourage children to think and talk about connections among concepts followed by an explanation and/or rationale ("Why?") for their thinking. This activity may require the use of visuals (picture/concept cards) to scaffold discussion of and thinking about abstract concepts in addition to modeling language use because children may require adult guidance to understand conceptual connections.*

### Informational Text: *How a Seed Grows*

Now it's time for our challenge questions. Let's put on our thinking caps to talk about everything that we have learned about plants and living things.

    a. *[Picture of leaves protruding from a long root]*

- What is the difference between a *root* and a *seed?*
- If you looked at a *plant* in a *garden,* would you see its roots? Why or why not?
- Why do *plants* need *roots?*

    b. *[Picture of soil with a few budding plants]*

- What is the difference between *soil* and a *root?*
- Would a seed that is growing be on top of the *soil?* Why or why not?
- Would *soil* need to be wet or dry for *plants* to grow? Explain why.

    c. *[Picture of four types of seeds: corn, bean seeds in a pod, seeds in a papaya, dry black-eyed peas]*

- What is the difference between a *seed* and *soil?*
- Could a *building* grow from a *seed?* Why or why not?
- What does a *seed* need to grow into a plant?

### 3. Provide an Instructional Task in Which Individual Children Have Opportunities to Talk About Words

*Provide an instructional task in which individual children have opportunities to talk about words. This activity also serves as a quick evaluation of students' ability to use target words to discuss concepts and life experiences with opportunities to model language use and extend students' responses. In the WORLD intervention, teachers implemented an activity referred to as "Magic Mirror," which allowed the teacher to talk about defining characteristics of a word by providing identifiable clues. This activity is similar to I Spy.*

[*The teacher looks into a handheld mirror.*] Let's look into our Magic Mirror to see what we can see about living things and plants. First I'll tell you what I see, and then some of you will have a turn to tell us what you see.

I see a little round thing in the ground that is covered with soil. It will grow into a plant. Does anyone know what the Magic Mirror is showing me?

Yes, Janet, I am looking at a seed! It is Janet's turn to come look into the mirror and tell us about the seed that she sees.

*The teacher assists Janet in describing an imaginary seed that she sees in the mirror by asking additional questions to help her think about the defining characteristics of a seed, perhaps prompting her to remember where she might see a seed.*

**Examples of Open-Ended Questions to Prompt Student Thinking and Responding**

    a. What kind of seed do you see? Is it a vegetable or flower seed?

    b. Describe the seed that you see. What is the color and shape of the seed?

    c. Where is the seed planted, and what does it need to grow?

### 4. Integrate Opportunities for Instructional Extensions Beyond the Book During the School Day

*Integrate opportunities for instructional extensions beyond the book during the school day. Provide one to two opportunities to use the content vocabulary knowledge beyond the shared book-reading experience to expand higher order thinking about connections between words and concepts—linking new information to previously learned knowledge. For example, children can work as a team at an instructional center or individually to engage in a learning experience that requires them to apply their understanding of the concept of change.*

*In the WORLD study, children talked about books that focused on changing seasons, changes in animal growth (e.g., animal hatching from an egg), changes in weather conditions (e.g., storms, tornados), changes in time, and changes in plant growth. After reading* Mr. Greg's Garden *for the second time, children would be ready to sort the current week's picture/concept cards and those from previous lessons by asking, "Which pictures show something changing? Which pictures show something that is not changing?" Because these higher cognitive tasks may require adult feedback and scaffolding, it is recommended to schedule children at such an instructional center when an adult might be present (e.g., an instructional aide, parent volunteer, teacher.). Table 5.2 lists other examples of center-based activities that encourage higher cognitive thinking while expanding their network of knowledge. Most activities require the use of picture/concept cards because they are inexpensive to create and can be reused for multiple purposes.*

**Table 5.2.** Examples of higher cognitive thinking center-based activities

*Science standard:* Demonstrate an understanding of the living world or "living things."

*Science theme:* Living things are plants, animals, and people.
Living things need water, air, and sunlight to help them grow.

*Topic:* plants

*Storybook: Mr. Greg's Garden*

*Vocabulary:* garden, plant

| | |
|---|---|
| *Classifying:* Children group and sort picture/concept cards from previous lessons, topics, and themes into categories for deep processing. This process assists young children to see how concepts are related. New picture/concept cards can also be included to expand children's knowledge. | Which pictures show living things? Why? Which pictures show nonliving things? Why? Enrichment: Categorize plants from two biomes—tropical rainforests and deserts. Which living things can be found in a desert? Why? Which living things can be found in a tropical rainforest? Why? |
| *Comparing:* Children look for differences and similarities. | Children work in small groups or individually to talk about what is similar or different by using thematic sets of two or three picture/concept cards. |
| *Additional thematic reading materials* | Children can look at additional storybooks and informational texts that are related to the current theme and topic. The school librarian can assist in locating these texts from the school library. |

## 5. Encourage Children to Use the Target Words at Home

*Encourage children to use the target words at home. This is another opportunity for children to engage in rich conversations using vocabulary related to the week's theme and topic with individuals beyond the school setting. Activities should be sequenced so that they are a continuation or extension of the home activities that were suggested during the first day of reading the storybook or informational text. The following examples demonstrate appropriate home and community extensions that support vocabulary learning and discussion. The family can:*

- Take a walk through the produce, seeds, and other gardening paraphernalia. Walk through the aisles and talk about what you see. Talk about how it relates to plants and growing, living things. In a thematic journal, draw a picture of two items that are used in gardening (e.g., a bag of fertilizer, a spade, a wheel barrow for transporting soil, gardening gloves).

- Take a walk through the produce section of a grocery store and talk about the fruits and vegetables that are displayed and how they grew from seeds. Buy a fruit (e.g., peach, apple, plum) and examine the seed(s) inside. Draw a picture of the seed in the thematic journal. Write the name of the fruit next to the picture. (Writing and labeling the name of the fruit can take place in the classroom.)

## SMALL-GROUP INSTRUCTION

The instructional format should also be considered when designing opportunities to maximize student engagement and adult–child interactions that facilitate a cycle of feedback and extended child responses. Although the typical practice of shared book reading occurs while reading to the entire class, WORLD preschool teachers taught small groups of five to six students while an instructional aide provided instructional support to the remaining students (e.g., learning center activities). A small-group format was preferred because previous studies have documented the intensity of small-group instruction (Vaughn & Linan-Thompson, 2003; Vaughn, Linan-Thompson, Kouzekanani, Pedrotty, Dickson, & Blozis, 2003), which can facilitate greater adult–child interactions during brief shared book-reading lessons (Simmons et al., 2008). For children who require more explicit and intensive instruction and acceleration, small-group instruction may be more beneficial than large-group or whole-class instruction because it provides opportunities for adults to model language usage extensively and provide individual feedback to children as they respond to and discuss critical science and social studies content (Simmons et al., 2008).

We acknowledge, however, that the realities of preschool settings (e.g., limited time, limited support, large classes) may impede reading and talking about books with smaller groups of children daily. An alternative approach is the implementation of shared book-reading content vocabulary instruction with the whole class while incorporating the assistance of instructional aides or parent volunteers who can sit next to smaller sections of students to monitor, provide feedback, and interact with children during shared book-reading discussions. In addition, preschool teachers can select specific science and/or social studies topics for whole-class instruction. Teachers can then continue with the topic with smaller groups of students who would benefit from more intensive instruction and a more interactive dialogic experience.

## WHOLE-CLASS, GROUP, PAIRED-PRACTICE, AND INDIVIDUAL RESPONSES

Whether shared book reading occurs with the whole class or within smaller groups, preschool teachers should strategically integrate opportunities for students to have individual turns to discuss and respond in order to maximize learning and adult–child interactions with feedback. Because it is not feasible to integrate opportunities for each individual child to respond in whole-class instruction, we recommend that some shared book-reading content be allocated for smaller-group discussions during the instructional day to increase opportunities for children to respond individually. This allows preschool teachers to informally assess students' mastery of vocabulary and concept knowledge, comprehension of book content, and ability to engage in higher-order thinking (i.e., associations and connections) during more challenging tasks (Simmons et al., 2008). Individual turns are essential because they allow preschool teachers to extend oral language responses so that students receive individual feedback or modeling of appropriate syntax and word usage.

Group and whole-class responses (e.g., choral responses, the entire group responding to a question) can be scheduled before, during, and after reading the book, allowing all children to participate and interact with the teacher and with each other. For example, prior to reading any book in the WORLD intervention, all children in the group would demonstrate their ability to connect the theme and topic to life experiences and to develop the background knowledge necessary for comprehending book content. Group responses also took place while reading a book to ensure that all children could identify and talk about vocabulary concepts depicted in book illustrations. In contrast, opportunities for individual responses were scheduled after reading the book to provide an opportunity for a child to review vocabulary concepts (e.g., Teacher: "Now it's your turn to tell us about the liquid that you see.").

Paired practice is another form of responding that allows children to participate in shared book-reading discussions with a peer or friend to demonstrate appropriate target word use and mastery of concept knowledge. Paired discussions allow teachers to listen to peer dialogues, observe language use, confirm responses, and provide feedback. In the WORLD intervention, these paired discussions were scheduled almost daily and occurred prior to reading a text for the first time so that students could use the text structure to make predictions:

Ms. Thomas:  Everyone, let's look at this page. On this page, we will learn about the new word, *soil*. What do you think you will learn about soil on this page? Turn and tell your friend what you will learn about the soil that you see on this page.

Paired discussions also occurred during the second reading of the book when teachers would stop on a book page and ask children to tell their friend what they learned about the vocabulary word/concept:

Ms. Thomas:  Look, we learned this word yesterday! Look at this picture. What is this? Yes, this is soil. Turn and tell your friend what you learned about the soil on this page.

Whenever paired practices are used, young children should be taught how to work in a pair, with the teacher demonstrating or modeling how to "talk to a friend."

## INTEGRATING A RANGE OF SIMPLE TO MORE COMPLEX TALKING AND THINKING OPPORTUNITIES

The suggestions in this chapter exemplify how vocabulary acceleration can be accomplished by varying the cognitive difficulty of instruction during the repeated reading process. In this approach to instruction, less complex skills, such as labeling or identifying (e.g., teacher points to picture in a book and says, "Where is the garden? Is this *soil*? This is a *bulb*.") and defining or explaining

**Table 5.3.** Be the teacher: Initial discussion on conceptual similarities and differences

| Vocabulary | Word meaning | Picture/concept card |
|---|---|---|
| Change | Change is to become different. | *Picture:* series of leaves that are changing in color from green to orange<br>*Big idea taught:* The leaves change colors and become different in the season of fall. |
| Blossom | A blossom is a flower on a tree. | *Picture:* white blossoms on a branch in the spring<br>*Big idea taught:* Blossoms are flowers that can appear on different plants. |
| Ripe | Ripe is when something is ready to eat or use. | *Picture:* photograph of two tomatoes on a branch. One tomato is green (not ripe), and the other one is red (ripe). An arrow was inserted on the picture that points to the red, ripe tomato.<br>*Big idea taught:* Both fruit are tomatoes, but the green tomato is not ready to be eaten yet. The red tomato can be eaten because it is ripe. Something that is not ripe, such as the tomato, can change and become ripe. |

(e.g., "A *seed* is a living thing from which plants grow. Here we see a tree *seed* and a flower *seed*.") are emphasized when children are learning new information and talking about the book for the first time. More analytical tasks and conversations occur after the second reading of the text when children are more familiar with target words and book content and are ready for in-depth discussions that require greater analytic and linguistic abilities.

Analytic discussions require the most instructional scaffolding during interactive shared book reading because children often require guidance, feedback, and teacher modeling of analytic thinking and language use in order to better respond to and discuss abstract concepts. In the following section, we discuss two instructional activities that were piloted in the WORLD study with preschool teachers.

## Be the Teacher

This is a carefully scaffolded activity in which individual children can talk about what is the same or different about two different visual representations of a vocabulary word or concept.

1. The entire group or class describes what is happening in the first vocabulary picture/concept card (e.g., leaves changing colors).

2. The teacher expands upon the group's or class's summary and talks about what is happening in the same picture (e.g., "The season is fall, and the weather is getting cooler, and the leaves are changing colors.").

3. An individual child has a turn to talk about what is happening in the same vocabulary picture with the teacher providing feedback.

4. The teacher shows a new picture of the same vocabulary word/concept and asks an individual child to describe what is happening in the picture with the teacher providing feedback.

5. The teacher both points to pictures and models how to talk about what is the same or different, depending on the instructional goal. For example, after rereading the information book *Colors of the Season* (Perez, 2004), children reviewed the three words listed in Table 5.3, which were taught in the book, and then participated in the following Be the Teacher discussion about the concept of *change*.

## Instructional Science Vignette: Seasons

### Discussion About the Target Word: *Change*

| | |
|---|---|
| Ms. Thomas: | *[Displaying a picture of leaves changing colors.]* Tell us what is happening here. |
| Children: | The leaves are changing. |
| Carlos: | The leaves are changing in the fall. |
| Ms. Thomas: | Yes, the season is fall, so the weather is getting cooler, there is less daylight, and the leaves are changing colors. |
| | It's Matt's turn to tell us something about change. |
| Matt: | Something is becoming different. |
| Ms. Thomas: | Good—what is becoming different? |
| Matt: | The leaves are becoming different. |
| Ms. Thomas: | Can you tell us how the leaves are becoming different? |
| Matt: | First they are all green. The leaves are becoming red and orange. |
| Ms. Thomas: | Good talking about how the leaves are changing colors and becoming different. |

*[The teacher then shows a new picture of change—the cycle of growth in which a caterpillar becomes a butterfly—and selects a child to be the teacher and talk about change as it occurs in the second picture.]*

| | |
|---|---|
| Ms. Thomas: | It's Luisa's turn to tell us what is happening to the caterpillar in this picture. |
| Luisa: | The caterpillar is small here. It gets big. That is a cocoon. |
| Ms. Thomas: | Yes, the little caterpillar is growing. When it is bigger, it forms a cocoon. |
| | What happens after the caterpillar forms a cocoon? What do you see in the picture? |
| Luisa: | A butterfly! |
| Ms. Thomas: | Say that with me: The caterpillar turns into a butterfly. |

*[The teacher models how to talk about what is the same about the two pictures last.]*

Ms. Thomas: What's the same about change in these two pictures? Hmm, these are both pictures of something that is becoming different *[pointing to both images]*.

The caterpillar is changing and becoming bigger until it becomes a cocoon and then a butterfly.

*[The teacher points to different phases of growth in the picture.]*

Here *[pointing to the pictures of leaves]*, the green summer leaves are changing colors and becoming different in the fall.

Both pictures show something that is changing and becoming different.

Ms. Thomas: Think. What is the same about these pictures?

Children: Changing!

Beatriz: Something is changing.

Luisa: Something is different!

The same instructional strategy was used to talk about the remaining vocabulary concepts in Table 5.4.

As children become adept in using the target words to talk about similarities, the instructional scaffolding and teacher modeling can gradually fade, and children can discuss similarities across three or four related words/concepts (e.g., picture of a green *plant* growing from a *seed*, a *sprouting bulb*, a *vine* growing from a bean *seed*). These are further examples of the concept of change and allow children to see connections among the previously taught vocabulary words/concepts *plant, seed, sprout, bulb,* and *vine.*

## Challenge Your Thinking

This is a variation of the previously discussed higher cognitive activity. In this interactive discussion, teachers develop a challenging question in which children talk about what is different between two vocabulary concepts with the

**Table 5.4.** Be the teacher: Advanced discussion on conceptual similarities and differences

| Vocabulary | First concept | Second concept | Similarities and differences |
| --- | --- | --- | --- |
| Blossom | *Picture 1:* white blossoms growing on a tree along a mountainside | *Picture 2:* tomato plant with white blossoms before the fruit appears on the vine | Both pictures show that blossoms are flowers whether they grow on trees or on vines. |
| Ripe | *Picture 1:* photograph of two tomatoes on a branch. One tomato is green (not ripe), and the other one is red (ripe). An arrow was inserted on the picture that points to the red, ripe tomato. | *Picture 2:* a ripe pumpkin on a vine | Both pictures show something (fruit) that is ripe and ready to use or eat whether they are grown on a vine or on a branch. |

objective of making connections among current content vocabulary and words/concepts that were taught in previous lessons when possible:

- "What is the difference between *spring* and *winter?*"
- "What is the difference between something *changing* and something *staying* the same?"
- "What is the difference between *summer* and *fall?*"
- "What is the difference between a *vine* and a *seed?*"

In addition, the teacher can develop a question that encourages children to challenge their thinking and talking about related life experiences. In these discussions, children are asked to provide a reason for their thinking:

- "Would it be very cold in the *summer?* Why or why not?"
- "Could you see a *raindrop* if it was snowing? Why or why not?"

Responding to challenging questions can generate critical thinking, especially when children are able to talk about exceptions. For example, when responding to the question, "Could we find a cow in the *city?*" there was always a child in the WORLD study who suggested that they saw a cow in the petting zoo in a large city. Such thinking and responding is applauded with the teacher emphasizing that a cow could be found in a city's petting zoo, but, for the most part, cows require larger areas of land or pastures for grazing. These pastures are found outside of a city where there is more land for raising farm animals. In this example, the teacher attends to an essential characteristic about cities—that cities have limited space (land) and may not be conducive to raising animals that require large land areas that can be found on ranches or farms. In the WORLD intervention, adult–child conversations that were analytical in nature were most associated with growth in children's vocabulary outcomes (Gonzalez, Pollard-Durodola, Simmons, Taylor, Davis, Fogarty, & Simmons, 2013). In other words, the more time preschool teachers spent on vocabulary-related association talk (e.g., "What is the difference between *frozen* water and *liquid?*"), the greater were children's general receptive vocabulary gains. Also, the more time preschool teachers spent in comprehension-related association talk (e.g., "Can you drink something that is *frozen?* Why or why not?"), the greater were the gains in generalized receptive vocabulary. In the end, these higher-level analytical discussions are dependent on the teacher's ability to extend oral responses and model extensive vocabulary usage (Dickinson, 2011).

## MULTIPLE OPPORTUNITIES TO EVALUATE STUDENT LEARNING VIA ORAL RESPONSES

In addition to providing a context for introducing and reviewing important vocabulary concepts within interactive thematic discussions, repeated text readings and intentional integration of opportunities to discuss and respond also facilitate multiple ways to informally evaluate student learning. In the WORLD intervention, students' linguistic and cognitive abilities were informally evaluated in interactive discussion opportunities with adult feedback that occurred throughout the lesson (e.g., after the first reading of a text, "Look at this picture in the book. What is this room under the house? How is a *basement* like other rooms in a house?"; during paired-discussions, "Turn and tell your neighbor what you learned about the *bulb* in this picture"; Ready, Set, Go!).

The 5th day of the instructional unit can be used to cumulatively review the week's topic and broader theme by discussing all target vocabulary and connected science and social concepts across complementary texts. Three activities that are appropriate for cross-text reviews are the Same Game, Classifications, and an extended Magic Mirror.

## The Same Game

This activity allows children to review the bigger theme and smaller topic in an instructional unit by discussing conceptual similarities across complementary texts. For example, after reading and discussing the storybook *No Jumping on the Bed!* (Arnold, 1987) and the complementary informational text *House* (Schaefer, 2003), children first retell what happened in the storybook and what new information they learned in the informational text. Then they identify and discuss conceptual similarities.

## Retell the Story with Book Pictures and Target Words

| | |
|---|---|
| Ms. Thomas: | This week, we read books and talked about places where people can live in a city. |
| | Look at this picture in the story *No Jumping on the Bed!* Tell us what happened to the character in the story. Try to use the word *apartment*. |
| | Now look at this picture [*character falling through the ceiling*], and tell us what happened in the story. Try to use the word *ceiling*. |
| Ms. Thomas: | Now let's look at our information book *House*. Tell us what you learned about *roof* on this page. |
| | Now look at this picture and tell us what you learned about *basements*. |

## Talk About Conceptual Similarities: Storybook and Informational Text

Now children describe similar attributes shared by apartments and homes:

| | |
|---|---|
| Ms. Thomas: | I want you to look carefully at the pictures from our books this week and talk about what is the same about apartments and homes. |

[*Children look carefully at a book page in the story that shows the main character jumping on the bed in a tall apartment that is part of a city skyline. Children compare this picture with a photograph of a home on the cover of the informational text.*]

Ms. Thomas:   Tell me what you see that is the same in these pictures of homes.

*[Children discuss the fact that both pictures depict city buildings—a home and an apartment building—in which people live and that both buildings contain lights, a roof, and windows. The teacher can reemphasize the idea that apartments and homes share similar features and that both buildings provide shelter from the weather.]*

## Magic Mirror

Another appropriate activity for a Day 5 cumulative review is the Magic Mirror (see Second Reading of the Book: Opportunities to Talk After Reading the Book), which would now include clues for all target words taught during the week. When designing this type of activity, provide brief clues that describe the critical features of the target word and also integrate the meaning of the word as it was taught in the shared book-reading experience. See the following examples:

Ms. Thomas:   I see a place that has lots of people and many tall and short buildings, street signs and stoplights, a lot of noise, many streets that are crowded with cars, and there are many places to work. Does anyone know what word the Magic Mirror is showing me?

*[Answer:* city, *a place with lots of people and buildings]*

Ms. Thomas:   I see someone who lives on my street or in my building and lives right next door to me. Does anyone know what word the Magic Mirror is showing me?

*[Answer:* neighbor, *a person who lives in a building or a house that is close to you]*

## Classification

In this activity, students are able to generalize knowledge about vocabulary and concepts beyond the context of the book. The teacher provides new examples of taught concepts, as well as nonexamples, and links concepts to previously taught information.

Ms. Thomas:   *[Showing a picture of a bowl of soup]* This is soup. Is this a *liquid*? Why or why not?

Ms. Thomas:   *[Showing a picture of shampoo]* This is shampoo. Is shampoo a *liquid*? Why or why not?

The teacher then can follow with two or three examples of target vocabulary from previous lessons.

Ms. Thomas:   *[Showing a picture of the ocean]* This is the *ocean*. Is an *ocean* a *liquid*? Why or why not?

Ms. Thomas:   *[Showing a picture of a river]* This is a *river*. Is a river a *liquid*? Why or why not?

Last, the teacher can include nonexamples from previous lessons.

Ms. Thomas: *[Showing picture of seeds]* These are *seeds*. Are *seeds* liquid? Why or why not?

Ms. Thomas: *[Showing picture of a meadow]* This is a *meadow*. Is a *meadow* a *liquid*? Why or why not?

## REVISED BLOOM'S TAXONOMY

Because the WORLD shared book-reading approach aimed to accelerate content learning through a range of task complexity, its continuum of instruction maps onto the Revised Bloom's Taxonomy (RBT; Anderson & Krathwohl, 2001; Pohl, 2001, 2006)—a model used to infuse more complex levels of thinking during academic learning. In the RBT, verbs are used in place of the original nouns (see Table 5.5) to describe the progression of cognitive thinking as an active and dynamic process (Pohl, 2001, 2006). In Table 5.5, we provide examples of WORLD instructional tasks that exemplify the continuum of basic to more complex thinking in the six-tiered RBT. (See http://www.utar.edu.my/fegt/file/Revised_Blooms_Info.pdf for further information on the six levels of thinking summarized in the RBT.)

## DESIGNING INSTRUCTION

In this chapter, we have provided examples of how instruction can be distributed across the week and before, during, and after reading the book. We also have provided examples of how to vary instruction from the first reading of the book to the second reading of the book to increase depth of learning with frequent opportunities to use new words to talk about book content and to make connections between new and previously learned concepts. Using the science and social studies standards and instructional planning from Chapters 3 and 4, you will continue to design a science and a social studies instructional unit. For each unit, you will do the following:

1. Create a content map to summarize how content vocabulary instruction will be sequenced and scheduled across the week (5 days) and implemented with the repeated reading of complementary texts. You can use simple headings such as *Before, While,* and *After Reading* to organize your instructional planning. See Figure 2.1 in Chapter 2 for an example of the WORLD content map for one instructional unit.

2. Develop open-ended questions to prime background knowledge before reading the book. Use *wh-* questions and avoid questions that can be answered with yes or no responses.

3. Develop open-ended postreading questions to talk about book content and life experiences while using new vocabulary. These questions can be used to informally evaluate children's comprehension of content and provide more time for in-depth discussions.

**Table 5.5.** Bloom's revised taxonomy and the WORLD approach

| Benjamin Bloom's original taxonomy | Revised Bloom's taxonomy (RBT) http://www.utar.edu.my/fegt/file/Revised_Blooms _Info.pdf | In the WORLD approach, preschool children do the following: |
|---|---|---|
| Level 1: knowledge | Remembering *Recalling, naming, and retrieving information* | Remember and recall vocabulary concepts and important prior knowledge before reading a text "Look at this picture *[garden]*. What is this?" |
| Level 2: comprehension | Understanding *Explaining concepts* | Demonstrate an understanding of book content (characters, what happened in the story, new facts learned about a topic in an informational text) and vocabulary concepts in after-reading discussions "Who are the characters in this storybook?" |
| Level 3: application | Applying *Applying and using information in a different situation* | Apply vocabulary and content knowledge to talk about life experiences beyond the book in after-reading discussions "Where have you seen a garden?" |
| Level 4: analysis | Analyzing *Exploring relationships among concepts by comparing and examining the smaller parts* | Explore relationships between semantically related content vocabulary and connected science and social studies concepts in challenge questions "What is the difference between a *root* and a *seed?*" Smaller part (scaffolding): "What do we know about roots?" |
| Level 5: synthesis | Evaluating (In the revised taxonomy, *evaluation* was used for the 5th level.) *Making judgments or justifying a decision* | Justify decisions by providing reasons (*why* questions) when thinking and talking about why concepts are or are not connected "Would a *seed* that is growing be on top of the *soil?* Why or why not?" |
| Level 6: evaluation | Creating (In the revised taxonomy, *synthesis* or *creating* was used for the 6th level.) *Encouraging new ways of seeing things* | See and talk about the world in new ways through the lens of new science and social studies knowledge |

*Key:* WORLD, Words of Oral Reading and Language Development.

4. Design review opportunities that integrate lower cognitive (e.g., brief word reviews) and higher cognitive skills (e.g., adult–child conversations that expand children's language use and knowledge through deep processing). Higher cognitive tasks should allow children to make important associations and connections between content vocabulary and concepts.

5. Design one home–community connection to encourage discussions between the child and family members.

6. Develop one center-based activity for the science and social studies instructional unit.

## RECOMMENDATIONS FOR ENGLISH LANGUAGE LEARNERS

Teachers of ELL children must be knowledgeable about language development in order to respond to children who may experience second-language difficulties while learning academic content knowledge in English (Fillmore & Snow, 2000; Wright, 2010). This means that ELL teachers 1) acknowledge the dual expectations (Gersten, 1996) placed on young language learners who are expected to quickly acquire English proficiency while mastering new academic content and 2) modify the language of instruction during challenging content learning as children demonstrate varied stages of language acquisition (Wright, 2010).

In order to make better decisions about how to provide language support during shared book-reading discussions, teachers of ELLs should know the following about second-language acquisition and instruction.

What Teachers Should Understand About Second-Language Acquisition:

1. There is evidence that it may take 2–4 years to develop oral English proficiency that is similar to that of native English speakers (Hakuta, Butler, & Witt, 2000) and even longer—5–8 years—for ELLs to develop and demonstrate English language proficiency that is appropriate for academic school discussions (Crawford & Krashen, 2007; Wright, 2010).

2. Academic language development includes the language used when talking about academic content (e.g., science, social studies, math, literature) and concepts as well as the language used to make school presentations, problem-solve with others, and so forth (Hamayan, Marier, Sánchez-López, & Damico, 2013).

3. Our understanding of preschool second-language acquisition and development is inconclusive because previous ELL studies often have included older school-age children and have not studied preschool children's second-language development independently (Genesee, 2010; Gutiérrez et al., 2010). Overall, there is limited research on child second-language development (Genesee, 2010).

What Teachers Should Understand About Second-Language Instruction

1. Prior to content learning, ELLs benefit from an introduction to or preview of content-related vocabulary and language (e.g., phrases, sentences) that are important for learning about a topic (Snow, Met, & Genessee, 1989). ELLs also need exposures to language unrelated to the text (e.g., verb tenses) that can assist children in discussing a topic (Hamayan et al., 2013; Snow et al., 1989).

2. Children from diverse linguistic backgrounds benefit from instructional conversations or dialogues that enhance children's oral language skills and provide a foundation for building complex vocabulary for higher order cognitive tasks (e.g., making inferences; Center for Research on Education, Diversity & Excellence, 2014; Tharp & Gallimore, 1991). See

*Instructional Conversations* at http://manoa.hawaii.edu/coe/crede/videos/ instructional-conversation.

The instructional implication of these big ideas on second-language acquisition and instruction is that young preschool ELL children may benefit from instructional support during shared book reading to enable them to discuss science and social studies concepts and book content while still developing academic English language proficiency. As discussed in Chapter 3, TESOL's (2006) English language proficiency standards summarize academic language proficiency as "being able to communicate for social, intercultural, and instructional purposes within the school setting and being able to communicate information, ideas, and concepts necessary for academic success in language arts, mathematics, science, and social studies" (Wright, 2010, p. 33).

Because it takes longer to *communicate* with an English proficiency that is sophisticated (e.g., syntax, vocabulary) enough to support academic learning, ELL children may initially experience difficulty using science and social studies vocabulary and concepts to discuss thematic shared book-reading content. For example, ELL Spanish-speaking children who participated in the English WORLD intervention entered preschool with limited English and Spanish language abilities (e.g., vocabulary, syntax structure) as indicated by their PreLAS (DeAvilia & Duncan, 2000) English and Spanish language proficiency scores at the beginning of the school year. During professional development sessions, bilingual teachers in the study discussed their concerns about children being able to participate in book discussions during the beginning of the school year when children were becoming acclimated to preschool and learning to speak in English.

Although there is no clear recipe for the type and amount of instructional support and scaffolding that should be integrated during brief shared book-reading sessions with ELLs, bilingual teachers in the WORLD ELL studies were taught to support and extend preschool children's oral language abilities in the following ways:

1. Teachers included multiple opportunities for ELL children to become familiar with the topic, concepts, and vocabulary prior to listening to thematic texts read in English (e.g., previewing vocabulary, priming background knowledge, hearing language modeled during topic immersion discussions).

2. Teachers used specific ESL strategies to facilitate language development (e.g., English as a second-language [ESL] strategies).

In this chapter, we have suggested ways (e.g., use of visuals, thematic posters, previewing vocabulary and the text) to familiarize young children with thematic topics, content-related vocabulary, and concepts before reading the book to build background knowledge and prepare children for listening to the text. Table 5.6 focuses on language strategies that can be used by teachers to

**Table 5.6.** Language-learning strategies that provide predictable ways for children to respond

| Description of language strategy | Examples from instruction |
|---|---|
| Sentence stems provide language patterns for starting a sentence. | 1. Magic Mirror activity: Describe vocabulary concepts. |
| | Ms. Thomas: Okay, Carla. Look into the magic mirror and tell us about the *waves* that you see. |
| | Say, "I see _____ in the Magic Mirror." |
| | "I see waves that are _____." |
| | 2. Make a prediction before reading a text. |
| | Ms. Thomas: Turn and tell your friend what you think will happen on this page with the ocean. |
| | Say, "I think _____." |
| | 3. Review previously taught information. |
| | Ms. Thomas: Look at the picture and say what is happening with the shark on this page. Tell your friend what you learned about the *shark* here. |
| | Say, "I learned that _____." |
| | Say, "The shark is _____." |
| Choral response is used to model appropriate language use (syntax, verb tense, etc.) with a group of children. The teacher models language use by saying a sentence in English and asking all children to repeat the sentence together. | 4. Postreading book discussion |
| | Ms. Thomas: What happens during the fall? Yes, the weather changes. |
| | Say this with me, "The weather changes during the fall." |
| | Ms. Thomas: Look at this picture. What happens in this garden in the spring? Yes, the plants grow. |
| | Say this with me, "The plants grow in the garden in the spring." |
| Paired practice is used to strategically have children talk and listen to each other. Pairs should be flexible and changed periodically to allow children to interact with different children. | Pair children by language abilities so that children who are less English proficient have opportunities to dialogue with children who are more English proficient. |

facilitate book discussions with ELL children with limited language abilities. These suggestions are similar to instructional practices implemented in early intervention studies that have relied on a range of language-learning strategies (e.g., use of gestures, sentence stems, native language support) to support language and literacy learning for young Spanish-speaking children (Collins, 2005; Mathes, Pollard-Durodola, Cárdenas-Hagan, Linan-Thompson, & Vaughn, 2007; Tong, Lara-Alecio, Irby, Mathes, & Kwok, 2008; Vaughn, Linan-Thompson, Pollard-Durodola, Mathes, & Cárdenas-Hagan, 2005).

In addition to scaffolding language use during difficult tasks with targeted language strategies, the use of visuals (e.g., WORLD picture/concept cards) with explicit teacher explanation is also a preferred method for teaching beginning language learners (Adelson-Goldstein, 1998). Using visual presentation strategies, however, do not ensure that learned words become included in children's active vocabularies, so there should be opportunities beyond the book- reading session to utilize the vocabulary in the primary language or in English.

In general, more research is needed to examine how shared book reading as an instructional tool can be implemented most effectively (e.g., length of intervention, language of instruction) with ELLs who have varied oral English language proficiency (Gutiérrez et al., 2010).

## SUGGESTED FURTHER READINGS

Pollard-Durodola, S.D., Gonzalez, J.E., Simmons, D.C., Simmons, L., & Nava-Walichowski, M. (2011). Using knowledge networks to develop preschoolers' content vocabulary. *The Reading Teacher, 65*(4), 259–269.

Wasik, B., & Iannone-Campbell, C. (2012). Developing vocabulary through strategic conversations. *The Reading Teacher, 66*(2), 321–332.

# Instruction in Practice

**6**

## Teaching Strategies in Action

**THE AIM OF THIS CHAPTER IS** to provide two instructional shared book-reading vignettes that exemplify how early childhood educators can accelerate content vocabulary knowledge via instruction that integrates the three design principles introduced in Chapter 1 and discussed in Chapters 3–5. In each vignette, we provide strategy suggestions (e.g., scaffolding, modeling appropriate language use) and specific activities (Ready, Set, Go!; Magic Mirror; Same Game; Challenge Questions) that were introduced in Chapter 5 as ways to enhance thematic content discussions. The first lesson includes a book discussion on plants. The second lesson is from a cumulative end-of-the-week discussion on seasons.

**KEY IDEAS |** The key ideas discussed in this chapter are as follows:

1. Provide plentiful opportunities for children to use their new vocabulary in a range of contexts (e.g., in the book, beyond the book).

2. Increase opportunities for language use through "turn and talk with your neighbor/partner." In this activity, each child is able to listen to and respond to his or her friend's comments while the teacher listens to each pair and provides feedback.

3. The most strategic way to correct student errors is to model the response to your question and then provide additional opportunities for children to respond.

4. There are many dimensions of language (e.g., receptive, expressive, single-word use, elaborated responses) that should be incorporated into shared book-reading discussions. How this is accomplished is dependent on the teacher's own instructional approach and strengths.

## CONTEXT FOR TWO WORDS OF ORAL READING AND LANGUAGE DEVELOPMENT SHARED BOOK-READING SCIENCE LESSONS: TEACHING STRATEGIES IN ACTION

The following instructional vignettes, both 20 minutes in length, illustrate shared book-reading lessons taught by Mrs. Espinosa and Ms. Lucia (pseudonyms), two preschool teachers in dual language (Spanish/English) classrooms in which Spanish-speaking children were acquiring English vocabulary instruction. We selected excerpts from their videotaped shared book-reading lessons because they were strong implementers of the WORLD pedagogical approach and made intentional attempts to scaffold instruction and model language use during challenging analytical tasks. These small-group dialogues are beneficial to early childhood educators because they offer examples of how to scaffold instruction, provide feedback, and encourage interactive discussions about content knowledge with children who are still acquiring language proficiency. These interactive conversations also would benefit native English-speaking preschool children through the same thoughtful modeling of oral language use and conceptual knowledge extensions.

Throughout the before, during, and after reading sequence in each shared book-reading vignette, we refer to specific and intentional strategies and steps implemented by the teacher to distribute thematic instruction and to enhance language engagement and content learning. These instructional strategies and steps parallel the sequence of suggestions summarized in Chapter 5 for distributing instruction across the repeated reading of complementary texts organized by science or social studies themes and topics.

WORLD teachers received basic lesson scripts to guide content learning and interactive discussions. We quickly learned, however, in the curriculum development process (summarized in Chapter 2) that a scripted approach only provides a framework, or a "plan," for sequencing instruction and offers limited suggestions for scaffolding instruction and responding to children. Both Mrs. Espinosa and Ms. Lucia exemplify two preschool teachers who "think on their feet" in response to children's knowledge level and oral abilities to create lively conversations that move beyond the framework of a prescribed lesson plan.

We have noted examples of when teachers scaffold instruction, extend student language or content knowledge, monitor paired discussions, and provide feedback or confirmation of student responses. We also note instances in which teachers might have provided additional information or clarification of concepts to increase students' content learning and use of more complex language. Keep in mind that these instructional vignettes depict adult–child conversational exchanges with children who are still developing English language proficiency while acquiring academic knowledge. The teaching behaviors reflect decisions made at the moment of instruction and often include the implementation of the language strategies discussed in Chapter 5 that *extend* children's oral abilities. These strategies are commonly used in classes in which English is taught as a second language (ESL):

- *Sentence stems:* Say, "I see a garden in the Magic Mirror."
- *Choral response:* Let's say this together . . .
- *Repetition of words, phrases, and sentences to ensure that students can understand what is being said or asked:* Tell me something that *you know* about a *bud*. What do you *know* about a *bud?* What can you *tell me* about a bud? Joseph?

## SCIENCE INSTRUCTIONAL VIGNETTE 1: MRS. ESPINOSA

Mrs. Espinosa is a preschool teacher who has 8 years of overall teaching experience with 1 year of teaching experience in a preschool setting. During this lesson, she is seated at a *u*-shaped table with six preschool students.

The lesson that she teaches is from an instructional unit on plants in the theme of *living things.* Mrs. Espinosa integrates multiple exposures to words and concepts via repeated readings of twin texts so that new information and words are introduced during the first reading of the text and reviewed in the second reading. On Days 1 and 2, specifically, Mrs. Espinosa reads the storybook *Planting a Rainbow* (Ehlert, 1988), introduces and reviews three related vocabulary words (*bulb, ground,* and *sprout*), and emphasizes the following concepts:

1. *Bulbs* are the round part of a plant that can be planted underground, such as a seed.
2. When *bulbs* are planted in the fall, they begin to *sprout,* or grow new parts, in the spring when the soil, or ground, is warm.
3. The *ground* is the part of the earth that people stand on and plants grow from.

Because concepts build on one another sequentially, on Day 3, the children learn more about plants via the informational text *Leaves* (Whitehouse, 2002), learn two new vocabulary words (*vine* and *bud*), and discuss the following concepts:

1. Leaves are parts of a plant and can grow on *vines,* which are long, curvy stems.
2. Leaves are important because they use sunlight, water, and air to make food for the plant and to help the plant breathe.
3. When a plant grows, new leaves appear inside the *bud.* The *bud* is the part of the plant that turns into a leaf or flower.

The following Day 4 instructional vignette illustrates how Mrs. Espinosa reviews concepts in the second reading of the information book *Leaves* and integrates higher cognitive questions in the postreading activities during her shared book-reading discussion. We summarize an excerpt of this discussion next.

## Discussion Before Rereading the Book *Leaves*

⭐ **TEACHING STRATEGY:** Review the theme and topic while pointing to examples of living things on the cover of the book.

Mrs. Espinosa: Okay, boys and girls. Remember that this week, we are learning about plants. Plants are living things because they need—what do plants need to grow?

Children: Water!

Hema: Sunlight!

Children: Air.

Mrs. Espinosa: Yes, plants are living things because they need water, air, and sunlight to grow tall. Remember that plants also need soil. *[Note: The word* soil *was taught in a previous lesson.]*

⭐ **TEACHING STRATEGY:** Use a new visual (picture/concept card) to review each vocabulary concept (*vine* and *bud*).

Mrs. Espinosa: Yesterday we read an information book called *Leaves.* Remember the book? We learned some new magic words. I am going to show you some new pictures of our new words. Everyone look—eyes here.

This is a *vine.* Everyone, what is this?

Children: *Vine!*

Mrs. Espinosa: Yes, it is a *vine.* Tell me something that you know about *vines.* What can you tell us about *vines?* Raise your hand. Victor, what can you tell us about a *vine? [The teacher emphasizes the word* vine *several times with her voice while pointing to* vine *in the picture.]*

Victor: I see the *vine.* It is a plant.

Mrs. Espinosa: Okay, a *vine* is the long stem of a plant. What else can you tell me about a *vine?* Remember when we talked about *vines?* What does a *vine* do? *[The teacher gestures with her finger to indicate that it spirals or curves.]* It does what? Letty?

Letty: It grows.

Mrs. Espinosa: Yes, it grows. But *how* does it grow *[still holding the picture of a vine and spiraling her finger in the air]*?

Miguel: Like a tree.

Mrs. Espinosa: It can grow up like a tree. But think, *what does it do [curving her finger while holding the picture of a vine]*?

| | |
|---|---|
| Children: | It curls. |
| Mrs. Espinosa: | Yes, it can curl or *curve* around a tree. |
| Rosa: | Or a pole! |
| Mrs. Espinosa: | Yes, it can grow around a pole, too! Good thinking. A *vine* helps the plant to grow long. In this new picture of a vine, we see that it can even grow along a wall. |
| | Now let's look at our other picture. This is a *bud*. What is this? |
| Children: | Bud! |
| Mrs. Espinosa: | Tell me something that you know about a *bud*. What can you tell me about a *bud*? Joseph? |
| Joseph: | I see a *bud*. It is a plant. |
| Mrs. Espinosa: | *A bud is a plant.* |
| | And what does a *bud* turn into? Guillermo, what does a *bud* turn into? |
| Rosa: | Flower! Flower! |
| Guillermo: | The *bud* is going to . . . to . . . to . . . close. |
| Mrs. Espinosa: | A *bud* can be closed. But what is going to happen to the *bud* in this picture *[gesturing with fingers, opening them like a bud]*? |
| Hema: | It opens. |
| Guillermo: | It opens. |
| Mrs. Espinosa: | Okay. Yes, it will open, and then it is going to turn into a what *[pointing to picture]*? |

**RECOMMENDED PRACTICE**

Use a visual, gestures, and more specific language to clarify word meaning. Mrs. Espinosa could clarify, "A vine can grow upward like a tree, but how does it grow around the tree? Look at this picture of the vine. What is the vine doing in this picture?"

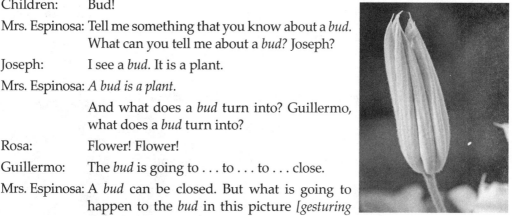

**RECOMMENDED PRACTICE**

Clarify the meaning of the word. Mrs. Espinosa could say, "A bud is not the entire plant. A bud is a *part* of a plant."

---

⭐ **TEACHING STRATEGY:** Model appropriate language use: "Yes, the bud is going to open. When it opens, what will it become?"

---

| | |
|---|---|
| Children: | A flower. |
| Mrs. Espinosa: | *Yes, the* bud *will turn into a flower!* *Excellent thinking.* |
| | The *bud* is going to turn into a flower. |

**RECOMMENDED PRACTICE**

Clarify the concept and model appropriate language use. Mrs. Espinosa could say, "Yes, a flower or leaf will grow from the bud."

Mrs. Espinosa: *So these are our two words.*

*[Showing the first picture again]*

This is *what*?

Children: *Vine.*

Mrs. Espinosa: Yes, *vine.* *[Showing the picture of the closed bud again]*

And this one is?

Children: *Bud*

Mrs. Espinosa: Yes, this is a *bud.* Let's say that together.

Mrs. Espinosa
and Children: This is a *bud.*

Mrs. Espinosa: Yes, this picture is a *bud.* Good, those are our two new words.

 **RECOMMENDED PRACTICE**

Provide an instructional objective. Mrs. Espinosa could say, "Let's practice the two words that we have reviewed today. What is this word?"

## Discussion While Rereading the Book *Leaves*

⭐ **TEACHING STRATEGY:** Read the book and stop to review each target word when it first appears on the page by generating a brief paired discussion on vocabulary concepts.

Mrs. Espinosa: Now we are going to read our information book called *Leaves.* This time, I want you to be ready to tell what you learned about plants on our magic word pages. I am going to ask you to tell what you learned about *vines* and *buds.*

*[The teacher reads the book, using her voice to emphasize key concepts while pointing to related items on the page. She stops before reading the sentence with the word vine.]*

Mrs. Espinosa: Look, this is an important page *[book content about and photograph of a vine].* I want you to look at the picture and tell what you *learned.* Now turn and tell your friend about what you learned on this page.

 **RECOMMENDED PRACTICE**

Be more specific when confirming the correct response. Mrs. Espinosa could say, "Good saying *vine* and *bud!*"

*[Children move close to their friend and begin to say, "I learned that _____."]*

⭐ **TEACHING STRATEGY:** Monitor the discussion by providing feedback to each pair of students while listening to their conversations.

Mrs. Espinosa: Say, "I learned _____." *[to another pair]* Okay, what curves here? What is that called? Okay, I heard "plant" but what is that *called? [to another pair] Very good! It is the stem of a plant [pointing to a book picture] and it curves around the tree in the picture.* So what is the magic word everyone?

Children: *Vine!*

Mrs. Espinosa: Excellent remembering! Now let's keep reading. First, I'll read the sentence about the *vine* and then I will keep reading.

*[The teacher continues to read and now reads about how leaves grow. She reads with expression, emphasizing key concepts that are written on the book page, such as "leaves need air, sunlight, and water"; "leaves begin to grow from inside seeds"; and so forth, while pointing to information depicted on the page.]*

Mrs. Espinosa: Ah, look at this. This is a page with our magic word. Look at the picture carefully and turn and tell your neighbor what you *learned.* Try to use the magic word. Talk to your friend *[using gestures to show children how to turn toward their friend]* about what you learned about this word *[pointing to picture].*

Mrs. Espinosa: Yes, it is closed. What is it called?

---

⭐ **TEACHING STRATEGY:** Listen to student responses, provide feedback to individual student pairs (pointing to book picture when needed), and model appropriate language use.

---

*[To another pair]* Yes, we see that it is closed, *but what is it?* Turn and tell your friend. It is a . . . I heard the magic word *bud!* Excellent thinking. *Say, "The bud is going to grow and open."* Yes, now you tell your friend about the bud. Look at each other when you talk.

*[To another pair]* Where? What is that called *[pointing to the picture of the bud in the book]?*

*[To another pair]* Okay, I heard the word *bud,* and I heard the word *plant.* Good using both words.

So everyone, what did you learn about *buds?*

Hema: The new leaves are inside the bud.

Mrs. Espinosa: Yes, Hema, the new leaves are inside the bud. *See, the leaves are going to pop out of the bud.*

**RECOMMENDED PRACTICE**

Mrs. Espinosa: Yes, we learned that the *buds* are now beginning to open during the spring when the weather is warm.

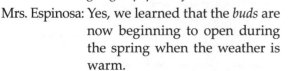

Extend learning. Mrs. Espinosa could say, "What else did we learn about *buds?*"

*[Mrs. Espinosa continues to read in the book about how animals use leaves for food and to build homes.]*

And that is the end of this information book called *Leaves.*

## Discussion After Rereading the Book *Leaves*

⭐ **TEACHING STRATEGY:** Use visuals (e.g., the same picture/concept cards) to cumulatively review words and concepts (present week and previous 2 weeks) quickly (1–2 minutes), as in Ready, Set, Go!

ACTIVITY

## Ready, Set, Go!—A Quick Cumulative Review of Concepts

Mrs. Espinosa: This is your favorite part. We are going to play Ready, Set, Go! Let's use the timer. You have 1 minute to tell me the name of each picture as fast as you can. You will tell me what the picture is, and we have to do this quickly. Now concentrate and listen carefully. [*She shuffles the cards to mix them up.*]

Mrs. Espinosa: Okay, ready, set, *go!*

[*She flashes two picture/concept cards for each vocabulary concept learned in the present week and in the previous 2 weeks. These cards have been randomly shuffled and are not presented in any specific order. See Table 6.1 for vocabulary concepts that children will review.*]

## Words and Concepts Cumulatively Reviewed in *Ready, Set, Go!*

⭐ **TEACHING STRATEGY:** Provide the correct information when children respond incorrectly or cannot identify the vocabulary concept depicted in the visual (e.g., "Everyone, this is _____. What is this?"), then recycle the card in the stack so that children will have another opportunity to identify the vocabulary concept correctly. Recycle it three cards back in the stack.

Mrs. Espinosa: Okay, let's look at these pictures for one more minute. I need to make sure that everyone really knows the information and new words.

Okay, eyes up here! Let's go. [*She flashes the cards again, using the 1-minute timer. All children are able to identify the words.*]

**Table 6.1.** Vocabulary concepts cumulatively reviewed in Ready, Set, Go!

| *Earth* topic | Vocabulary concepts |
| --- | --- |
| Land and water | Sea, shark, ocean, wave, underwater, coral |
| | |
| *Living things* topic | |
| Plants | Garden, plant, seed, soil, root |
| | |
| Plants | Bulb, sprout, ground, bud, vine |

**Challenge Questions: Talking About Differences Among Concepts**

⭐ **TEACHING STRATEGY:** Use higher cognitive questions to deeply process content vocabulary and related concepts as in Challenge Questions in which students first talk about conceptual differences prior to focusing on the "big-kid question."

Mrs. Espinosa: Okay, let's look at this picture, and I am going to ask some questions [holding picture of vine].

What is the *difference* between a *vine* and a *seed?*

[Silence.]

Rosa: Not the same!

Mrs. Espinosa: Yes, Rosa, difference means that something is not the same. How are the *vine* and the *seed* not the same?

Rosa: Because one needs water.

Mrs. Espinosa: Does the *vine* need water?

Children: Yes!

Mrs. Espinosa: Does the *seed* need water?

Children: Yes!

Mrs. Espinosa: Then a *vine* and a *seed* are the same because they need water. How is the *seed* different from a *vine?* Think, how are they *not the same?*

[Silence.]

The seed is what?

[Silence.]

⭐ **TEACHING STRATEGY:** Use visuals of the vocabulary concepts to help children remember that a plant grows from a seed.

Mrs. Espinosa: Okay, *let's look at this picture of a seed.*

Remember we learned about *seeds* in the storybook *How a Seed Grows.* What is growing from the *seed* in this picture?

Joseph: A plant grows from a *seed.*

Mrs. Espinosa: Good, Joseph. Everyone, what do you think? Does a *seed* need water to *grow?*

Children: Yes!

Mrs. Espinosa: Yes, a seed needs water to grow. Does a *vine* need water?

Children:     Yes!

Mrs. Espinosa: Then that is something that is the *same about a vine and a seed.*

---

⭐ **TEACHING STRATEGY:** Extend learning about what is the same by connecting open-ended questions to the theme (living things; e.g., "A *vine* and a *seed* need water because they are living things, and living things need water.")

---

Mrs. Espinosa: Let me help you understand the *difference* between a *vine* and a *seed*. In this picture of a *seed*, we see that the *seed* is the thing that this plant is growing from. In this picture of vine, we see that a *vine* is different from a seed because it is the long curvy stem of a plant. . . . But the *vine* is not the *seed*. It can grow *from* a seed. So the difference between a *vine* and a seed is that the *vine* is a long, curvy stem and a *seed* is the thing that plants grow from.

## An Opportunity for Reflection: What Are the Minimal Differences Between a Seed and a Vine?

In this episode of the lesson, it was difficult for children to talk about the difference between a seed and a vine. Although Mrs. Espinosa used a visual to review the concept *seed*, which was introduced in the previous week, additional scaffolding and clarification was required so that children could better understand the critical attributes of a seed and a vine and how the two concepts are different.

When children could not talk about the difference between a seed and a vine, Mrs. Espinosa attempted to scaffold instruction first by encouraging the children to think about what is the *same* about a vine and a seed. She did this by asking if a vine and a seed needed water. Although it may be beneficial first to talk about *conceptual similarities* before discussing *conceptual differences*, this strategy clearly is not implemented in this lesson, which began with a discussion on differences.

What is also missing is a clear understanding of the *minimal differences* between a seed and a vine. We suggest that students' learning could be enhanced if Mrs. Espinosa used visuals to point out the *minimal differences* between the two concepts.

Here is an example of how Mrs. Espinosa could turn this conversation around with instructional scaffolding when children cannot talk analytically. She can use visuals of both concepts to focus on and point to the minimal differences between a seed and a vine while reviewing what children have learned about vines and seeds in previous shared book-reading lessons. See Figure 6.1 for an example of instructional scaffolding.

---

**An Example of Instructional Scaffolding to Clarify Conceptual Differences**

| | |
|---|---|
| Mrs. Espinosa: | Let's look at this picture of a seed *[pointing to a picture of a seed with a sprouting plant].* |
| | Remember we learned about seeds in the storybook *How a Seed Grows.* |
| | In this picture, we see that *the seed is the part of the plant "before" it starts to grow.* |
| | *[Pointing to this part]* |
| | Let's say this together, "The *seed* is the part of the plant before it starts to grow." |
| Mrs. Espinosa and children: | The *seed* is the part of the plant before it starts to grow. |
| Mrs. Espinosa: | Look at this picture of a *vine.* The *vine* is part of the plant *after it has grown.* |
| | *[Pointing to this part of the plant in the picture of the vine]* |
| | It is a long and curvy stem. Let's say this together, "The *vine* is the part of the plant after it has grown. It is a long and curvy stem." |
| Mrs. Espinosa and children: | The *vine* is the part of the plant after it has grown. It is a long and curvy stem. |
| Mrs. Espinosa: | In this picture, we see that a vine is different from a seed because it is the *plant that is growing.* The *seed is the part that the plant grows from.* The difference between a *vine* and a *seed* is that the vine is a long, curvy stem of a plant and a seed is the thing that plants grow from. |

**Figure 6.1.** Mrs. Espinosa's challenge question: What is the difference between a vine and a seed?

## Continuation of Mrs. Espinosa's Postreading Discussion of *Leaves*

### Big Kid Question—Relating the Concepts to Life

Mrs. Espinosa: Here is our big kid question for today: What would happen if we didn't have any flower *buds?* If we just had a plant, and we didn't have any *buds.*

Would we have flowers?

Letty: No. We need *buds* to have flowers.

Rosa: If we don't have *buds,* the flowers can't grow.

Mrs. Espinosa: Does everyone agree with Letty and Rosa?

Children: Yes!

Mrs. Espinosa: Remember that a *bud* is the part of the plant that turns into a leaf or flower.

ACTIVITY

## Magic Mirror

⭐ **TEACHING STRATEGY:** Provide opportunities like Magic Mirror for individual children to talk about words so that you can informally evaluate students' ability to use vocabulary to discuss concepts and life experiences.

Mrs. Espinosa: Okay, it's time to look into the Magic Mirror! Is everyone ready for the Magic Mirror?

Children: Yes!

Mrs. Espinosa: I'll tell you what I see, then some of you will have a turn to tell us what you see.

*[She looks into a mirror that she is holding.]*

I see a *living thing that has many stems*—all of the stems are very curvy. The stems are wrapped around a tree outside. Does anyone know what the Magic Mirror is showing to me?

Joseph: A tree!

Mrs. Espinosa: Yes, I see that the curvy stems are growing around a tree. What I see is curvy *[using gestures]* and it grows around the tree. Hmm, what is that called?

Children: *Vine! Vine! Vine!*

Mrs. Espinosa: Good! Joseph, tell us about the vine that you see in the Magic Mirror. What do you see?

Joseph: I see . . .

⭐ **TEACHING STRATEGY:** Model appropriate language use.

Mrs. Espinosa: *Yes, start by saying, "I see a."*

Joseph: I see a *vine.*

Mrs. Espinosa: Good, Joseph used the word *vine.*

⭐ **TEACHING STRATEGY:** Extend learning by asking additional open-ended questions (e.g., "Tell us about the *vine.* Where is it? Where is it growing?")

Joseph: I see.

Mrs. Espinosa: A *vine* is a part of a plant. Where do you see this *vine* growing?

Joseph: *[Silent]*

Mrs. Espinosa: Is it growing around a building? What do you see in the Magic Mirror?

Joseph: I see a *vine* growing on a *house.*

Mrs. Espinosa: Okay, that is possible because some *vines,* like ivy, grow along walls and around windows or doors on houses. Good telling us about the *vine* that you see.

Now I see something *new* in the Magic Mirror. I see a living thing growing on a stem. It is small and closed up. It is part of a plant. It will grow into a pretty flower. Does anyone know what the Magic Mirror is showing me? It is the small and closed part on the plant. What am I looking at [*gesturing with fingers to form a small* bud]?

Children: *Bud!*

Mrs. Espinosa: Yes, I see a *bud.* Rosa, tell us about the *bud* that you see in the Magic Mirror.

What is happening to the *bud?*

Rosa: I see a . . .

Mrs. Espinosa: *What does it look like? What is the* bud *doing?*

**RECOMMENDED PRACTICE**

Rosa: I see that the *bud* is closed.

Mrs. Espinosa: Very good, Rosa. The *bud* is closed, and when it grows, it will open into a what?

Scaffold instruction by using more specific language. Mrs. Espinosa could say, "What do you notice about the *bud?*"

Rosa: A flower. I see a flower *bud.* I see a flower *bud* and it is closed.

Mrs. Espinosa: Good describing the *bud* that you see, Rosa. When it grows it will turn into a beautiful flower. *What color is the flower?*

Rosa: Pink! It will grow into a pink flower *blossom.*

Mrs. Espinosa: Wow—you remembered the word *blossom!* So the *bud* was closed, and Rosa saw it opening into a pink flower *blossom.* Thanks, Rosa, for sharing what you saw in the Magic Mirror today!

## Final Lesson Review

⭐ **TEACHING STRATEGY:** Use visuals to quickly review vocabulary concepts, and encourage children to use the target words at home.

Mrs. Espinosa: Today we learned about two magic words. What is this everyone [*Showing a picture of a* bud.*]*?

Children: *Bud!*

Mrs. Espinosa: And what is this word [*showing a picture of a* vine]?

Children: *Vine!*

Mrs. Espinosa: Today we learned about *vines* and *buds*. Now try to use these magic words at school and at home.

## An Opportunity for Reflection: Mrs. Espinosa Actively Stimulates Paired-Practice Interactions

What stands out in Mrs. Espinosa's shared book-reading lesson is the exemplary way in which she has taught the children to participate in paired discussions and the attentiveness with which she listens to and extends individual child responses during these peer conversations. While reading the book, she stops on a book page and asks children to "turn and talk to their friend" by gesturing with her hands how to physically turn and look at their partner. Mrs. Espinosa then directs each child to talk to their friend about what they learned about vines and then to talk later about buds. In these examples, Mrs. Espinosa is actively engaged as listener, and based on what children say to their partner, she asks additional prompting questions as facilitator (e.g., "What is that called? What curves here? What did you learn about bud? Yes, we see that it is closed but *what* is it?"). In this process, she notices when individual children have difficulty responding and provides a sentence stem for that child (e.g., "Say, 'I learned that ____.'") or models appropriate language use (e.g., "Say, 'the *bud* is going to grow and open.'") Mrs. Espinosa is both proactive, anticipating possible obstacles and having a plan in mind, and responsive, differentiating feedback based on the ability and knowledge of each individual child. Small-group instruction facilitates Mrs. Espinosa's approach to teaching and monitoring of student learning. This vignette illustrates Mrs. Espinosa's instructional approach to breathing life into the WORLD lessons.

## SCIENCE INSTRUCTIONAL VIGNETTE 2: MS. LUCIA

Ms. Lucia has 13 years of teaching experience, all of which are in preschool settings. In her Day 5 cumulative review, book-reading content focuses on what children have learned about seasons from the *nature* theme. Two information books were read in this instructional unit because a thematically related storybook with appropriate content (science) vocabulary could not be found. On Days 1 and 2, children listened to *Changing Seasons* (Smith, 2009), learned three new words (*seasons, winter,* and *fall*), and discussed the following concepts:

1. A *season* is a time of year.
2. There are four *seasons:* winter, spring, summer, and fall.
3. Because the weather changes in different *seasons,* people wear different clothing and may do different things.
4. Many plants lose their leaves in the *winter,* the coldest season, because it is difficult for plants to remain alive.
5. The leaves on some plants may change color during the *fall* when the weather gets cooler.

On Days 3 and 4, children listened to *Colors of the Seasons* (Perez, 2004), learned three new words (*change, spring,* and *summer*), and discussed the following concepts:

1. When something *changes,* it becomes different. When the seasons *change,* we see different colors in nature.
2. *Spring* is a time of year when it rains and plants start to grow.
3. Flowers of different colors grow in the *spring.*
4. Summer is the time of year when it is hot.
5. In the *summer,* the trees grow green leaves and the grass becomes green again during the warmer weather.

The following Day 5 instructional vignette reflects how Ms. Lucia reviewed vocabulary and connected concepts across the week's twin texts, *Changing Seasons* and *Colors of the Season.* In this cumulative lesson review, she is seated at a small table with five students. Ms. Lucia uses a timer to keep track of the 20-minute lesson.

## Cumulative Review of Thematic Content and Vocabulary Using the Week's Complementary Thematic Texts

⭐ **TEACHING STRATEGY:** Use pages and pictures from each book that were used during the week to review and talk about vocabulary concepts.

## Review of *Changing Seasons*

Ms. Lucia:      Today we are going to review what we have learned about seasons. First we are going to look at our information book *Changing Seasons.* This time, I am not going to read the book, but you are going to talk about what happened on our magic word pages. Remember to use the words *season, winter,* and *fall* when we talk about this book.

*[She turns to a book page that shows the four seasons.]*

Tell us what you learned on this page.

Manuel:      *Seasons.*

| | |
|---|---|
| Lisa: | *Seasons.* |
| Children: | *Seasons.* |
| Ms. Lucia: | What did you *learn about* seasons? |
| Beatriz: | That . . . *[The student has difficulty expressing her thoughts.]* |
| Ms. Lucia: | Say, "I learned . . ." |
| Children: | I learned . . . |
| Ms. Lucia: | What did you learn about seasons, Beatriz? |
| Beatriz: | I learned about fall, winter, spring, and summer. |
| Ms. Lucia: | Very good, those are the four seasons, but what did you *learn* about the seasons? |
| | What happens in the winter? |
| Bruce: | The leaves falling down. |
| Ms. Lucia: | The leaves are falling in the winter? |
| Children: | No, the *fall,* the *fall!* |
| Ms. Lucia: | Very good. In the fall, the leaves fall from the trees. But what happens in the winter, Bruce? |
| Bruce: | It's cold. |
| Ms. Lucia: | Say, "It's cold in the winter." |
| Bruce: | It's cold in the winter. |
| Ms. Lucia: | So the *seasons change,* right? In the picture, we see that there are four times of the year when the seasons change. |

*[She turns to a book page that depicts the next target word,* winter.*]*

| | |
|---|---|
| Ms. Lucia: | Here is a picture of winter. It is a cold season. Tell me more about what we learned about this cold season. |
| Carlos: | It's a lot of snow and snowflakes. |
| Ms. Lucia: | Good. Can you say, "I learned that in the winter, there is a lot of snow and snowflakes"? |
| Ms. Lucia and Carlos: | I learned . . . that in winter . . . there is a lot of snow . . . and snowflakes. |
| Ms. Lucia: | Good job, Carlos! Now, I want to hear from *all of you.* What else did you learn about winter? |
| Bruce: | You can make a snowman. |
| Manuel: | You can play! |
| Children: | You can make a snow man! |
| Ms. Lucia: | Okay, when you go outside in the winter, you can play and you can make a snowman because it is cold. What would you *use* to make a snow man? |
| Children: | Snow. |

| | |
|---|---|
| Ms. Lucia: | Or what do you wear? |
| Bruce: | You wear a jacket. |
| Ms. Lucia: | Why do you wear a jacket in the winter? |
| Lisa: | Because it is so, so, so, so cold! |
| Ms. Lucia: | Yes, in the winter we can play outside and use balls of snow to make a snowman. We would wear a jacket to stay warm. |

*[She turns to a book picture of the fall season.]*

| | |
|---|---|
| Ms. Lucia: | What did you learn about this page? |
| Bruce: | Summer! |
| Ms. Lucia: | Hmm, let's look again at the picture. |
| Bruce: | Oh, *fall*. |
| Children: | It's *fall*. |
| Ms. Lucia: | How do we know that it is fall in this picture? |
| Beatriz: | Colors! Lots of yellow and red colors! |
| Ms. Lucia: | Beatriz, can you say, "The leaves are changing colors." |
| Children with Beatriz: | The leaves are changing colors. |
| Ms. Lucia: | And we learned that in the *fall* the leaves change colors, and they fall from the trees. Here we see the brown, bright red, and yellow leaves falling from the trees. |
| | How is the weather in the *fall?* |
| Bruce: | It starts to get a little cold. I need a sweater. |
| Ms. Lucia: | Yes, the warm weather changes and becomes cooler in the *fall*. And yes you might use a sweater because the weather is cooler. |

## Review of *Colors of the Season*

| | |
|---|---|
| Ms. Lucia: | Now we are going to look at our information book *Colors of the Season*. You are going to tell about what you learned on our magic word pages. Remember to use the words *change, spring,* and *summer*. |

*[She turns to page that depicts change.]*

| | |
|---|---|
| | What did you learn about on this page? |
| Children: | *Seasons!* |
| Ms. Lucia: | Yes, but what did you learn about the seasons? |
| Lisa: | *Change their colors.* |

⭐ **TEACHING STRATEGY:** Confirm student's response (e.g., "Yes, we see different colors when the seasons change.").

| | |
|---|---|
| Ms. Lucia: | And when something *changes,* what happens? |
| Bruce: | It's different. |

⭐ **TEACHING STRATEGY:** Scaffold to help students understand that the weather also changes.

| | |
|---|---|
| Ms. Lucia: | Okay, *we learned that when something changes, it becomes different. So yes, we see that colors of the leaves in this picture change with the seasons. But what else changes with the seasons? Who can describe how the weather also changes?* |
| Children: | It's hot. |
| Manuel: | It's hot in the *summer.* |
| Ms. Lucia: | Yes, it's hot in the *summer.* Look here—how is the weather in the winter? |
| Children: | It's cold. |
| Ms. Lucia: | So the weather can change from hot to cold when the seasons change. What else *changes during winter?* |
| Lisa: | No leaves on the tree. It is too cold. |
| Ms. Lucia: | Yes, *the trees change, too,* because now they have ice hanging from the branches. Everything looks *frozen.* |

### An Opportunity for Reflection: What Changes During the Winter?

In this episode of Ms. Lucia's shared book-reading lesson, she encouraged children to review what they learned during the week about seasonal changes. She asked, "What *changes* during the winter?" She next confirmed, "The trees change, too, because now they have ice hanging from the branches." This response, however, provides *partial knowledge* about why the trees have changed. Learning can be extended by responding with greater details as indicated here:

| | |
|---|---|
| Ms. Lucia: | Yes, the trees change too because *they have lost their leaves when the weather became colder. It is too cold for any leaves to live on these trees.* Now ice hangs from the tree branches because it is very cold outside. Everything looks frozen. |

Providing more information about why changes occur assists children in understanding cause and effect—higher cognitive thinking that is important for listening and text comprehension.

### Continuation of Cumulative Review of Thematic Content and Vocabulary Discussion

| | |
|---|---|
| Ms. Lucia: | *[Turning to a picture of spring]* Here is another magic word page. What did you learn about in this picture? Try to use a magic word. |

| Children: | *Spring!* |
|---|---|
| Ms. Lucia: | Yes, this is *spring,* and it is a season. What did you learn about *spring?* |
| Beatriz: | They are rainy. |
| Carlos: | There are lots of flowers. |
| Ms. Lucia: | Good thinking! It rains in the spring, and there are lots of flowers growing outside. Everything in this picture looks green. Good, Beatriz, for saying that it rains in the spring. Say that with me. |
| Beatriz: | It rains in the *spring.* |
| Ms. Lucia: | And good, Carlos, for saying that there are a lot of flowers in the *spring.* Here in the picture, we see buds opening and flowers blooming. We see things come alive in the spring. |
| Ms. Lucia: | Everyone say, "There are many flowers growing in the spring." |
| Children: | There are many flowers growing in the *spring.* |
| Ms. Lucia: | *[Turning to a picture of summer]* What did you learn about here? Try to use a magic word. |
| Children: | *Summer!* |
| Ms. Lucia: | Yes, this is *summer. Summer* is also a season. What did you learn about *summer?* |
| Bruce: | You can play. |
| Ms. Lucia: | You can play *where?* |
| Manuel: | The sand. The water beach! I like water. |
| Ms. Lucia: | Why can you play in the water at the beach? |
| Carlos: | Because it's *summer.* |
| Beatriz: | Because it is hot. |
| Ms. Lucia: | Yes, it's very hot in the *summer,* and some people play in the water at the beach to stay cool! Very good, children! We've learned a lot about the seasons! |

## ACTIVITY The Same Game

⭐ **TEACHING STRATEGY:** Review thematic content by discussing conceptual similarities across complementary texts.

| Ms. Lucia: | Now we are going to play the Same Game. Look carefully at this page *[Colors of the Season]* and the cover of this book *[Changing Seasons].* Tell me what you see that is the same in these pictures of seasons. Look carefully, and use your new words to talk about what is the *same.* |
|---|---|

| | |
|---|---|
| Lisa: | *Winter* and *winter*. |
| Ms. Lucia: | Lisa said she sees *winter* on the book cover and on this page. What else do we see that is the same? |
| Carlos: | They have the *spring* and the *fall*. |

**RECOMMENDED PRACTICE**

Clarify the concept. Ms. Lucia could say, "And you see the leaves on the trees change *in each season.*"

| | |
|---|---|
| Ms. Lucia: | Yes, we see examples of trees growing green leaves during the *spring* and losing their leaves in the *fall*. What else do you see? |
| Beatriz: | I see summer too. |
| Ms. Lucia: | Yes, both pictures show trees during the summer. Show me here, in both pictures, where is the summer. *[The children point to summer in both pictures.]* |
| | Good finding what is the same in the pictures. So we see trees that are *changing*. |
| | What do we call these four things that we see in the pictures? |

**RECOMMENDED PRACTICE**

Clarify conceptual similarities with greater details to enhance learning. Ms. Lucia could say, "Yes, the seasons look the same in each picture or the colors of the trees' leaves look the same in the seasons that we see in each book."

| | |
|---|---|
| Children: | *Seasons!* |
| Ms. Lucia: | Yes, they are seasons! And you see the trees changing in each season. |
| Manuel: | And they're *the same*. |
| Ms. Lucia: | Yes, *they are the same in each picture*. |

## Cumulative Review of Vocabulary and Concepts from Previous 3–4 Weeks

⭐ **TEACHING STRATEGY:** Use visuals (picture/concept cards) to review vocabulary from the previous weeks in 1–2 minutes, as in Ready, Set, Go!

ACTIVITY **Ready, Set, Go!**

| | |
|---|---|
| Ms. Lucia: | I want you to name each picture as fast as you can. Let's see what you remember about the words we have learned. When I start this timer, then go. |

> ⭐ **TEACHING STRATEGY:** Provide the correct information when children respond incorrectly or cannot identify the vocabulary concept depicted in the visual (e.g., "Everyone, this is _____. What is this?") Recycle the card back into the stack so that children will have an additional opportunity to review and identify the vocabulary/concept. Recycle the card three cards back into the stack.

*[In this cumulative review lesson, Mrs. Espinosa reviews picture/concept cards for 21 target words, which were taught in the current and previous three weeks in the nature theme. See Table 6.2 for vocabulary concepts that children will review.]*

**Table 6.2.** Words and concepts cumulatively reviewed in Ready, Set, Go!

| Nature theme | Vocabulary concepts |
| --- | --- |
| Water | Pour, puddle, liquid, frozen, solid |
| Snow | Snow, melt, cloud, snowflake |
| Storms | Storm, raindrop, lightning, wind, spin, tornado |
| Seasons | Season, winter, fall, spring, summer, change |

ACTIVITY

# Magic Mirror

> ⭐ **TEACHING STRATEGY:** Provide opportunities, such as Magic Mirror, for individual children to talk about words so that you can informally evaluate students' ability to use vocabulary to discuss concepts in the context of life experiences.

The following are two examples of clues provided for vocabulary that were reviewed in the Magic Mirror activity.

Ms. Lucia: I'll tell you what I see in the Magic Mirror, and then some of you will have a turn to tell us what you see.

*[She looks into a mirror that she is holding.]*

I see a time of the year when things are very cold outside. People have to wear coats and hats to stay warm. Does anyone know what word the Magic Mirror is showing me?

Children: *Winter.*

Ms. Lucia: Now Beatriz, tell me about the *winter that you see.* Here, you look into the mirror.

Beatriz: I can make a snowman.

Ms. Lucia: *You can make a snowman. What else can you tell me about the winter that you see?*

| | |
|---|---|
| Beatriz: | I see a lot of ice. |
| Ms. Lucia: | You see a lot of ice, Beatriz? Do you see a place that is hot or cold? |
| Beatriz: | It is cold. There are snowflakes. There is frozen ice. |
| Ms. Lucia: | Okay, you see snowflakes and frozen ice in the *winter* because it is cold. Can you say, "I see frozen ice because it is cold in the *winter.*" |
| Beatriz: | I see frozen ice because it is cold in the *winter.* |
| Ms. Lucia: | Good talking about the *winter* that you saw in the Magic Mirror. |
| | I am looking into the mirror again. This time I see something happening: The sun was out, and it was hot outside, but now it is cold. The weather is different from before. Does anyone know what word the Magic Mirror is showing me? It is now *different* from before. |
| Carlos: | Summer! |
| Lisa: | Winter! |
| Ms. Lucia: | I want you to listen very carefully. It was very hot outside, but now it is very cold *[pretending to shiver]*. Something is *different* from before. What is the mirror showing me? |
| Bruce: | *Change!* |
| Ms. Lucia: | Good! Now tell me about the change that you see in the Magic Mirror. |
| Bruce: | I see a baby. |
| Ms. Lucia: | You see a baby that is changing. He is growing . . . |
| Bruce: | Large. The baby can crawl. |
| Ms. Lucia: | Wow, you saw a crawling baby. First, the baby was little but now he is larger; he is growing and *changing.* He will continue to grow until one day the baby will walk. Good thinking. Everyone, let's say, "I see a baby that is *changing.*" |
| Children: | I see a baby that is *changing.* |
| Ms. Lucia: | Good talking about seeing the baby that is *changing* in the Magic Mirror. |

> **RECOMMENDED PRACTICE**
>
> Extend thinking by asking additional questions. Ms. Lucia could say, "Do you see yourself making a snow man? What else can you do in the winter?"

## Wrap-Up: Final Review of the Week's Theme

---

⭐ **TEACHING STRATEGY:** Use a thematic poster as a visual prompt to review important concepts.

---

Ms. Lucia: *[Holding a poster with a collage of pictures that represent different types of nature]* This week we learned about nature. Let's look at this picture, and tell me about the nature that you see.

Carlos: I see water.

Lisa: Winter.

Ms. Lucia: You see the winter. Good. What else do you see?

Bruce: I see mountains.

Miguel: The sun. I see the sun.

Beatriz: I see the sky and a storm.

Ms. Lucia: Good being able to find these examples of nature in our picture.

## Encourage Children to Use the Target Words at Home

Ms. Lucia: Today we learned more about our magic words: *season, winter, fall, spring, summer,* and *change.* Now I want you to try to use these magic words at school and at home. Good job participating today!

### An Opportunity for Reflection: Ms. Lucia Teaches Children to Think Deeply

What stands out in Ms. Lucia's shared book-reading lesson is her exemplary ability to turn the conversation around with the use of open-ended questions to prompt children to *think deeper* about a concept. This is a preschool teacher who consistently asks a general question about a concept and then follows with a more specific probing question to encourage deeper processing. Here are some examples of her scaffolding approach as she facilitates a discussion on seasons:

1. Seasons
   a. First question: What did you learn about the seasons? (Response: Change their colors)
   b. Probing Question 1: And when something changes *what happens?* (Response: It's different. [Ms. Lucia: The leaves change and are different.])

    c.  Probing Question 2: But *what else* changes with the seasons? (This leads to a discussion on *weather.*)

2.  Summer

    a.  First question: What did you learn about here? (Response: Summer!)

    b.  Probing Question 1: *What* did you *learn* about the summer? (Response: You can play.)

    c.  Probing Question 2: You can play *where?* (Response: The water beach!)

    d.  Probing Question 3: *Why* can you play in the water at the beach? (This leads to a discussion on hot weather and the desire to stay cool.)

Although Ms. Lucia starts with a basic question supplied in the WORLD lesson plan (i.e., "What did you learn about summer?"), she transforms this lesson to integrate multiple opportunities to extend knowledge, language, and learning in ways that are beneficial for children who are developing their English proficiency. Her instructional approach, however, is beneficial for all children and is indicative of her ability to breathe life into the WORLD lessons.

## A SUMMATIVE REFLECTION

### What Did These Teachers Do Well? What Could They Improve Upon?

**Strengths**  Both Mrs. Espinosa and Ms. Lucia respond to and extend children's language abilities and reasoning skills by asking additional open-ended questions that require children to provide more information about science concepts while encouraging target word use. Both teachers facilitate conversations in which there is a cycle of feedback and oral language modeling contrary to simply asking open-ended questions and accepting children's responses without providing any feedback. They are responsive to individual children's needs and adjust strategies (e.g., use gestures, visuals, repeat the question while emphasizing similarities and/or differences) for children whose oral language abilities were more limited. Both teachers also use strategies to highlight the critical differences or similarities between vocabulary concepts (e.g., the difference between a vine and a bud).

**Areas for Improvement**  Sometimes there are missed opportunities to extend children's brief responses, and this may reflect the realities of actual conversations during shared book reading—children sometimes excitedly shout out responses all at once, so the conversation progresses really quickly, and it is easy to overlook a teaching moment. In addition, it would be helpful if teachers used more specific language to clarify conceptual understanding and model appropriate language use. Overall, both instructional vignettes provide examples of how typical shared book-reading practices can be intensified and used to accelerate content vocabulary learning in brief, daily lessons.

## "What Do Children Need to Learn?"

Reflect on the following guiding questions to determine where content-shared book-reading instruction should begin.

1. Which social studies concepts do children need to learn?
2. Which science concepts do children need to learn?
3. Which oral language abilities do children need to develop?

## Oral Language Objectives

These may also include TESOL and/or WIDA Objectives.

A.  Simple language expectations

Objective 1:


Objective 2:


Objective 3:


B.  More complex language expectation

Objective 4:


## Science Standard and Theme

Smaller topic:

1.  Select twin texts.
    a.  Storybook
        - Title and author:


        - Three semantically related content words/concepts and definitions: *Note the book page on which the target word is first discussed and/or visually represented.*


    b.  Informational text
        - Title and author:


        - Three semantically related content words/concepts and definitions: *Note the book page on which the target word is first discussed and/or visually represented.*

*(continued)*

2. Summarize three or four big ideas or key concepts that children will learn in the instructional unit.

   a.

   b.

   c.

   d.

## Social Studies Standard and Theme

Smaller topic:

1. Select twin texts
   a. Storybook
      - Title and author:

      - Three semantically related content words/concepts, and definitions: *Note the book page on which the target word is first discussed and/or visually represented.*

   b. Informational text
      - Title and author:

      - Three semantically related content words/concepts and definitions: *Note the book page on which the target word is first discussed and/or visually represented.*

2. Summarize three or four big ideas or key concepts that children will learn in the instructional unit.

   a.

   b.

   c.

   d.

## Theme 1: Science

| Week/topic | Book/author | Vocabulary | Definition |
|---|---|---|---|
| 1 Topic: | Storybook title/Author | 1. 2. 3. | |
| | Informational text title/Author | 1. 2. 3. | |
| 2 Topic: | Storybook title/Author | 1. 2. 3. | |
| | Informational text title/Author | 1. 2. 3. | |
| 3 Topic: | Storybook title/Author | 1. 2. 3. | |
| | Informational text title/Author | 1. 2. 3. | |

## Theme 1: Social Studies

| Week/topic | Book/author | Vocabulary | Definition |
|---|---|---|---|
| 1 Topic: | Storybook title/Author | 1. 2. 3. | |
| | Informational text title/Author | 1. 2. 3. | |
| 2 Topic: | Storybook title/Author | 1. 2. 3. | |
| | Informational text title/Author | 1. 2. 3. | |
| 3 Topic: | Storybook title/Author | 1. 2. 3. | |
| | Informational text title/Author | 1. 2. 3. | |

## CRITICAL FEATURES ANALYSIS

- *What is working:* I feel most confident about . . .


- *What needs attention:* I have difficulty with . . .


## LESSON ACTIVITIES

- *Activities that are fluent:* I feel most confident with . . .


- *Activities that need improvement:* I still have difficulty with . . .


- *Ways children are successful:* Children are able to . . .


- *Ways children are not successful:* Children have difficulty with . . .


## SHARPENING OUR FOCUS

List three goals that will strengthen your content related shared book-reading practices. These goals can be evaluated and modified to reflect your professional growth.

Goal 1:


Goal 2:


Goal 3:

# What Lies Ahead

## Inspiring a Paradigm Shift in Thinking and Teaching

**THIS CONCLUDING CHAPTER PROVIDES** final suggestions for supporting teachers' shared book-reading practices in ways that are conducive to vocabulary and oral language development. We focus on moving beyond potential obstacles to effective shared book-reading instruction: 1) false assumptions about how young children learn, 2) professional development practices that require rapid instructional changes in brief time periods, 3) children's misinterpretation of visual information (e.g., book illustrations, pictures) during shared book-reading episodes, and 4) teachers' oral language abilities. We also introduce two tools (i.e., Getting Started and Self-Reflection Prompt) to support teachers' content vocabulary instruction.

**KEY IDEAS** | The key ideas discussed in this chapter are as follows:

1. Intensifying typical shared book-reading practices to accommodate content vocabulary learning may require incremental changes in teachers' behaviors so that teachers have adequate time to try out new strategies and reflect on, modify, and adjust instruction, as needed, based on what works and student needs (ELL and non-ELL needs).

2. The self-reflection prompt can be used as an ongoing PD tool for teachers to monitor their progress, check for understanding, and grow professionally. This self-reflection can also allow teachers to anticipate possible barriers to student success and be proactive in more effectively addressing these concerns prior to teaching the shared book-reading lesson.

3. There is strength in working together to change teaching practices. This collaboration between teachers and coaches and/or mentors can occur in planned self-reflective discussions and opportunities that involve large groups of teachers, smaller groups of teachers with an instructional target, and individual teachers who study their own practices with the emotional support, feedback, and instructional expertise of a wise coach and/or mentor.

4. Taking advantage of those natural "teaching moments" that occur throughout the day is important for vocabulary acceleration and oral language development. These experiences, however, should not supplant intentional and explicit instructional planning with thoughtful consideration of how lower and higher cognitive skills can be integrated in content vocabulary learning.

## SUPPORTING TEACHERS' CONTENT VOCABULARY INSTRUCTION

In this text, we have gradually introduced and invited early childhood educators to reflect on three research-based instructional design principles or goals for developing thematic shared book-reading practices. We first introduced the importance of aligning vocabulary instruction with preschool content and language standards as a starting point for instructional design. This step was followed by a discussion on the second instructional design principle: create frequent exposures to semantically related words and connected thematic concepts via varied text genres. The third instructional design principle was then introduced with suggestions for how to integrate multiple adult–child conversations about high-priority topics and themes into the shared book-reading lesson.

Our purpose in this gradual progression of curricular discussions was to "scaffold" the instructional design process for early childhood educators by making recommendations that are feasible to accomplish within the daily time constraints of early childhood settings. These design principles are important, therefore, because they provide a starting point for curriculum development and instructional decisions about how content vocabulary knowledge can be embedded in literacy experiences. Overall, published preschool curricular materials provide limited guidance on recommended practices for vocabulary instruction and knowledge development for young children. Early childhood educators, therefore, must be knowledgeable about instructional design principles and how they can be used to design more effective early childhood instruction (Neuman & Wright, 2013).

We do not suggest that shared book reading is the only context for providing content-rich vocabulary instruction for preschool children, because there is ample evidence to suggest that children from high-poverty settings require vocabulary instruction and opportunities for language development throughout the preschool day and across multiple contexts (i.e., in the book, outside of the book; Schickedanz & Collins, 2012; Wasik et al., 2006). Shared book reading, however, is a commonly implemented practice in early childhood classrooms and, when intensified with research-based practices (e.g., repeated reading, interactive dialogues, brief in-context definitions), has the potential to accelerate the oral language abilities and world knowledge of young children.

One key challenge is how to support early childhood educators in ways that will result in practices that affect young children's vocabulary and oral language learning (Dickinson, 2011). Shifting the quality of teachers' shared book-reading practices in ways that are conducive to content vocabulary acceleration and oral language development may first require a shift in thinking about some commonly accepted notions about how children learn.

## A SHIFT IN THINKING: MOVING TOWARD SCIENTIFIC EVIDENCE

In the following sections, we discuss three myths about young children's learning with the goal of inspiring a shift in thinking toward a more research-based framework in instructional design. We encourage early childhood practitioners to reconsider misconceptions about incidental vocabulary learning, small-group instruction, and children's ability to successfully engage in higher cognitive discussions—especially in the context of providing content-rich shared book-reading instruction. These myths have been commonly accepted and also addressed by other researchers (Brenneman, 2013; Neuman & Wright, 2013, p. 8).

### Misconception 1

*Incidental vocabulary learning via "teachable moments" (Neuman & Wright, 2013, p. 8) is sufficient for learning new words and concepts.*

Although informal opportunities to use and talk about new words throughout the school day are important, they do not provide sufficient repeated exposures to new information, which can only take place through explicit intentional planning. Carefully selecting vocabulary that is important for talking about complex ideas during academic learning is important and cannot be left to chance (Neuman & Wright, 2013). Teachers must decide in advance which content words to teach to accelerate domain knowledge (Hirsch, 2003). In addition, teachers must create intentional, planned conversations in which children have multiple opportunities to use new vocabulary when responding to open-ended questions followed by strategic feedback to extend language and knowledge (Wasik & Iannone-Campbell, 2012). The most effective instructional strategy is to integrate both implicit (i.e., incidental learning) and intentional, or explicit, instruction so that words and concepts learned via planned instruction are utilized in meaningful ways beyond the book-reading session (Neuman & Wright, 2013). In the WORLD study, we highlighted the importance of explicit and intentional vocabulary instruction in the initial professional development of preschool teachers. We wanted teachers to understand that although incidental learning is important, children require specific opportunities to engage in conversations about books with their peers and with an adult. These important activities cannot be left to chance.

### Misconception 2

*Small-group instruction is not appropriate for young preschool children.*

A small group size is beneficial because it facilitates the use of open-ended questions during adult–child interactions. The frequency of language stimulation techniques (e.g., the use of open-ended questions) may occur more during small-group instructional formats because teachers can monitor and respond to individual children (van de Pol, Volman, & Beishuizen, 2010). Center time is an example of an effective use of small-group instructional time that is appropriate for young children. Center time generally can be used to intentionally build opportunities for purposeful and strategic conversations because children can interact in small groups, listen to each other talk, use vocabulary in a meaningful context, and listen to and interact with an adult who can scaffold the conversation (Wasik & Iannone-Campbell, 2012). In the WORLD study, we supported teachers' use of small-group shared book-reading instruction by providing suggestions for the physical arrangement of the group (e.g., small, *u*-shaped tables allowed teachers to better manage materials so that children would have access to visual supports) and the use of the instructional aide who monitored the remaining students in the class (e.g., usually rotating through planned center activities). When schools were limited in the availability of instructional aides, principals were supportive in making sure that there was instructional support (e.g., a school volunteer) during the 20-minute shared book-reading intervention. Preschool teachers did not report that a small-group format was inappropriate for preschool learning.

## Misconception 3

*Preschool science instruction should only emphasize concepts that children can experience in a direct way, because preschoolers cannot think abstractly.*

There is increasing evidence that young children can learn much more than previously believed, and this learning can take place in settings beyond natural play (Brenneman, 2013; Gelman & Brenneman, 2004; Ginsburg & Golbeck, 2004). Emerging theorists emphasize inherent mental structures that direct and guide the acquisition of knowledge in young children. Underlying this framework of thinking are two beliefs: 1) Because concepts and vocabulary are connected to each other within a domain of knowledge, abstract thinking is facilitated by generalizing and making inferences from "known cases to novel cases" (Gelman & Brenneman, 2004, p. 152). 2) Language (e.g., vocabulary) plays an important role in abstract thinking because it allows children to talk about knowledge connections (Gelman & Brenneman, 2004, p. 152). Overall, explicit instruction on these knowledge connections with instructional scaffolding facilitates abstract thinking in young children. As an example of this approach to explicit and intentional teaching, WORLD preschool teachers found it beneficial to preview upcoming higher cognitive shared book-reading tasks and to anticipate ways to scaffold content instruction to teach abstract concepts and ideas (e.g., "What would humans do if they didn't have *plants*?"). The instructional implication for content learning is that young children can engage in some abstract high cognitive thinking during content instruction when it is at an appropriate level and there is adult guidance (Brenneman, 2013).

Moving beyond these myths is an important step in designing high-quality instruction for children from high-poverty settings. The next important consideration is how to support teachers' instructional decisions through more responsive PD.

## A SHIFT IN TEACHING: MOVING TOWARD RESPONSIVE PROFESSIONAL DEVELOPMENT APPROACHES

PD is generally more effective and demonstrates ecological validity when it is 1) situated in the context of genuine work experiences (Webster-Wright, 2009), 2) emphasizes content-specific instruction (NRP, 2000), and 3) allows teachers to translate new knowledge into real classroom practices (Snow, Griffin, & Burns, 2005). In reality, however, teachers often are expected to change several domains of their instructional behaviors at once or to modify their instructional practices significantly after attending brief PD workshops. Our collaboration with WORLD preschool teachers taught us that a more effective and ecological PD approach to shifting teachers' shared book-reading behaviors may be to 1) limit "the range of . . . strategies" that teachers are required to focus on (Dickinson, 2011, p. 967) customize PD in response to varied levels of teacher expertise and experience, and 3) provide sustained (e.g., across the year) instructional support with feedback and opportunities for self-reflection on one's teaching practice. In the following section, we provide suggestions for how this PD approach can be applied to initiate instructional change in a more pragmatic framework.

### Incremental Change

Getting Started is one PD tool that can be used to gradually intensify typical shared book-reading practices to include targeted vocabulary instruction via high-priority content themes and topics. Getting Started is a modified version of the comprehensive WORLD multidimensional approach that can be used daily for the first 4 weeks as teachers are learning to implement novel shared book-reading practices. During this time, teachers can gradually build their shared book-reading expertise by skillfully implementing a smaller range of shared book-reading strategies before gradually integrating higher cognitive tasks in the 20-minute lesson. This PD approach, therefore, schedules intentional time for teachers and students to engage in interactive discussions within a *simpler book-reading routine* with fewer complex oral language activities and materials to manage. These 4 weeks serve as a formative period in which teachers can reflect on their ability to listen to and extend children's oral abilities, model core instructional tasks (e.g., make predictions, engage in paired discussions), provide feedback to child responses, and reflect on what works and areas of concern that may require support. Through self-reflection (discussed later in this chapter), peer discussions, and reflective conversations with an instructional coach or mentor, this incremental shift in teaching occurs in the context of the preschool classroom. In the following example of Getting Started, we provide suggestions for how preschool teachers can incorporate novel strategies while gradually becoming more proficient and self-confident in their ability to implement their content-related shared book-reading practices.

## Getting Started: Week 1

*During the first week of Getting Started, teachers generate interactive thematic book discussions by primarily encouraging children to do the following:*

- Identify and recall important content information: "This week we are studying about nature. What are some things in nature that you see in this picture? This is a *tornado*. This is *wind*. What is this picture? What is the *tornado* doing in this picture?"

- Define and describe vocabulary concepts: "A *storm* is when the *wind* and rain are very strong. In this picture, we see rainstorms and snowstorms. Let's talk about the lightning in this picture."

These lower cognitive skills and questions occur before, during, and after reading the book (see Table 7.1).

## Getting Started: Weeks 2 and 3

*During the 2nd and 3rd week of Getting Started, preschool teachers continue with the modified WORLD shared book-reading sequence in addition to adding the following instructional opportunities:*

1. Model how to make a prediction before reading the story.

2. Model how to participate in a paired discussion.

These more challenging tasks and behaviors occur before, during, and after reading the book, as indicated in the following examples.

### Discussion Before Reading the Text

⭐ TEACHING STRATEGY: Model how to make predictions about book content during a picture walk. Have students make predictions with you during the picture walk. In a paired-practice session, encourage students to make predictions about what they will learn.

Ms. Thomas:    Let's look at the pictures to find out what happens in the *ocean*. I think the *sharks* will swim in the *ocean*. I think the *sharks* will find other fish in the *ocean*. Let's keep looking at the pages. What do you think will happen here? *[Place students in pairs.]* Now look at your partner. Tell your partner what you think will happen here.

**Table 7.1.** Getting started: Week 1

|  | Day 1: storybook | Day 2: storybook | Day 3: informational text | Day 4: informational text | Day 5: cumulative review |
|---|---|---|---|---|---|
| **Dialogue before reading the book** (5–7 minutes) | Use a visual (picture/concept card) to build background knowledge while introducing the theme, a smaller topic, and an instructional objective. | Review the thematic topic, vocabulary, and concepts using the same visual. | Review the theme and related background knowledge using a new visual. | Review the thematic topic, vocabulary, and concepts using the same Day 3 visual. | Use the visuals from the week to review theme and topic, referring to vocabulary concepts. *Magic Mirror:* Review all four words by providing important clues. Demonstrate how to look into the mirror and talk about a word that you see. Encourage children to use the magic mirror to describe what they see. |
| **Dialogue while reading the book** (7 minutes) | Introduce the title and author of the text. While reading the book, stop to talk about two semantically related words and related concepts while pointing to pictures in the book that depict those vocabulary words. | Reread the book and stop briefly on selected book pages that depict the vocabulary. *As a group,* talk about what children learned about the vocabulary concept. | Introduce the title and author of the text. While reading the book, stop to talk about two semantically related words and related concepts while pointing to pictures in the book that depict those vocabulary words. | Reread the book and stop briefly on selected book pages that depict the vocabulary. *As a group,* talk about what children learned about the vocabulary concept. |  |
| **Dialogue after reading the book** (5–7 minutes) | Discuss the big thing that happened in the story while making connections to vocabulary concepts using appropriate book pages. | Review vocabulary with picture/concept cards during Ready, Set, Go! | Discuss new information that was learned about the theme/topic using appropriate book pages. | Review vocabulary with picture/concept cards during Ready, Set, Go! |  |

## Discussion Before Rereading the Text

⭐ **TEACHING STRATEGY:** Stop on a book page with a vocabulary concept, and model how to talk with a student about what you learned. Encourage students to talk about what they learned using vocabulary words in a paired practice.

Ms. Thomas: Yesterday I learned, on this page, that when the *sharks* swim around the *ocean,* one of the *sharks* will get hurt. What else did we learn on this page about *sharks? [Assign partners.]* Now turn and look at your partner. Tell your partner what you learned on this page about sharks.

## Getting Started: Week 4

*In the 4th week of Getting Started, teachers may feel more proficient in implementing the lower cognitive strategies and tasks from the first 3 weeks and ready to add more cognitively challenging associating vocabulary tasks ("Could there be a sea in a city? Why or why not?") within the modified shared book-reading sequence. These activities occur after rereading the book on the next day. This week is important because teachers can practice scaffolding instruction during more challenging discussions and reflect on what works or areas that may require coaching support.*

## Discussion After Rereading the Text

Ms. Thomas:   What is the difference between a *sea* and a *stream?*

⭐ **TEACHING STRATEGY:** First model how to talk about connections between words and concepts before encouraging children to talk about conceptual connections.

Ms. Thomas:   I remember that a *sea* is a place with lots of salty water and it is big. I also remember that a *stream* is a little bit of water that moves slowly. A difference between a *sea* and a *stream* is that a *stream* is smaller than a *sea*. Also, the *sea* has salty water and a *stream* does not. Now who can tell us, what is the difference between a sea and a stream?

During these 4 weeks of curriculum initiation and acclimation, teachers can share their concerns with other teachers and/or an instructional coach or mentor, discuss ways to extend children's oral abilities during interactive book discussions, and engage in self-reflection on their content-related shared book-reading practices.

### Self-Reflection and Sharpening Our Focus

In the WORLD study, we first observed videotaped segments of teachers' shared book-reading lessons and then met with teachers in large and small groups (five to six teachers) or individually to provide feedback on their instructional practices. During these hour-long meetings, we also discussed teachers' concerns about intervention implementation. Using a self-reflection prompt (see Appendix 6C) in large group discussions, teachers analyzed the critical features of their shared book-reading practices in addition to lesson activities and experiences that were either successful or unsuccessful.

We now provide real examples of teachers' self-reflections during two WORLD meetings toward the beginning of the study during which researchers and coaches used the self-reflection prompt as a guide for discussing what was working and what wasn't working in teachers' shared book-reading practices.

# Self-Reflection

## CRITICAL FEATURES ANALYSIS

- What's working: I feel most confident about . . .

  **Examples:**

  - "I feel confident when introducing new information prior to reading the book."
  - "I feel confident manipulating the materials, and I have a small easel for displaying the picture/concept cards during instruction."
  - "I feel great using a 1-minute hour glass for timing Ready, Set, Go!"

- What needs attention: I'm having difficulty with . . .

  - "I'm having difficulty getting the children to sit still while seated cross-legged on the floor."
  - "I'm having difficulty pacing. I think I am moving too quickly through the lesson and just asking questions without creating a discussion."

## LESSON ACTIVITIES

- Activities that are fluent: I feel most confident about . . .

  - "I feel most confident when reviewing past vocabulary (the last 4 weeks of lessons) in Ready, Set, Go!"
  - "I feel most confident when reading the book and stopping to talk about the vocabulary."

- Activities that need attention: I'm still having difficulty with . . .

  - "I'm having difficulty during the picture walk. I am spending too much time previewing the book pages. How long should this take?"
  - "I'm having difficulty getting the children to talk to each other during the paired activity."
  - "I'm having difficulty during the Challenge Questions. I can't think of a good way to scaffold to help the children talk about 'why' or the difference between concepts."

- My children are successful: Children are able to . . .

  - "My children are able to identify the big thing that happened in the storybook."
  - "My children are able to use the words at home. One boy told me that he saw his mom *pour* a *liquid* into the *drain*."
  - "My children like the informational text on the ocean."

- My children are not successful: Children have difficulty when . . .
  - "One girl is having difficulty describing what she sees in the Magic Mirror."
  - "In one informational text, the children are having difficulty focusing on the key concepts because there are too many distracting pictures on the page (e.g., types of farm animals, places that are in a city, types of fish)."

After our large-group teacher meetings, we then identified three or four goals for strengthening future book-reading practices. We referred to these "universal" (Becker, Darney, Domitrovich, Keperling, & Ialongo, 2013, p. 217) goals as *Sharpening Our Focus* because their intent was to strengthen teachers' shared book-reading vocabulary practices by targeting three or four specific areas that would benefit all teachers. What follows are examples of Sharpening Our Focus goals that were established after our first and second meeting with teachers as they were becoming acclimated to the WORLD shared book–reading approach.

## Sharpening Our Focus Goals

### FIRST WORDS OF ORAL READING AND LANGUAGE DEVELOPMENT FEEDBACK MEETING

- Model how to make a prediction. Model how to tell "your partner" what you learned.
- Provide confirmation of children's responses, and when children respond incorrectly, model a correct response and/or redirect questions with feedback or ask additional guiding or clarifying questions. Responding with "yes" for incorrect responses can lead to conceptual confusions.
- Redirect Spanish responses by modeling English statements for students who need some support during discussions.
- Encourage children to ask questions.

### SECOND WORDS OF ORAL READING AND LANGUAGE DEVELOPMENT FEEDBACK MEETING

- Prepare for the lesson by reading it and the materials in advance. Use the 20 minutes to teach this information until mastery is achieved.
- Use a timer to manage your time so that you are not moving too quickly or slowly through the lesson—especially during Ready, Set, Go!
- Ready, Set, Go! 1-minute rule: If children cannot respond automatically as a group with a correct response, they have not learned the concepts well. This is not an opportunity to "teach" the concepts but an opportunity to quickly evaluate and reflect on whether the children have learned the concepts successfully.

Overall, these goals focus on procedural issues because teachers were learning to implement the WORLD pedagogical approach and needed suggestions for managing materials and adjusting their pacing so that they spent sufficient time on different lesson components within the total 20-minute lesson. Teachers, however, may face different instructional challenges with the progression of time and feel that they need more guidance in scaffolding higher cognitive tasks.

We feel this self-reflection process and discussion prompt (see Appendix 6C) can be used effectively as an ongoing professional development tool. As preschool teachers develop and implement their own thematic shared book–reading lessons, they can be encouraged to reflect on their instructional practice by using the self-reflection prompt or keeping a journal. Both tools allow teachers to record brief, reflective notes about their implementation of shared book-reading features (e.g., before, during, after reading sequence), specific lesson activities, and general challenges related to accelerating children's oral language abilities throughout the preschool day. These self-reflections can be shared in traditional, weekly grade-level meetings with other teachers, with an instructional coach or mentor, and within a supportive, professional learning community of early childhood educators who meet routinely to reflect on instructional issues related to a chosen topic (e.g., how literacy experiences can be used to integrate science and social studies learning). Although these discussions are crucial during the initial 4 weeks of *Getting Started*, this self-reflective process should be ongoing—guiding decisions for more customized PD (e.g., do teachers require opportunities to observe other teachers or a coach implement a specific strategy?) in response to teachers' varied levels of teaching expertise.

## Differentiating Professional Development Opportunities

In a collective case study of seven preschool teachers who implemented the Spanish WORLD shared book-reading intervention (Pollard-Durodola et al., 2012), we observed that preschool teachers entered school with a range of prior knowledge and skills that may have influenced the quality of their shared book-reading vocabulary instruction. Specifically, some teachers seemed to require more opportunities to learn how to build background knowledge, whereas others needed greater support in integrating higher cognitive skills (e.g., tasks that emphasize abstract thinking) during interactive discussions.

From this collective case study, we learned that PD models must be able to adjust and distribute support more responsively when it is evident that individual teachers require more intensive support than others (Becker et al., 2013; Pollard-Durodola et al., 2012). Although traditional workshops may augment teachers' knowledge about curricular content or a novel pedagogical approach, these brief PD experiences may not be intensive enough to shift teachers' typical classroom practices (Fixsen, Naoom, Blase, Friendman, & Wallace, 2005). In addition, these workshops do not reflect the reality that "one size does not fit all" (Klingner, 2004, p. 252).

Differentiating instructional support allows PD to be more responsive and proactive with regard to preschool teachers' entry-level teaching quality and abilities. A more responsive and proactive PD model may include an initial "universal" (Becker et al., 2013, p. 217) approach in which feedback, modeling of instructional tasks, and recommendations are provided to all teachers to address common implementation concerns. A more customized (Becker et al., 2013) PD approach, however, is appropriate when providing feedback to 1) smaller groups of teachers with similar instructional needs and 2) individual teachers who require more intensive support via classroom coaching experiences. Both universal and more customized PD practices can be facilitated with the assistance of an instructional coach or mentor and the use of videotaped shared book-reading vignettes.

## Instructional Coaching

Coaching can be defined as providing continuous guidance to support the development of teaching behaviors (Noell et al., 2005). Instructional coaches can be supportive mentor teachers—those who have greater expertise and are able to employ a variety of formative strategies (e.g., modeling exemplary instruction or specific book-reading strategies, team teaching) to support and extend teachers' instructional practices with feedback. Although this one-to-one coaching experience may be more effective when individualized feedback and instructional demonstrations are situated in real classroom experiences, coaches also can gauge teachers' level of instructional proficiency via informal observations of preschool teachers' shared book-reading lessons. These informal observations may be conducted in person or by viewing videotaped shared book-reading lessons followed by reflective conversations on teachers' strengths and areas in which they can improve. This is the process that was implemented in the WORLD study with teachers of ELLs.

## Videotaped Lessons

Coaches may encourage individual preschool teachers to conduct a self-study of their teaching practices by viewing videotaped segments of their instruction several times to engage in self-reflection in ways that are not possible during actual teaching episodes (Brophy, 2004; Seidel, Stürmer, Blomberg, Kobarg, & Schwindt, 2011; van de Pol et al., 2010). This process, however, is only effective when teachers are taught how to identify what is important in the videos and how to analyze, think about, and discuss instructional patterns (van Es & Sherin, 2008).

When the teacher and coach view instructional segments together, the coach can prompt analytical thinking by pausing the videotape to ask probing questions such as the following:

1. What were you thinking and doing in this segment of the lesson?
2. What were you thinking when the students did not respond?

3. What were you thinking when the wrong answer was provided?

4. How might you have responded differently here?

5. What concepts did children not understand here? How could you scaffold instruction here?

These are questions that we actually used in a WORLD ELL case study while interviewing a smaller subset of bilingual preschool teachers to better understand how teachers made instructional decisions (e.g., scaffolding during a difficult task, providing feedback) during the shared book-reading process (Pollard-Durodola, Gonzalez, Saenz, & Soares, 2013). These, or similar probing questions, can be used to initiate a reflective conversation between the coach and individual teacher to highlight ways of thinking and teaching that may not be beneficial for child learning. Sharpening Our Focus goals can then be established after these discussions.

Table 7.2 recommends a PD model that includes three levels of instructional support, which progress from responding to general instructional concerns to individualized assistance and coaching. This PD model shares some similarities with a two-tiered approach (Tier 1: Universal PD and feedback, followed by Tier 2: Individualized PD and feedback) developed by Becker et al. (2013).

**Table 7.2.** General versus more customized instructional support and feedback

| Level | Guiding questions for a coach or mentor | Type(s) of instructional support |
|---|---|---|
| *Level 1:* whole-group self-reflection discussions with feedback | 1. What are consistent patterns of teacher concerns? <br><br> 2. Which individual teachers express a need for instructional support? <br><br> 3. Which concerns should be addressed using smaller groups of teachers or individual coaching? | Provide general feedback to the entire group with 3–4 recommendations for strengthening instructional practices. |
| *Level 2:* flexible small-group self-reflection discussions with feedback | Based on observations of teachers' instruction, conversations, and shared book-reading practices, which strategies should be addressed within a small group of teachers with similar instructional needs or through individual coaching? | Provide feedback by addressing instructional areas of improvement that are common for smaller groups of teachers. <br><br> Group membership is flexible so that the instructional focus changes in response to new areas of teacher concern. Teachers may be observed informally in person or via sessions that are videotaped by a coach or peer mentor. |
| *Level 3:* individualized self-study discussions with feedback | 1. Which strategies should be modeled for a small group of teachers with similar instructional needs? <br><br> 2. Which teachers would benefit from individual coaching? | An individual teacher and coach work together to strengthen shared book-reading vocabulary practices. This may include opportunities for self-reflection and/or discussions of videotaped observations. Observations are formative and informal. |

## POTENTIAL OBSTACLES TO STUDENT SUCCESS

Our teacher collaborations, discussions, and observations of the WORLD intervention implementation for the past 8 years have led us to identify and reflect on three potential obstacles to student's language development and content learning during the shared book-reading process. For example, misinterpretation of book illustrations and visuals can be related to children's overreliance on their own limited life experiences (Schickedanz & Collins, 2012). Other potential problems derive from teachers' use of open-ended questions and their own oral language abilities. In the following sections, we discuss these three barriers to child learning with recommendations from our research or from previous shared book-reading investigations.

### Misunderstandings of Pictures and Visuals

In our intervention, we found that pictures—in the book and outside of the book—could quickly be reused in varied ways during the shared book-reading experience to scaffold difficult tasks, enhance comprehension, and introduce and review content vocabulary concepts. Some experts, however, note that pictures can lead to misunderstandings about book content (Beck & McKeown, 2001; Schickedanz & Collins, 2012). This misinterpretation of book illustrations, pictures, and visuals, in general, may be due to the fact that children must integrate information from a variety of sources (e.g., prior knowledge, details in the text) to correctly understand what is taking place in a picture (Beck & McKeown, 2001; Schickedanz & Collins, 2012). To better understand the source of young children's confusions during shared book-reading discussions, Schickedanz and Collins (2012) observed how teachers responded to children's misinterpretations of book illustrations and noted some basic sources of confusion.

These researchers noted that misunderstandings can be due to the following:

1. Confusions about an illustration
2. An overreliance on insufficient background knowledge
3. The teacher's limited or lack of response to children's comprehension errors

In addition, teachers' brief statements in response to child errors may not provide enough clarifying information for children to understand why their response was incorrect. An example is the following teacher response in which children in the shared book-reading small group identify a picture of the *ocean* as a *pond:*

Ms. Thomas
Response:      This is an *ocean* and not a *pond.*

This statement does not clarify the *minimal differences* between the two bodies of water. A more informative response could be the following:

Ms. Thomas
Response:    *[Scaffolding with picture/concept cards]* This is an *ocean*. Remember an ocean is a large body of salty water that covers the earth. This is not a *pond*. Remember, a *pond* is water with ground or land all around it in which animals can live. In this picture of *pond*, we see that it is surrounded by grass growing in the *meadow*. When I look at this picture of the ocean, I see waves *[pointing]* and a long sandy beach *[pointing]*. A *pond* is smaller than an *ocean*.

In this response, the teacher provides clarifying feedback and models her reasoning as she points to features of the ocean and the pond in the picture/concept cards.

To avoid some of these misinterpretations of visuals, Schickedanz and Collins (2012) recommend that teachers assist children in learning what to expect from book illustrations (e.g., objects and characters can appear in multiple ways on the same page), point to important details in the picture while providing an explanation, and reread the text for clarification (Collins, 2010; Schickedanz & Collins, 2012). Although young children may require deeper life experiences beyond the book to avoid some of their confusions, children's misinterpretations should not be overlooked but addressed using specific clarifying and probing language during the shared book-reading experience. The instructional implication is that teachers should not allow children to rely on personal experience alone in lieu of learning how to use details in the picture and text to facilitate comprehension.

## Open-Ended Questions

Open-ended questions foster students' abilities to use more complex grammatical structures to expand critical and abstract thinking, such as making predictions and inferences (Lee & Kinzie, 2012; Wasik et al., 2006). Children's responses to open-ended questions allow teachers to informally evaluate learning and to adjust instruction and strategy use (van de Pol et al., 2010). There is some evidence that group size may influence the effectiveness of open-ended questions, with smaller group sizes allowing more frequent use of these questions when the instructional tasks are directed toward individual children (van de Pol et al., 2010, p. 860).

It is misleading, however, to believe that open-ended questions inevitably lead to interactive adult–child discussions. In the WORLD preschool intervention, we have observed individual preschool teachers ask an open-ended question, wait for children to respond, and then proceed to the next question without taking the time to extend children's responses, ask clarifying questions (e.g., "Can you tell me more about. . . . ? Why do you think. . . . ?"), and create a genuine back-and-forth *dialogue* using *wh-* questions (e.g., who, why, where). In the latter years of our ELL studies, we began to evaluate intervention implementation by preschool teachers' ability to generate this back-and-forth quality in adult–child book conversations. After observing a videotaped instructional vignette, we posed the global question, "Was the dialogue with the children *interactive* during the shared book-reading lesson?" We then reflected on the following specific questions to evaluate the interactivity of the shared book-reading experience:

1.  Does the teacher employ a cycle of open-ended questions that result in a *conversation* about vocabulary and connected content in ways that are appropriate for young learners?

2.  Does the teacher attempt to push students' conversational abilities *beyond* customary interactions?

3.  Does the teacher *extend* children's oral responses or model oral responses to create a conversation?

Overall, our recommendation is that early childhood educators should be attentive to opportunities during shared book reading for using open-ended questions as a conversational springboard to promote rich discussions about life connections to science and social studies concepts. The purpose of using open-ended questions is to move beyond single-word and sparse responses.

## Preschool Teachers' Language Use

Children's language use and development may also be related to their teacher's *conversational abilities* (Justice, McGinty, Zucker, Cabell, & Piasta, 2012; Wasik et al., 2006). This includes teachers' use of complex or simple grammatical structures (Piasta et al., 2012) and the frequency of teacher talk about word meanings (Dickinson, 2011).

Due to the bidirectionality of adult–child interactions, children who interact with teachers who use more complex language may demonstrate richer conversational abilities than children who are taught by teachers who use more simple syntax (grammar) patterns (Piasta et al., 2012). In addition, the frequency of teacher talk about target vocabulary can vary considerably from teacher to teacher. In one study of preschool Head Start teachers, for example, researchers compared one teacher who used only six utterances to talk about a target word to another teacher who used 268 utterances (Dickinson, 2011). In the WORLD study, we also noted that for some teachers, extensive conversations were more difficult to facilitate due to their own language use and abilities.

There is some evidence that preschool teachers may benefit from oral language or discourse strategies (e.g., using elaborate language, promoting active listening) to engage in more interactive dialogues or conversations with children during shared book reading (Wasik et al., 2006). Preschool teachers, however, may require sustained PD opportunities with modeling and coaching to benefit from this type of instructional support (see Wasik et al., 2006 for further details). The implication is that early childhood educators may need sufficient time to develop proficiency in novel conversational strategies and practices.

## CONCLUSION

In the 2011 spring issue of *American Educator*, James Heckman, a Nobel Memorial Prize winner in economics, uses multiple examples to confirm the importance of early childhood instruction and intervention as a starting point for equalizing the playing field of young children from varied socioeconomic backgrounds. Heckman emphasizes that high-quality early childhood instruction serves as a catalyst for children's specific skill development and general academic achievement (Heckman, 2011). "Achievement," however, is based on *knowledge*, and knowledge is *acquired*. If children enter schools with varying degrees of word and world knowledge determined in part by family resources and socioeconomics, early childhood educators must be motivated and equipped to intervene early by providing multiple opportunities for children to learn and see the world around them in new ways through strategic content instruction.

Being equipped, however, may mean that early childhood educators must be able to provide higher cognitive task instruction with thoughtful scaffolding to make difficult content easier to understand, talk about, and relate to real-life child experiences. Few studies, however, have examined the use of instructional scaffolding during shared book reading in preschool settings; researchers in one study (Pentimonti & Justice, 2010) concluded that preschool teachers may not always provide the appropriate level of scaffolding (e.g., high support versus low support scaffolding strategies) during challenging read-aloud tasks. In the WORLD ELL studies, we are only beginning to examine instructional scaffolding during more analytical content-related shared book-reading episodes (e.g., challenge questions) with Spanish-speaking children. In general, more knowledge in this area is needed to better understand how teachers can be both proactive and responsive to children's language and conceptual abilities during shared book-reading interactions.

In conclusion, because word learning is a complex and incremental process, vocabulary acceleration will invariably take time (Nagy & Scott, 2000) and intentional, thoughtful planning. This includes sufficient time for children to acquire and use new knowledge and sufficient time for preschool teachers to become proficient in implementing novel content-related vocabulary practices in relevant and thoughtful ways.

## SUGGESTED FURTHER READINGS

Beauchat, K.A., Blamey, K.L., & Walpole, S. (2009). Building preschool children's language and literacy one storybook at a time. *The Reading Teacher, 63*(1), 26–39.

Pinkman, K., & Neuman, S.B. (2012). *Knowledge development in early childhood: Sources of learning and classroom implications.* New York, NY: Guilford Press.

Schickedanz, J., & Collins, M.F. (2012). For young children, pictures in storybooks are rarely worth a thousand words. *The Reading Teacher, 65*(8), 539–549.

# References

Adams, M.J. (1990). *Beginning to read: Thinking and learning about print—a summary.* Urbana-Champaign: University of Illinois, Center for the Study of Reading, The Reading Research and Education Center.

Adelson-Goldstein, J. (1998). Developing active vocabulary: Making the communicative connection. *ESL Magazine, 1*(3), 10–14.

Anderson, L.W., & Krathwohl, D.R. (2001). *A taxonomy for learning, teaching, and assessing: A revision of Bloom's taxonomy.* New York, NY: Longman.

Anderson, R.C., & Freebody, P. (1981). Vocabulary knowledge. In J. Guthrie (Ed.), *Comprehension and teaching: Research reviews* (pp. 77–117). Newark, DE: International Reading Association.

Anderson, V., & Roit, M. (1996). Linking reading comprehension instruction to language development for language-minority students. *The Elementary School Journal, 96*(3), 295–309. doi:10.1086/461829

Anderson, V., & Roit, M. (1998). Reading as a gateway to language proficiency for language-minority students in the elementary grades. In R.M. Gersten & R.T. Jiménez (Eds.), *Promoting learning for culturally and linguistically diverse students: Classroom applications from contemporary research* (pp. 42–54). New York, NY: Wadsworth.

Armbruster, B.B., & Nagy, W.E. (1992). Reading to learn: Vocabulary in content area lessons. *The Reading Teacher, 45*(7), 550–551.

Arnold, D.H., & Whitehurst, G.J. (1994). Accelerating language development through picture book reading: A summary of dialogic reading and its effect. *Bridges to Literacy, Children, Families, and Schools, 1,* 103–128.

Arnold, T. (1987). *No jumping on the bed!* New York, NY: Puffin Books.

Arnold, T. (1987). *¡No se salta en la cama!* New York, NY: Puffin Books.

Asch, F. (1999). *La sombra de Moonbear.* New York, NY: Aladdin Books.

Asch, F. (1999). *Moonbear's shadow.* New York, NY: Aladdin Books.

August, D. (2003). *Supporting the development of English literacy in English language learners: Key issues and promising practices.* Baltimore, MD: Center for Research on the Education of Students Placed at Risk.

August, D., Carlo, M., Dressler, C., & Snow, C. (2005). The critical role of vocabulary development for English language learners. *Learning Disabilities: Research and Practice, 20*(1), 50–57.

August, D., & Shanahan, T. (2006). *Developing literacy in second-language learners: A report on the National Literacy Panel on Language Minority Children and Youth.* Mahwah, NJ: Lawrence Erlbaum Associates.

Baker, S.K., Simmons, D.C., & Kame'enui, E.J. (1998). Vocabulary acquisition: Research bases. In D.C. Simmons & E.J. Kame'enui (Eds.), *What reading research tells us about children with diverse learning needs* (pp. 183–218). Mahwah, NJ: Lawrence Erlbaum Associates.

Ballantyne, K.G., Sanderman, A.R., & Levy, J. (2008). *Educating English language learners: Building teacher capacity.* Washington, DC: National Clearinghouse for English Language Acquisition. Retrieved from http://www.ncela.us/files/uploads/3/EducatingELLsBuildingTeacherCapacityVol1.pdf

Bannan-Ritland, B. (2003). The role of design in research: The integrative learning design framework. *Educational Researcher, 32*(1), 21–24.

Barbarin, O., Bryant, D., McCandies, T., Burchinal, M., Early, D., Clifford, R., & Pianta, R. (2006). Children enrolled in public pre-K: The relation of family life, neighborhood quality, and socio-economic resources to early competence. *American Journal of Orthopsychiatry, 76*, 265–267.

Barracca, D., & Barracca, S. (1990). *The adventures of Maxi the taxi dog.* New York, NY: Penguin Books.

Barracca, D., & Barracca, S. (1990). *Las aventuras de Maxi el perro taxista.* New York, NY: Penguin Books.

Beane, J.A. (1995). *Toward a coherent curriculum.* Alexandria, VA: Association for Supervision and Curriculum Development.

Beck, I.L., & McKeown, M.G. (2001). Text talk: Capturing the benefits of read-aloud experiences for young children. *The Reading Teacher, 55*(1), 10–20.

Beck, I.L., & McKeown, M.G. (2007). Increasing young low-income children's oral vocabulary repertoires through rich and focused instruction. *The Elementary School Journal, 107*(3), 251–271.

Beck, I.L., McKeown, M.G., & Kucan, L. (2002). *Bringing words to life: Robust vocabulary instruction.* New York, NY: Guilford Press.

Beck, I.L., McKeown, M.G., & Kucan, L. (2013). *Bringing words to life: Robust vocabulary instruction* (2nd ed.). New York, NY: Guilford Press.

Beck, I.L., McKeown, M.G., & Omanson, R.C. (1987). The effects and uses of diverse vocabulary instructional techniques. In M.G. McKeown & M.E. Curtis (Eds.), *The nature of vocabulary acquisition* (pp. 147–163). Mahwah, NJ: Lawrence Erlbaum Associates.

Beck, I.L., Perfetti, C.A., & McKeown, M.G. (1982). The effects of long-term vocabulary instruction on lexical access and reading comprehension. *Journal of Educational Psychology, 74*, 506–521.

Becker, K.D., Darney, D., Domitrovich, C., Keperling, J.P., & Ialongo, N.S. (2013). Supporting universal prevention programs: A two-phased coaching model. *Clinical Child Family Psychology Review, 16*, 213–228.

Becker, W.C. (1992). Direct instruction: A twenty year review. In R.P. West & L.A. Hamerlynck (Eds.), *Designs for excellence in education: The legacy of B.F. Skinner* (pp. 71–112). Longmont, CO: Sopris West.

Berger, M. (1996). *Amazing water.* New York, NY: Newbridge Educational Publishing.

Biemiller, A. (2003). Vocabulary: Needed if more children are to read well. *Reading Psychology, 24*, 323–335.

Blok, H. (1999). Reading to young children in educational settings: A meta-analysis of recent research. *Language Learning, 49*, 343–371.

Borba, M. (2007). Rediscovering shred reading for social studies instruction. *Social Studies Review, 47*(1), 54–56.

Bradley, B.A., & Reinking, D. (2011). Enhancing research and practice in early childhood through formative and design experiments. *Early Child Development and Care, 81*(3), 305–319. doi:10.1080/03004430903357894

Brennan, A. (2006). *Mr. Greg's garden.* New York, NY: National Geographic Society.

Brenneman, K. (2013). *Science, math, literacy, and socio-emotional development in early childhood—Can we do it all?* Denver, CO: Marsico Institute, Morgridge College of Education at the University of Denver.

Brophy, J. (1992). Probing the subtleties of subject-matter teaching. *Educational Leadership, 49*(7), 4–8.

Brophy, J. (2004). *Advances in research on teaching: Using video in teacher education.* New York, NY: Elsevier.

Brown, M.W. (1942). *The runaway bunny.* New York, NY: Harper & Row.

Brownell, R. (2000). *Expressive One-Word Picture Vocabulary Test manual.* Novato, CA: Academic Therapy Publications.

Cabell, S.Q., Justice, L.M., Vukelich, C., Buell, M.J., & Han, M. (2008). In L.M. Justice, & C. Vukelich (Eds.), *Achieving excellence in preschool literacy instruction* (pp. 198–220). New York, NY: Guilford Press.

Calderón, M., August, D., Slavin, R., Durán, D., Madden, N., & Cheung, A. (2005). Bringing words to life in classrooms with English-language learners. In E. H. Hiebert & M. L. Kamil (Eds.), *Teaching and learning vocabulary: Bringing research to practice* (pp. 115–136). Mahwah, NJ: Lawrence Erlbaum Associates.

Carnine, D.W. (1994). Introduction to the mini-series: Diverse learners and prevailing, emerging, and research-based educational approaches and their tools. *School Psychology Review, 23*, 341–350.

Carroll, J. (1963). A model for school learning. *Teachers College Record, 64*, 723–733.

Center for Research on Education, Diversity & Excellence (CREDE). (2014). *Instructional conversations.* Manoa: University of Hawaii. Retrieved from http://manoa.hawaii.edu/coe/crede/videos/instructional-conversation

Charlesworth, R., & Lind, K.K. (2013). *Math and science for young children* (7th ed.). Belmont, CA: Wadsworth.

Christie, J.F. (2008). The scientifically based reading research approach to early literacy instruction. In L.M. Justice & C. Vukelich (Eds.), *Achieving excellence in preschool literacy instruction* (pp. 25–40). New York, NY: Guilford Press.

Cobb, P., Confrey, J., diSessa, A., Lehrer, R., & Schauble, L. (2003). Design experiments in educational research. *Educational Researcher, 32*(1), 9–13.

Cohen, L.E., Kramer-Vida, L., & Frye, N. (2012a). Implementing dialogic reading with culturally, linguistically diverse preschool children. *NHSA Dialog: A Research-to-Practice Journal for the Early Childhood Field, 15*(1), 135–141.

Cohen, L.E., Kramer-Vida, L., & Frye, N. (2012b). Using dialogic reading as professional development to improve students' English and Spanish vocabulary. *NHSA Dialog, 15,* 59–80.

Collins, A., Joseph, D., & Bielaczyc, K. (2004). Design research: Theoretical and methodological issues. *The Journal of the Learning Sciences, 13*(1), 15–42.

Collins, M.F. (2005). ESL preschoolers' English vocabulary acquisition from storybook reading. *Reading Research Quarterly, 40,* 406–408.

Collins, M.F. (2010). ELL preschoolers' English vocabulary acquisition from storybook reading. *Early Childhood Research Quarterly, 25,* 84–97.

Cook-Gumperz, J. (1993). The relevant text: Narrative, storytelling, and children's understanding of genre. *Linguistics and Education, 5,* 149–156.

Core Knowledge Foundation. (2013). *Core knowledge for development of preschool topic sequences.* Charlottesville, VA: Author.

Covey, R. (2013). *The 7 habits of highly effective people: Powerful lessons in personal change.* New York, NY: Simon and Schuster.

Coyne, M.D., McCoach, D.B., & Kapp, S. (2007). Vocabulary intervention for kindergarten students: Comparing extended instruction to embedded instruction and incidental exposure. *Learning Disability Quarterly, 30,* 74–88.

Crawford, J., & Krashen, S. (2007). *English learners in American classrooms: 101 questions, 101 answers.* New York, NY: Scholastic.

Cummins, J. (1979). Linguistic interdependence and the educational development of bilingual children. *Review of Educational Research, 49,* 222–251.

DeAvila, E.A., & Duncan, S.E. (2000). *Pre-LAS2000: English and Spanish technical notes.* Monterey, CA: CTB/McGraw-Hill.

de Temple, J., & Snow, C.E. (2003). Learning words from books. In A. van Kleeck, S.S.A. Stahl, & E.B. Bauer (Eds.), *On reading books to children: Parents and teachers* (pp. 16–36). Mahwah, NJ: Lawrence Erlbaum Associates.

Diamond, K.E., Justice, L.M., Siegler, R.S., & Snyder, P.A. (2013). *Synthesis of IES research on early intervention and early childhood education.* (NCSER 2013–3001). Washington, DC: U.S. Department of Education, Institute of Education Sciences, National Center for Special Education Research. Retrieved from http://ies.ed.gov/ncser/pubs/20133001

Dickinson, D.K. (2001). Book reading in preschool classrooms: Is recommended practice common? In D.K. Dickinson & P.O. Tabors (Eds.), *Beginning literacy with language: Young children learning at home and school* (pp. 175–203). Baltimore, MD: Paul H. Brookes Publishing Co.

Dickinson, D.K. (2011). Teachers' language practices and academic outcomes of preschool children. *Science, 333,* 964–967.

Dickinson, D.K., & Keebler, R. (1989). Variation in preschool teachers' styles of reading books. *Discourse Processes, 12,* 353–375.

Dickinson, D.K., & Smith, M.W. (1994). Long-term effects of preschool teachers' book readings on low-income children's vocabulary and story comprehension. *Reading Research Quarterly, 29,* 104–122.

Dickinson, D.K., & Tabors, P.O. (2001). Fostering language and literacy in classrooms and homes. *Young Children, 57*(2), 10.

Duke, N.K. (2000). 3.6 minutes per day: The scarcity of informational texts in first grade. *Reading Research Quarterly, 35,* 202–224.

Duke, N.K. (2003). Reading to learn from the very beginning: Information books in early childhood. *Young Children, 58,* 14–20.

Duke, N.K. (2004). The case for informational text. *Educational Leadership, 61*(6), 40–41.

Duke, N.K., & Bennett-Armistead, V.S. (2003). *Reading and writing informational text in the primary grades.* New York, NY: Scholastic.

Duke, N.K., Bennett-Armistead, V.S., & Roberts, E.M. (2003). Filling the nonfiction void: Why we should bring nonfiction into the early-grade classroom. *American Educator, 27*(1), 30–34, 46.

Duke, N.K., & Kays, J. (1998). "Can I say 'once upon a time'?": Kindergarten children developing knowledge of informational text language. *Early Childhood Research Quarterly, 13*(2), 295–318.

Dunn, L.M., & Dunn, D.M. (1997). *Peabody Picture Vocabulary Test* (3rd ed.). Circle Pines, MN: American Guidance Service.

Durán, L.K., Roseth, C.J., & Hoffman, P. (2010). An experimental study comparing English-only and transitional bilingual education on Spanish-speaking preschoolers' early literacy development. *Early Childhood Research Quarterly, 25,* 207–217.

Duschl, R.A., Schweingruber, H.A., & Shouse, A.W. (2007). *Taking science to school: Learning and teaching science in grades k–8.* Washington, DC: National Academies Press.

Early, D.M., Iruka, I.U., Ritchie, S., Barbarin, O.A., Winn, D.C., Crawford, G.M., . . . Pianta, R.C. (2010). How do pre-kindergarteners spend their time? Gender, ethnicity, and income as predictors of experiences in pre-kindergarten classrooms. *Early Childhood Education Quarterly, 25,* 177–193.

Ehlert, L. (1988). *Planting a rainbow.* Singapore: Tien Wah.

Elleman, A.M., Lindo, E.J., Morphy, P., & Compton, D.L. (2009). The impact of vocabulary instruction on passage-level comprehension of school-age children: A meta-analysis. *Journal of Research on Educational Effectiveness, 2,* 1–44.

Emberley, R. (1990). *Caminando.* New York, NY: Scholastic.

Emberley, R. (1990). *Taking a walk.* New York, NY: Scholastic.

Emmett, J. (2004). *Ruby in her own time.* New York, NY: Scholastic.

Espinosa, L. (2010). Classroom teaching and instruction "Best Practices" for young English language learners. In E.E. García & E.C. Frede (Eds.), *Young English language learners: Current research and emerging directions for practice and policy* (pp. 143–164). New York, NY: Teachers College Press.

Ezell, H.K., & Justice, L.M. (2005). *Shared storybook reading: Building young children's language and emergent literacy skills.* Baltimore, MD: Paul H. Brookes Publishing Co.

Farkas, G., & Beron, K. (2004). The detailed age trajectory of oral vocabulary knowledge: Differences by class and race. *Social Science Research, 33,* 464–497.

Fillmore, I.W., & Snow, C.E. (2000). *What teachers need to know about language.* Washington, DC: Clearinghouse on Languages and Linguistics.

Fixsen, D., Naoom, S., Blase, K., Friendman, R., & Wallace, F. (2005). *Implementation research: A synthesis of the literature.* Tampa, FL: National Implementation Research Network, Louis de la Parte Florida Mental Health Institute, University of South Florida.

Flynn, K.S. (2011). Developing children's oral language skills through dialogic reading. *Teaching Exceptional Children, 44,* 8–16.

Foorman, B.F., Seals, L., Anthony, J., & Pollard-Durodola, S.D. (2003). Vocabulary enrichment project. In B.F. Foorman (Ed.), *Preventing and remediating reading difficulties: Bringing science to scale* (pp. 419–441). Timonium, MD: York Press.

French, L. (2004). Science as the center of a coherent, integrated early childhood curriculum. *Early Childhood Research Quarterly, 19,* 138–149.

Gelman, R., & Brenneman, K. (2004). Science learning pathways for young children. *Early Childhood Research Quarterly, 19,* 150–158.

Genessee, F. (2010). Dual language development in preschool children. In E.E. García & E.C. Frede (Eds.), *Young English language learners* (pp. 59–79). New York, NY: Teachers College Press.

Gersten, R. (1996). Special issue: The language-minority student in transition. *The Elementary School Journal, 96*(3), 227–244.

Gersten, R., & Baker, S. (1998). Real world use of scientific concepts: Integrating situated cognition with explicit instruction. *Exceptional Children, 65*(1), 23–35.

Gersten, R., & Baker, S. (2000). What we know about effective instructional practices for English-language learners. *Exceptional Children, 66*(4), 454–470.

Gersten, R., Baker, S.K., Shanahan, T., Linan-Thompson, S., Collins, P., & Scarcella, R. (2007). *Effective literacy and English language instruction for English learners in the elementary grades: A practice guide.* (NCEE 2007-2011). Washington, DC: National Center for Education Evaluation and Regional Assistance, Institute of Education Sciences, U.S. Department of Education. Retrieved from http://www.p12

.nysed.gov/biling/bilinged/documents/el_practice_guide.pdf

Gersten, R., Fuchs, L.S., Williams, J.P., & Baker, S. (2001). Teaching reading comprehension strategies to students with learning disabilities: A review of research. *Review of Educational Research, 71*(2), 279–320.

Ginsburg, H.P., & Golbeck, S.L. (2004). Thoughts on the future of research on mathematics and science learning and education. *Early Childhood Research Quarterly, 19,* 190–200.

Gonzalez, J.E., Pollard-Durodola, S.D., Simmons, D., Taylor, A., Davis, M., Fogarty, M., & Simmons, L. (2013). Enhancing preschool children's vocabulary: Effects of teacher talk before, during and after shared reading. *Early Childhood Research Quarterly, 29,* 214–226.

Gonzalez, J.E., Pollard-Durodola, S.D., Taylor, A., Simmons, D.C., Davis, M., & Simmons, L. (2011). Developing low income preschoolers' social studies and science vocabulary through content-focused shared book reading. *Journal of Research on Educational Effectiveness, 4,* 25–52.

Gorard, S., Roberts, K., & Taylor, C. (2004). What kind of creature is a design experiment? *British Educational Research Journal, 30*(4), 577–590.

Graves, M.F., August, D., & Mancilla-Martinez, J. (2013). *Teaching vocabulary to English language learners.* New York, NY: Teachers College Press.

Gutiérrez, K.D., Zepeda, M., & Castro, D.C. (2010). Advancing early literacy learning for all children: Implications of the NELP report for dual-language learners. *Educational Researcher, 39*(4), 334–339.

Hakuta, K., Butler, Y.G., & Witt, D. (2000). *How long does it take English learners to attain proficiency?* Policy report 2000-1. University of California Linguistic Minority Research Institute.

Hamayan, E., Marier, B., Sánchez-López, C., & Damico, J. (2013). *Special education considerations for English language learners: Delivering a continuum of services.* Philadelphia, PA: Caslon Publishing.

Hancin-Bhatt, B., & Nagy, W.E. (1994). Lexical transfer and second language morphological development. *Applied Psycholinguistics, 15*(3), 289–310.

Hargrave, A.C., & Sénéchal, M. (2000). A book reading intervention with preschool children who have limited vocabularies: The benefits of regular reading and dialogic reading. *Early Childhood Research Quarterly, 15,* 75–90.

Hart, B., & Risley, T.R. (1995). *Meaningful differences in the everyday experience of young American children.* Baltimore, MD: Paul H. Brookes Publishing Co.

Heckman, J. (2011). The economics of inequality: The value of early childhood education. *American Educator, 35*(1), 31–47.

Herczog, M.M. (2010). Using the NCSS national curriculum standards for social studies: A framework for teaching, learning, and assessment to meet state social studies standards. *Social Education, 74*(4), 217–222.

Hickman, P., & Pollard-Durodola, S.D. (2009). *Dynamic vocabulary read-aloud strategies for English learners: Building language and literacy in the primary grades.* Newark, DE: International Reading Association.

Hiebert, E.H., & Cervetti, G.N. (2012). What differences in narrative and informational texts mean for learning and instruction of vocabulary. In E.J. Kame'enui & J.F. Baumann (Eds.), *Vocabulary instruction: Research to practice* (2nd ed., pp. 322–344). New York, NY: Guilford Press.

Hirsch, E.D. (2003). Reading comprehension requires knowledge of the words and the world. *American Educator, 27*(1), 10–14.

Hirsch, E.D. (2006). Building knowledge: The case for bringing content into the language arts block and for a knowledge-rich curriculum core for all children. *American Educator, 30*(1), 8–18.

Horst, J.S., Parsons, K.L., & Bryan, N.M. (2011). Get the story straight: Contextual repetition promotes word learning from storybooks. *Frontiers in Psychology, 2,* 1–11.

Huttenlocher, J., Vasilyeva, M., Cymermann, E., & Levine, S. (2002). Language input and child syntax. *Cognitive Psychology, 45,* 337–374.

Jordan, H.J. (2006). *How a seed grows.* New York, NY: Harper Collins Publishers.

Justice, L.M., McGinty, A.S., Zucker, T., Cabell, S.Q., & Piasta, S.B. (2013). Bi-directional dynamics underlie the complexity of talk in teacher-child play-based conversations in classrooms serving at-risk pupils. *Early Childhood Research Quarterly, 28,* 496–508.

Justice, L.M., Meier, J., & Walpole, S. (2005). Learning new words from storybooks: An efficacy study with at-risk kindergartners. *Language, Speech, and Hearing Services in Schools, 36,* 17–32.

Kame'enui, E.J., Dixon, R.C., & Carnine, D.W. (1987). Issues in the design of vocabulary instruction. In M.G. McKeown & M.E. Curtis (Eds.), *The nature of vocabulary acquisition* (pp. 129–145). Mahwah, NJ: Lawrence Erlbaum Associates.

Kelly, A.E. (2003). Research as design. *Educational Researcher, 32*(1), 3–4.

Klingner, J.K. (2004). The science of professional development. *Journal of Learning Disabilities, 37,* 248–255.

Klingner, J.K., Vaughn, S., & Schumm, J.S. (1998). Collaborative strategic reading during social studies in heterogeneous fourth-grade classrooms. *The Elementary School Journal, 99*(1), 3–22.

Kuhn, D., & Pearsall, S. (2000). Developmental origins of scientific thinking. *Journal of Cognition and Development, 1,* 113–129.

Landauer, T.K., & Dumais, S.T. (1997). A solution to Plato's problem: The latent semantic analysis theory of acquisition, induction, and representation of knowledge. *Psychological Review, 104, 2,* 21–40.

Lareau, A. (2003). *Unequal childhoods: Class, race, and family life.* Berkeley, CA: University of California Press.

Lee, Y., & Kinzie, M.B. (2012). Teacher question and student response with regard to cognition and language use. *Instruction Science, 40,* 857–874.

Leung, C.B. (2008). Preschoolers' acquisition of scientific vocabulary through repeated read-aloud events, retellings, and hands-on science activities. *Reading Psychology, 29,* 165–193.

Lonigan, C.J., Shanahan, T., & Cunningham, A. (2008). Impact of shared reading interventions on young children's early literacy skills. In *Developing early literacy: Report of the national early literacy panel.* Washington, DC: National Early Literacy Panel. Retrieved from http://lincs.ed.gov/publications/pdf/NELPReport09.pdf

Maduram, I. (2000). Playing possum: A young child's responses to information books. *Language Arts, 77*(5), 391–397.

Malouf, D.B., & Schiller, E.P. (1995). Practice and research in special education. *Exceptional Children, 61*(5), 414–419.

Mantzicopoulus, P., & Patrick, H. (2011). Reading picture books and learning science: Engaging young children with informational text. *Theory into Practice, 50*(4), 269–276.

Marulis, L.M., & Neuman, S.B. (2011). How do vocabulary interventions affect young at-risk children's word learning: A meta-analytic review. *Review of Educational Research, 80,* 300–335.

Marulis, L.M., & Neuman, S.B. (2013). How vocabulary interventions affect young children at risk: A meta-analytic review. *Journal of Research on Educational Effectiveness, 6,* 223–262. doi:10.1080/19345747.2012.755591

Mathes, P., Pollard-Durodola, S.D., Cárdenas-Hagan, E., Linan-Thompson, S., & Vaughn, S. (2007). Teaching struggling readers who are native Spanish speakers: What do we know? *Language Speech and Hearing Services in Schools, 38,* 260–271.

McCardle, P., Chhabra, V., & Kapinus, B. (2008). *Reading research in action: A teacher's guide for student success.* Baltimore, MD: Paul H. Brookes Publishing Co.

McGee, L.M., & Schickedanz, J.A. (2007). Repeated interactive read-alouds in preschool and kindergarten. *Reading Teacher, 60,* 742–752. doi:10.1598/RT.60.8.4

McKeown, M., and Curtis, M.E. (1987). *The nature of vocabulary acquisition.* Hillsdale, NJ: Lawrence Erlbaum Associates.

McLoyd, V. (1990). The impact of economic hardship on black families and children: Psychological distress, parenting, and socio-emotional development. *Child Development, 61,* 311–346.

McTighe, J., & Wiggins, G. (1998). *Understanding by design.* Alexandria, VA: Association for Supervision and Curriculum Development.

Meyer, B.F.J., Brandt, D.M., & Bluth, G.J. (1980). Use of top-level structure in reading in text: Key for reading comprehension in 9th grade students. *Reading Research Quarterly, 16*(1), 72–103.

Mindes, G. (2005). Social studies in today's early childhood curricula. *Beyond the Journal: Young Children on the Web.* Retrieved from https://www.naeyc.org/files/yc/file/200509/MindesBTJ905.pdf

Mol, S.E., & Bus, A.G. (2011, March). To read or not to read: A meta-analysis of print exposure from infancy to early adulthood. *Psychological Bulletin, 137*(2), 267–296. doi:10.1037/a0021890

Mol, S.E., Bus, A.G., & de Jong, M.T. (2009). Interactive book reading in early education: A tool to stimulate print knowledge as well as oral language. *Review of Educational Research, 79,* 979–1007.

Mol, S.E., Bus, A.G., de Jong, M.T., & Smeets, D.J.H. (2008). Added value of dialogic parent–child book readings: A meta-analysis. *Early Education & Development, 19*, 7–26.

Montelongo, J.A., Hernández, A.C., Herter, R.J., & Cuello, J. (2011). Using cognates to scaffold context clue strategies for Latino ELLs. *The Reading Teacher, 64*(6), 429–434.

Nagy, W.E. (1988). *Teaching vocabulary to improve reading comprehension.* Newark, DE: International Reading Association.

Nagy, W.E. (2005). Why vocabulary instruction needs to be long-term and comprehensive. In E.H. Hiebert & M.L. Kamil (Eds.), *Teaching and learning vocabulary* (pp. 27–44). Mahwah, NJ: Lawrence Erlbaum Associates.

Nagy, W.E. (2007). Metalinguistic awareness and the vocabulary–comprehension connection. In R.K. Wagner, A.E. Muse, & K.R. Tannenbaum (Eds.), *Vocabulary acquisition: Implications for reading comprehension* (pp. 52–77). New York, NY: Guilford Press.

Nagy, W.E., García, G.E., Durgunoglu, A.Y., & Hancin-Bhatt, B.J. (1993). Cross-language transfer of lexical knowledge: Bilingual students' use of cognates. *Journal of Reading Behavior, 25*, 241–259.

Nagy, W.E., & Scott, J.A. (2000). Vocabulary processes. In M.L. Kamil, P.B. Mosenthal, P.D. Pearson, & R. Barr (Eds.), *Handbook of reading research* (Vol. 3, pp. 269–284). Mahwah, NJ: Lawrence Erlbaum Associates.

National Association for the Education of Young Children. (1998). *Learning to read and write: Developmentally appropriate practices for young children.* Retrieved from http://www.naeyc.org/files/naeyc/file/positions/PSREAD98.PDF

National Association for the Education of Young Children. (2002). *Early learning standards: Creating the conditions for success.* Washington, DC: Author.

National Association for the Education of Young Children. (2011). *The Common Core state standards: Caution and opportunity for early childhood education.* Washington, DC: Author.

National Clearinghouse for English Language Acquisition. (2011, January). *Key demographics & practice recommendations for young English learners.* Retrieved from http://www.ncela.us/files/uploads/9/EarlyChildhoodShortReport.pdf

National Council for Social Studies. (2007). *Social studies in the era of No Child Left Behind: A position statement of National Council for Social Studies.* Silver Spring, MD: Author. Retrieved from http://www.socialstudies.org/positions/nclbera

National Council for Social Studies. (2010). *National curriculum standards for social studies: A framework for teaching, learning, and assessment.* Silver Spring, MD: Author.

National Early Literacy Panel. (2009). *Developing early literacy: Report of the National Early Literacy Panel, a scientific synthesis of early literacy development and implications for intervention.* Washington, DC: National Institute for Literacy.

National Reading Panel. (2000). *Teaching children to read: An evidence-based assessment of the scientific research literature on reading and its implications for reading instruction.* Washington, DC: National Institute of Child Health and Human Development.

Neuman, S.B. (1999). Books make a difference: A study of access to literacy. *Reading Research Quarterly, 34*, 286–311.

Neuman, S.B. (2006). The knowledge gap: Implications for early education. In S.B. Neuman & D.K. Dickinson (Eds.), *Handbook of early literacy research* (pp. 29–40). New York, NY: Guilford Press.

Neuman, S.B. (2010). Lessons from my mother: Reflections on the National Early Literacy Panel report. *Educational Researcher, 39*, 301–304.

Neuman, S.B., & Celano, D. (2001). Access to print in middle- and low-income communities: An ecological study of four neighborhoods. *Reading Research Quarterly, 36*, 8–26.

Neuman, S.B., & Dwyer, J. (2009). Missing in action: Vocabulary instruction in preschool. *The Reading Teacher, 62*, 384–392.

Neuman, S.B., & Dwyer, J. (2011). Developing vocabulary and conceptual knowledge for low-income preschoolers: A design experiment. *Journal of Literacy Research, 43*, 103–129.

Neuman, S.B., & Roskos, K. (2005). The state of state pre-kindergarten standards. *Early Childhood Research Quarterly, 20*, 125–145.

Neuman, S.B., & Roskos, K. (2007). *Nurturing knowledge.* New York, NY: Scholastic.

Neuman, S.B., & Wright, T.S. (2013). *All about words: Increasing vocabulary in the Common Core classroom, prek–2.* New York, NY: Teachers College Press.

Nevárez-La Torre, A.A. (1999). Developing voice: Teacher-research in bilingual classrooms. *Bilingual Research Journal, 23*(4), 451–470.

NICHD Early Child Care Research Network. (2005). *Childcare and child development: Results from the NICHD study of early childcare and youth development.* New York, NY: Guilford Press.

Noell, G.H., Witt, J.C., Slider, N.J., Connell, J.E., Gatti, S.L., Williams, K.L., . . . Duhon, G.J. (2005). Treatment implementation following behavioral consultation in schools: A comparison of three follow-up strategies. *School Psychology Review, 34,* 87–106.

Odlin, T. (1989). *Language transfer: Cross-linguistic influences in language learning.* New York, NY: Cambridge University Press.

Pappas, C.C. (2006). The informational text genre: Its role in integrated science literacy research and practice. *Reading Research Quarterly, 41,* 226–250.

Pappas, C., & Pettegrew, B.S. (1998). The role of genre in the psycholinguistic guessing game of reading. *Language Arts, 75,* 36–44.

Parker, V. (2006). *Light.* Chicago, IL: Heinemann Library.

Parker, V. (2006). *Luz.* Chicago, IL: Heinemann Library.

Patrick, H., Mantzicopoulus, P., Samarapungavan, A., & French, B.F. (2008). Patterns of young children's motivation for science and teacher-child relationship. *Journal of Experimental Education, 76*(2), 121–144.

Penno, J., Wilkinson, A., & Moore, D. (2002). Vocabulary acquisition from teacher explanation and repeated listening to stories: Do they overcome the Matthew effect? *Journal of Educational Psychology, 86,* 139–153.

Pentimonti, J.M., & Justice, L.M. (2010). Teachers' use of scaffolding strategies during read alouds in the preschool classroom. *Early Childhood Education Journal, 37,* 241–248.

Perez, M. (2004). *Colors of the seasons.* Pelham, NY: Benchmark Education.

Perfetti, C., & Lesgold, A. (1979). Coding and comprehension in skilled reading and implications for reading instruction. In L.B. Resnick & P. Weaver (Eds.), *Theory and practice of early reading* (Vol. 1, pp. 2–44). Mahwah, NJ: Lawrence Erlbaum Associates.

Pianta, R.C., LaParo, K.M., Payne, C., Cox, M.J., & Bradley, R. (2002). The relation of kindergarten classroom environment to teacher, family, and school characteristics and child outcomes. *Elementary School Journal, 102,* 225–238.

Piasta, R.C., Justice, L.M., Cabell, S.Q., Wiggins, A.K., Turnbull, K.P., & Curenton, S.M.

(2012). Impact of professional development on preschool teachers' conversational responsivity and children's linguistic productivity and complexity. *Early Childhood Research Quarterly, 27*(3), 387–400.

Pohl, M. (2001). *Learning to think—thinking to learn: Models and strategies to develop a classroom culture of thinking.* Heatherton, Australia: Hawker Brownlow Education.

Pohl, M. (2006). *Still learning to think—thinking to learn: Into Bloom's taxonomy and beyond.* Heatherton, Australia: Hawker Brownlow Education.

Pollard-Durodola, S.D., Gonzalez, J.E., Saenz, L.M., & Soares, D. (2013). *Analysis of pre-school teachers' scaffolding decisions while providing feedback during a content-rich shared book reading intervention with ELLs.* Paper presented as part of a symposium, "Observations of teachers' instructional support during early literacy/language instruction," organized by S.D. Pollard-Durodola for the Literacy Research Association annual conference, Dallas, TX.

Pollard-Durodola, S.D., Gonzalez, J.E., Simmons, D.C., Kwok, O., Taylor, A.B., Davis, M.J., . . . Simmons, L. (2011). The effects of an intensive shared book reading intervention for preschool children at-risk for vocabulary delay. *Exceptional Children, 77,* 161–183.

Pollard-Durodola, S.D., Gonzalez, J.E., Simmons, D.C., Taylor, A.B., Davis, M., Simmons, L., & Nava-Walichowski, M. (2012). An examination of preschool teachers' shared book reading practices in Spanish: Before and after instructional guidance. *Bilingual Research Journal, 35*(1), 5–31.

Provensen, A. (2008). *A book of seasons.* New York, NY: Random House.

Purcell-Gates, V., & Duke, N.K. (2001, 24–26 August). *Explicit explanation/teaching of informational text genres: A model for research.* Paper presented at the National Science Foundation Conference, "Crossing Borders: Connecting Science and Literacy," Baltimore, MD.

Reading to Kids. (2002). *The picture walk.* Retrieved from http://readingtokids.org/ReadingClubs/TipPictureWalk.php

Reese, E., Cox, A., Harte, D., & McAnally, H. (2003). Diversity in adults' styles of reading books to children. In A. van Kleeck, S.A. Stahl, & E.B. Bauer (Eds.), *On reading books to children* (pp. 37–57). Mahwah, NJ: Lawrence Erlbaum Associates.

Roberts, T., & Neal, H. (2004). Relationships among preschool English language learners' oral proficiency in English, instructional experience and literacy development. *Contemporary Educational Psychology, 29,* 283–311.

Saçkes, M., Trundle, K.C., & Flevares, L.M. (2009). Using children's literature to teach standard-based science concepts in early years. *Early Childhood Education Journal, 36*(5), 415–422.

Saunders, W.M., & Goldenberg, C. (1999). Effects of instructional conversations and literature logs on limited-and-fluent-English-proficient students' story comprehension and thematic understanding. *The Elementary School Journal, 99*(4), 277–301.

Scarborough, H.S. (2001). Connecting early language and literacy to later reading (dis) abilities: Evidence. In S.B. Neuman & D.K. Dickinson (Eds.), *Handbook of early literacy research* (pp. 97–110). New York, NY: Guilford Press.

Scarborough, H.S., & Dobrich, W. (1994). On the efficacy of reading to preschoolers. *Developmental Review, 14,* 245–302.

Scarcella, R. (2003). *Academic English: A conceptual framework* [Technical report]. Irvine, CA: University of California Linguistic Minority Research Institute.

Schickedanz, J.A., & Collins, M.F. (2012). For young children, pictures in storybooks are rarely worth a thousand words. *The Reading Teacher, 64*(8), 539–549.

Seidel, T., Stürmer, K., Blomberg, G., Kobarg, M., & Schwindt, K. (2011). Teacher learning from analysis of videotaped classroom situations: Does it make a difference whether teachers observe their own teaching or that of others? *Teaching and Teacher Education, 27,* 259–267.

Sénéchal, M. (1997). The differential effect of storybook reading on preschoolers' acquisition of expressive and receptive vocabulary. *Journal of Child Language, 24,* 123–138.

Sénéchal, M., Thomas, E., & Monker, J. (1995). Individual differences in 4-year-old children's acquisition of vocabulary during storybook reading. *Journal of Educational Psychology, 87,* 218–229.

Schaefer, L.M. (2003). *Casa.* Chicago, IL: Heineman Library.

Schaefer, L.M. (2003). *House.* Chicago, IL: Heineman Library.

Shanahan, T., & Beck, I. (2006). Effective literacy teaching for English-language learners. In D. August & T. Shanahan (Eds.), *Developing literacy in second-language learners: A report on the National Literacy Panel on Language Minority Children and Youth* (pp. 415–488). Mahwah, NJ: Lawrence Erlbaum Associates.

Silverman, R.D. (2007). Vocabulary development of English-language and English-only learners in kindergarten. *The Elementary School Journal, 107*(4), 365–383.

Simmons, D.C., Pollard-Durodola, S.D., Gonzalez, J.E., Davis, M., & Simmons, L. (2008). Shared book reading interventions. In S.B. Neuman (Ed.), *Educating the other America: Top experts tackle poverty, literacy, and achievement in our schools* (pp. 187–211). Baltimore, MD: Paul H. Brookes Publishing Co.

Smith, S. (2009). *Changing seasons.* Chicago, IL: Heinemann Library.

Snow, C.E., Burns, M.S., & Griffin, P. (1998). *Preventing reading difficulties in young children.* Washington, DC: National Academies Press.

Snow, C., Griffin, P., & Burns, M.S. (2005). *Knowledge to support the teaching of reading: Preparing teachers for a changing world.* San Francisco, CA: Jossey-Bass.

Snow, M.A., Met, M., & Genessee, F. (1989). A conceptual framework for the integration of language and content in second language instruction. *TESOL Quarterly, 23,* 201–217.

Spycher, P. (2009). Learning academic language through science in two linguistically diverse kindergarten classes. *The Elementary School Journal, 109*(4), 359–379.

Stahl, S.A. (1991). Beyond the instrumentalist hypothesis: Some relationships between word meanings and comprehension. In P.J. Schwanenflugel (Ed.), *The psychology of word meanings* (pp. 157–186). Mahwah, NJ: Lawrence Erlbaum Associates.

Stahl, S.A. (2003). How words are learned incrementally over multiple exposures. *American Educator, 27*(1), 18–19, 44.

Stahl, S.A., & Nagy, W.E. (2006). *Teaching word meanings.* Mahwah, NJ: Lawrence Erlbaum Associates.

Stipek, D. (2006). No Child Left Behind comes to preschool. *The Elementary School Journal, 106*(5), 455–466.

Storch, S.A., & Whitehurst, G.J. (2002). Oral language and code-related precursors to reading: Evidence from a longitudinal structural model. *Developmental Psychology, 38,* 934–947.

Sudol, P., & King, C.M. (1996). A checklist for choosing nonfiction trade books. *The Reading Teacher, 49*(5), 423–424.

Swanson, E., Vaughn, S., Wanzek, J., Petscher, Y., Heckert, J., Cavnaugh, C., . . . Tackett, K. (2011). A synthesis of read-aloud interventions on early reading outcomes among preschool through third graders at risk for reading difficulties. *Journal of Learning Disabilities, 44*, 258–275.

Swingley, D. (2010). Fast mapping and slow mapping in children's word learning. *Language Learning and Development, 6*, 179–183.

Teachers of English to Speakers of Other Languages, Inc. (2006). Prek–12 English language proficiency standards: Augmentation of the world-class instructional design and assessment (WIDA) consortium English language proficiency standards. Alexandria, VA: Author.

Tharp, R., & Gallimore, R. (1991). *The instructional conversation: Teaching and learning in social activity*. (Research Report 2). Santa Cruz, CA: National Center for Research on Cultural Diversity and Second Language Learning, University of California.

Tong, F., Lara-Alecio, R., Irby, B., Mathes, P., & Kwok, O. (2008). Accelerating early academic oral English development in transitional bilingual and structured English immersion programs. *American Education Research Journal, 45*(4), 1011–1044.

Trumbauer, L. (2004). *Trees are terrific!* Bloomington, MN: Red Brick Learning.

Trundle, K.C., & Saçkes, M. (2012). Science and early learning. In R.C. Pianta (Ed.), *Handbook of early childhood education* (pp. 240–258). New York, NY: Guilford Press.

van de Pol, J., Volman, M., & Beishuizen, J. (2010). Scaffolding in teacher-student interaction: A decade of research. *Educational Psychology Review, 22*, 271–296.

van Es, E.A., & Sherin, M.G. (2008). Mathematics teachers' learning to notice: In the context of a video club. *Teaching and Teacher Education, 24*, 244–276.

van Kleeck, A. (2003). Research on book sharing: Another critical look. In A. van Kleeck, S.A. Stahl, & E.B. Bauer (Eds.), *On reading books to children* (pp. 272–320). Mahwah, NJ: Lawrence Erlbaum Associates.

van Kleeck, A. (2008). Providing preschool foundations for later reading comprehension: The importance of and ideas for targeting inferencing in storybook-sharing interventions. *Psychology in the Schools, 45*(7), 627–643. doi:10.1002/pits.20314

Varelas, M., & Pappas, C.C. (2006). Intertextuality in read-alouds of integrated science-literacy units in urban primary classrooms: Opportunities for the development of thought and language. *Cognition and Instruction, 24*(2), 211–259. doi:10.1207/s1532690xci2402_2

Vaughn, S., & Linan-Thompson, S. (2003). Group sizes and time allotted to intervention: Effects for students with reading difficulties. In B. Foorman (Ed.), *Preventing and remediating reading difficulties: Bringing science to scale* (pp. 275–320). Baltimore, MD: York Press.

Vaughn, S., Linan-Thompson, S., Kouzekanani, K., Pedrotty, B., Dickson, S., & Blozis, S.A. (2003). Reading instruction grouping for students with reading difficulties. *Remedial and Special Education, 24*(5), 301–315.

Vaughn, S., Linan-Thompson, S., Pollard-Durodola, S.D., Mathes, P., & Cárdenas-Hagan, E. (2005). Effective interventions for English language learners (Spanish/English) at-risk for reading difficulties. In D.K. Dickinson & S.B. Neuman (Eds.), *Handbook of early literacy research* (Vol. 2, pp. 185–197). New York, NY: Guilford Press.

Vaughn-Shavuo, F. (1990). Using story grammar and language experience for improving recall and comprehension in the teaching of ESL to Spanish-dominant first-graders. (Unpublished doctoral dissertation, Hofstra University, NY.)

Verhoeven, L. (2011). Second language reading acquisition. In M.L. Kamil, P.D. Pearson, E.B. Moje, & P.P. Afflerback (Eds.), *Handbook of reading research* (Vol. 4, pp. 661–683). New York, NY: Routledge.

Verhoeven, L., & Perfetti, C.A. (2011). Introduction to this special issue: Vocabulary growth and reading skill. *Society for the Scientific Study of Reading, 15*(1), 1–7.

Vygotsky, L.S. (1987). Thinking and speech. In R.W. Rieber & A.S. Carton (Eds.), *The collected works of L.S. Vygotsky: Vol. 1. Problems of general psychology* (N. Minick, Trans., pp. 37–285). New York, NY: Plenum. (Original work published 1934.)

Wallace, C. (2007). Vocabulary: The key to teaching English language learners to read. *Reading Improvement, 44*(4), 189–193.

Walsh, K. (2003). Basal readers: The lost opportunity to build background knowledge that propels comprehension. *American Educator, 31*, 25–27.

Wasik, B.A., & Bond, M.A. (2001). Beyond the pages of a book: Interactive book reading and language development in a preschool classroom. *Journal of Educational Psychology, 93,* 243–250.

Wasik, B.A., Bond, M.A., & Hindman, A. (2006). The effects of language and literacy intervention on Head Start children and teachers. *Journal of Educational Psychology, 98,* 63–74.

Wasik, B.A., & Iannone-Campbell, C. (2012). Building vocabulary through purposeful, meaningful conversations. *The Reading Teacher, 66*(4), 321–332.

Webster-Wright, A. (2009). Reframing professional development through understanding authentic professional learning. *Review of Educational Research, 79*(2), 702–739.

What Works Clearinghouse. (2006). *Intervention report: Shared book reading.* Retrieved from http://ies.ed.gov/ncee/wwc/intervention report.aspx?sid=458

Whitehouse, P. (2002). *Leaves.* Chicago, IL: Heinemann Library.

Whitehurst, G.J., Falco, F.L., Lonigan, C.J., Fischel, J.E., DeBryshe, B.D., Valdez-Menchaca, M.C., & Caulfied, M. (1988). Accelerating language development through picture book reading. *Developmental Psychology, 24,* 552–559.

Whitehurst, G.J., & Lonigan, C.J. (1998). Child development and emergent literacy. *Child Development, 69,* 848–872.

Wisconsin Center for Education Research. (2014a). *Can do descriptors for WIDA's levels of English language proficiency.* Madison, WI: School of Education, University of Wisconsin-Madison, World-Class Instructional Design and Assessment (WIDA).

Wisconsin Center for Education Research. (2014b). *Early English language development (E-ELD).* Madison, WI: School of Education, University of Wisconsin-Madison, World-Class Instructional Design and Assessment (WIDA).

Wright, T.S. (2012). What classroom observations reveal about oral vocabulary instruction in kindergarten. *Reading Research Quarterly, 47*(4), 353–355.

Wright, T.S. (2013). From potential to reality: Content-rich vocabulary and informational text. *The Reading Teacher, 67*(5), 359–367.

Wright, W.E. (2010). *Foundations for teaching English language learners: Research, theory, policy, and practice.* Philadelphia, PA: Caslon Publishing.

Zehler, A.M., Fleischman, H.L., Hopstock, P.J., Stephenson, T.G., Pendzick, M.L., & Sapru, S. (2003). *Descriptive study of services to LEP students and LEP students with disabilities.* Research report submitted to the U.S. Department of Education, OELA. Arlington, VA: Development Associates Inc.

Zevenbergen, A.A., & Whitehurst, G.J. (2003). Dialogic reading: A shared picture book reading intervention for preschoolers. In A. van Kleeck, S.A. Stahl, & E.B. Bauer (Eds.), *On reading books to children* (pp. 177–200). Mahwah, NJ: Lawrence Erlbaum Associates.

# List of Vignettes

A

# List of Storybooks and Informational Texts

## STORYBOOKS

Arnold, T. (1987). *No jumping on the bed!* New York, NY: Puffin Books.

Arnold, T. (1987). *¡No se salta en la cama!* New York, NY: Puffin Books.

Asch, F. (1999). *La sombra de Moonbear.* New York, NY: Aladdin Books.

Asch, F. (1999). *Moonbear's shadow.* New York, NY: Aladdin Books.

Barracca, D., & Barracca, S. (1990). *The adventures of Maxi the taxi dog.* New York, NY: Penguin Books.

Barracca, D., & Barracca, S. (1990). *Las aventuras de Maxi el perro taxista.* New York, NY: Penguin Books.

Brennan, A. (2006). *Mr. Greg's garden.* New York, NY: National Geographic Society.

Brown, M.W. (1942). *The runaway bunny.* New York, NY: Harper & Row.

Emmett, J. (2004). *Ruby in her own time.* New York, NY: Scholastic.

## INFORMATIONAL TEXTS

Berger, M. (1996). *Amazing water.* New York, NY: Newbridge Educational Publishing.

Ehlert, L. (1988). *Planting a rainbow.* Singapore: Tien Wah.

Emberley, R. (1990). *Caminando.* New York, NY: Scholastic.

Emberley, R. (1990). *Taking a walk.* New York, NY: Scholastic.

Jordan, H.J. (2006). *How a seed grows.* New York, NY: Harper Collins Publishers.

Parker, V. (2006). *Light.* Chicago, IL: Heinemann Library.

Parker, V. (2006). *Luz.* Chicago, IL: Heinemann Library.

Perez, M. (2004). *Colors of the seasons.* Pelham, NY: Benchmark Education.

Provensen, A. (2008). *A book of seasons.* New York, NY: Random House.

Provensen, A. (2008). *Un libro de estaciones.* New York, NY: Random House.

Schaefer, L.M. (2003). *Casa.* Chicago, IL: Heineman Library.

Schaefer, L.M. (2003). *House.* Chicago, IL: Heineman Library.

Smith, S. (2009). *Changing seasons.* Chicago, IL: Heinemann Library.

Trumbauer, L. (2004). *Trees are terrific.* North Mankato, MN: Capstone.

Whitehouse, P. (2002). *Leaves.* Chicago, IL: Heinemann Library.

# Index